Essential Paris

by Elisabeth Morris

Above: *lanterns against the façade of Notre-Dame*

AAA Publishing
1000 AAA Drive, Heathrow, Florida 32746

Above: *a French breakfast*

Front cover AA World Travel Library/James Tims: *Eiffel Tower*
Back cover AA World Travel Library/James Tims: *Le Louvre*

Find out more about AAA Publishing and the wide range of services that AAA provides by visiting our website at aaa.com

Written by Elisabeth Morris

Edited, designed and produced by AA Publishing

The contents of this publication are believed correct at the time of printing. Nevertheless, the publishers cannot accept responsibility for errors or omissions or for changes in details given. We are always grateful to readers who let us know of any errors or omissions they come across, and future printings will be updated accordingly.

Library of Congress Catalog Card Number: on file

ISBN 1–59508–0279

Published in the United States by AAA Publishing,
1000 AAA Drive,
Heathrow, Florida 32746
Published in the United Kingdom By AA Publishing

A02164

Colour separation: BTB Digital Imaging Ltd,
Whitchurch, Hampshire
Printed and bound in Italy by Printer Trento S.r.l.

The weather chart on **page 118** of this book is calibrated in °C. For conversion to °F simply use the following formula:

$$°F = 1.8 \times °C + 32$$

Contents

About this Book

KEY TO SYMBOLS

Throughout the guide a few straightforward symbols are used to denote the following categories:

- map reference to the maps in the What to See section
- address or location
- telephone number
- opening times
- restaurant or café on premises or near by
- nearest underground train station
- nearest bus/tram route
- nearest overground train station
- nearest ferry stop
- facilities for visitors with disabilities
- admission charge
- other places of interest near by
- other practical information
- ➤ indicates the page where you will find a fuller description

This book is divided into five sections to cover the most important aspects of your visit to Paris.

Viewing Paris pages 5–14
An introduction to Paris by the author
Paris's Features
Essence of Paris
The Shaping of Paris
Peace and Quiet
Paris's Famous

Top Ten pages 15–26
The author's choice of the Top Ten places to see in Paris, each with practical information.

What to See pages 27–90
Two sections: Paris and Ile de France, each with its own brief introduction and an alphabetical listing of the main attractions
Practical information
Snippets of 'Did You Know...' information
4 suggested walks
3 suggested tours
2 features

Where To... pages 91–116
Detailed listings of the best places to eat, stay, shop, take the children and be entertained.

Practical Matters pages 117–24
A highly visual section containing essential travel information.

Maps
All map references are to the individual maps found in the What to See section of this guide.
For example, Notre-Dame has the reference 29E2 – indicating the page on which the map is located and the grid square in which the cathedral is to be found. A list of the maps that have been used in this travel guide can be found in the index.

Prices
Where appropriate, an indication of the cost of an establishment is given by € signs:
€€€ denotes higher prices, €€ denotes average prices, while € denotes lower charges.

Star Ratings
Most of the places described in this book have been given a separate rating:

✪✪✪	Do not miss
✪✪	Highly recommended
✪	Worth seeing

Viewing Paris

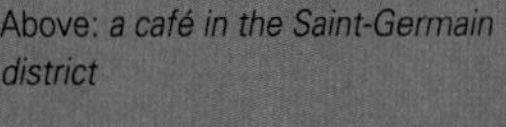

Above: *a café in the Saint-Germain district*

Elisabeth Morris's Paris

Paris never leaves me indifferent. It has the power to rouse strong feelings in me, whatever mood I am in: admiration, exhilaration, irritation and even frustration, but above all fascination as time and again I am bewitched by its charm and diversity.

Paris may seem straightforward and orderly to the first-time visitor as it unfolds its wealth of stately monuments, but it is in fact a complex city and its beauty has many facets; besides the vast open vistas there are picturesque villages like Saint-Germain-des-Prés, Le Marais or Montmartre where you may suddenly come across a tiny square steeped in a romantic old-world atmosphere or be confronted with a bold modern sculpture defiantly competing with a medieval masterpiece. What never ceases to amaze me, however, is the overall sense of harmony that pervades these contrasting features and confers on the city a unique homogeneity.

Paris is a melting-pot of new, daring, even outrageous ideas in the fields of art, fashion, architecture, cuisine, lifestyle, politics and sociology. Living in the midst of this continuous creative outburst is tremendously stimulating, but I also enjoy standing back and relaxing at lunchtime in the peaceful Jardins du Palais-Royal, at the heart of the city, or taking a stroll along the river at sunset when Parisians set aside their hurried daily pursuit of an elusive happiness and unashamedly give in to their inclination for enjoyment. Paris then seems more alive and exciting than ever.

'Villages' such as St-Germain-des-Prés (above) and the conviviality of café life (below) are just part of Paris's charm

Bistros and Cafés

You may think that *bistro* is just another name for *café* but there is a subtle difference. Cafés were traditionally the haunt of fashionable society and artists. Bistros are cafés of modest appearance where locals meet regularly for a drink, a game of dice and sometimes a snack. The number of cafés and bistros has decreased considerably in recent years.

Paris's Features

Geography

• Situated at the heart of northern France, some 250km from the sea, Paris lies on the banks of the meandering River Seine.

The City

• The city is small and compact, entirely surrounded by the boulevard périphérique, a congested 35km-long dual carriageway. Green spaces cover an area of 366ha excluding the Bois de Boulogne and Bois de Vincennes and there is one tree for every four Parisians.

Greater Paris

• The surrounding area, known as the *banlieue*, includes densely populated suburbs, dormitory towns and traditional villages scattered through the green belt, as well as several new towns. The whole region enjoys a reasonably dry climate, fairly cold in winter, hot and sunny in summer.

An unmistakeable skyline – the Tour Eiffel beyond the pont Neuf

Administration

• Paris is a municipality administered by a council and a mayor like any other town in France, but it is also a *département* (county) headed by a *préfet*.

• Paris is divided into 20 *arrondissements* numbered from 1 to 20 starting from the Louvre in the historic centre.

Population

• The city has just over 2 million inhabitants but nearly 11 million people, almost one-fifth of the French population, live in Greater Paris.

The Oldest...

• The oldest bridge is the pont Neuf (New Bridge!) dating from 1578.

• The oldest church is St-Germain-des-Prés, built in the 11th century.

• The oldest houses date from the 15th century; the Musée de Cluny is one of them (➤ 62).

• The oldest tree, planted in 1601, stands in the square Viviani, on the Left Bank opposite Notre-Dame.

Paris's Highest Monuments

Tour Eiffel: 317m
Tour Montparnasse: 209m
Grande Arche de la Défense: 110m
Dôme des Invalides: 105m
Panthéon: 83m
Sacré-Coeur: 80m`
Notre-Dame: 69m
Arc de Triomphe: 50m

Paris to...by Road

Amsterdam: 504km
Berlin: 1,069km
Brussels: 308km
Geneva: 538km
London: 343km
Luxembourg: 376km
Madrid: 1,310km
Rome: 1,417km

Essence of Paris

Paris is order, harmony, beauty and elegance...the result of bold town planning that was particularly successful in marrying tradition and innovation, sometimes with stunning effects, as in the case of the stark glass pyramid erected in front of the Louvre.

Paris is also passion, youthful energy and a stimulating cultural life.

But Paris is above all the capital of good living: the best of French cuisine, an enticing choice of gastronomic specialities from various countries, the glamorous world of *haute couture* and eccentric fashion, and a sparkling nightlife.

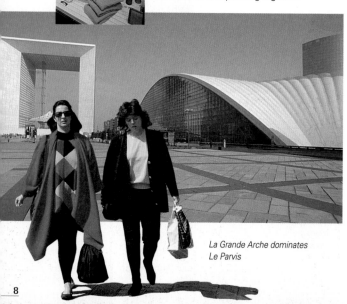

La Grande Arche dominates Le Parvis

THE 10 ESSENTIALS

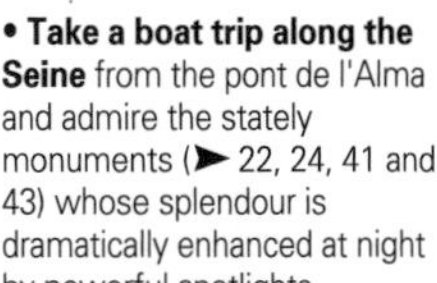

If you have only a short time to visit Paris and would like to take home unforgettable memories, here are the essentials:

A trip along the Seine is an ideal way to see many of the city's sights

- **Take a boat trip along the Seine** from the pont de l'Alma and admire the stately monuments (➤ 22, 24, 41 and 43) whose splendour is dramatically enhanced at night by powerful spotlights.
- **Climb to the top of the Tour Eiffel** for an aerial view of Paris (➤ 25); guaranteed thrill from the panoramic lift.
- **Take a morning walk through the Jardin du Luxembourg** and stand beside the romantic Fontaine de Médicis (➤ 12).
- **Sit outside Les Deux Magots Café** in boulevard St-Germain, on the Left Bank, and watch the world go by. Street bustle peaks around lunchtime and from 6PM (➤ 71).
- **Stand on the pont de la Tournelle** near Notre Dame: look downriver for panoramic views of 'old Paris' (Ile de la Cité and beyond) and upriver for contrasting views of 'new Paris' (Bercy and Institut du Monde Arabe, ➤ 54).
- **Stroll along the quais** and browse through the *bouquinistes*' stock of old prints and books (➤ 24).
- **Take the funicular to Sacré Coeur** at the top of Montmartre for stunning views of the city (➤ 70).
- **Go to the colourful Moulin-Rouge** show and discover the glamour of traditional Parisian entertainment (➤ 58).
- **Stand on the place de la Concorde** at night and look up the Champs-Elysées. The illuminated avenue, gently rising towards the Arc de Triomphe, offers one of the most perfect urban vistas in the world (➤ 17).
- **Mingle with Parisians** doing their daily shopping in street markets along the rue Mouffetard (Quartier Latin), or on Sundays, buying organic food on boulevard Raspail.

Place de la Concorde, the great square at one end of the Champs-Elysées

The Shaping of Paris

***c*250 BC**
A Celtic tribe, called the Parisii, settles on the Ile de la Cité.

52 BC
The Parisii are defeated by the Romans.

2nd century AD
Building of the Gallo-Roman city of Lutetia.

***c*300**
Lutetia is renamed Paris.

508
Clovis, king of the Franks, chooses Paris as his capital.

845
First Viking raid on Paris.

***c*1100**
Abélard teaches in Paris and meets Héloïse. The Quartier Latin spreads to the left bank.

1163–1245
Building of Notre-Dame Cathedral.

1215
Foundation of the Paris University.

***c*1220**
The Royal Palace of Le Louvre is completed.

1358
The merchants of Paris, headed by Etienne Marcel, rebel against royal authority and call for tax reforms.

1408
During the Hundred Years' War, Paris is occupied by the English.

1431
King Henry VI of England is crowned king of France in Notre-Dame.

1437
Charles VII liberates Paris.

***c*1470**
The first printing-press is set up in the Sorbonne.

1559
Foundation of the French Reformed Church.

1594
King Henri IV enters Paris, cheered by the population, and thus puts an end to the Wars of Religion.

1570–1610
The Louvre is extended.

Napoleon I dressed in his coronation robes

1605
The building of the place Royale (now place des Vosges), Paris's oldest square, leads to the development of the Marais district.

1660–70
The Louvre is extended once more.

***c*1670**
The first cafés become popular.

1680
Foundation of the Comédie-Française, France's most prestigious theatre. Louis XIV leaves Paris for Versailles.

1755–75
Building of the place Louis XV (now place de la Concorde).

1783
First-ever balloon flight by Pilâtre de Rozier.

1789
The fall of the Bastille marks the beginning of the French Revolution.

1804
Napoleon is crowned emperor in Notre-Dame Cathedral.

1816
Gas lighting is installed in the city. The first steamships sail along the Seine.

General Eisenhower in liberated Paris, 1944

1852–70
Baron Haussmann reshapes Paris.

1870
Paris is besieged by the Prussians and is forced to capitulate. The Hôtel de Ville is burnt down and is rebuilt in under 10 years.

1889
The Tour Eiffel is the main attraction at the World Fair.

1900
The first métro line is inaugurated.

1914
Paris is saved from German occupation by the Battle of the Marne.

1919
Inauguration of the world's first commercial airline between Paris and London.

1940
Paris is occupied by German troops.

1944
Paris is liberated.

1947
First-ever fashion parade, organised by Christian Dior.

1968
Series of student demonstrations followed by a general strike.

1973
The boulevard périphérique is completed.

1977
The office of Mayor is reinstated after 100 years; Jacques Chirac is elected. Centre Georges Pompidou is inaugurated.

1986
Inauguration of the Musée d'Orsay.

1989
The Grand Louvre, the Opéra-Bastille and the Grande Arche de la Défense are inaugurated for the bicentenary of the Revolution.

1996
Opening of the new Bibliothèque Nationale.

1998
The football World Cup final takes place in the newly built Stade de France in St-Denis – and is won by France.

2000
The Eiffel Tower is revamped with glittering halogen lighting.

2002
Euro notes and coins introduced.

Peace & Quiet

Paris is a compact, densely populated city and the pace of life is notoriously hectic. Fortunately, the city has its quiet spots, full of charm and mystery, ideal for relaxing after a head-spinning shopping spree in boulevard Haussmann or a marathon visit to the Louvre.

Paris's green spaces cover an area of about 2,000ha. They come in all shapes and sizes, from the tiny square du Vert Galant on the Ile de la Cité to the imposing Bois de Boulogne on the outskirts of town. Names vary according to size: *squares* are small gardens, often occupying the centre of a square such as the square Louis XIII in the place des Vosges; *jardins* are larger and usually formal in design, such as the Jardin des Tuileries; *parcs* are freer in style: they can be romantic like the parc Monceau or futuristic like the parc André Citroën. Whether you wish to take a brief pause or are longing for a day away from it all, you should find what you are looking for in the selection below.

Jardin du Luxembourg, popular with students as a retreat from the nearby Sorbonne

In the City Centre

Square du Vert Galant – this triangular green patch, situated at the western end of the Ile de la Cité, offers a splendid view of the Louvre.

Arènes de Lutèce – surrounded by greenery, the ruins of the city's Gallo-Roman amphitheatre form a picturesque setting at the heart of the busy Quartier Latin.

Square Viviani – adjacent to the small medieval church of St-Julien-le-Pauvre, on the Left Bank, it shelters Paris's oldest tree. Admire the delightful view of Notre-Dame.

Jardin du Luxembourg – situated a stone's throw from the Sorbonne, this attractive French-style garden is traditionally the favourite haunt of students and lovers, who particularly favour the area surrounding the Fontaine de Médicis, named after Marie de Médicis, who commissioned the Palais du Luxembourg (now the Senate) and the gardens.

Jardin du Palais-Royal – walking under the arches into the garden is like taking a journey back in time: the noise of traffic fades away and the visual impression is one of 18th-century elegance and harmony.

Parc Monceau – this English-style park is scattered with 18th-century follies. Combine a quiet stroll here with a visit to the nearby Musée Nissim de Camondo (➤ 63) and Musée Cernuschi (➤ 39).

Further Out

Parc des Buttes-Chaumont – complete with lake, rocky island, bridges and waterfall, this was the first park to be laid out in the city's northern districts.

Parc André-Citroën – this ultra-modern park in the 15th *arrondissement* combines architecture with nature and experiments with colours, metals and water to create different impressions and striking contrasts.

Bois de Boulogne and Bois de Vincennes – landscaped in the English style at the end of the 19th century with artificial lakes, lawns, woodland areas, footpaths and tracks for horse-riding and bicycling, these offer an ideal one-day break from city life. The Bois de Boulogne boasts two racecourses as well as cafés and restaurants while the Bois de Vincennes has a racecourse, a zoo and a working farm open to the public.

Top: *Bois de Vincennes, an extensive area of parkland on the edge of the city*
Above: *floating wooden boats in the Jardin des Tuileries, a popular pastime with Parisian children*

Paris's Famous

Molière

The son of an upholsterer established near Les Halles, Molière turned down a promising career in law to become an actor. His first attempts at directing his own company ended in disaster and...prison! However he persevered and success finally came in 1659 with *Les Précieuses ridicules*, the first of many incisive comedies in which he satirised human nature in general and French society in particular. He worked and lived near the Palais-Royal, where the Comédie-Française is now established; the armchair in which Molière was playing the rôle of the *Malade imaginaire* when he collapsed and died in 1673, is inside.

André Le Nôtre

André Le Nôtre was Louis XIV's (the Sun King) famous landscape gardener. He conceived his gardens along architectural lines and showed an extraordinary flair for harmonious proportions. He not only designed the magnificent parks of Vaux-le-Vicomte and Versailles, but also left his mark on Paris by redesigning the Jardin des Tuileries and creating the vast vista leading up to the Arc de Triomphe, later to become the Champs-Elysées.

Baron Haussmann

During the second half of the 19th century, Baron Haussmann's brilliant town planning transformed Paris from a squalid medieval town into a spacious, modern city. The Ile de la Cité underwent major surgery, to an extent which seems excessive today, and several wide arteries were opened up along the left and right banks; the place de l'Etoile and its 12 radiating avenues were created, and green spaces were provided all over the town centre.

Jacques Chirac

Jacques Chirac was mayor of Paris from 1977 to 1995. During that time, he continued the work of his famous predecessors, including the systematic cleaning of the town's monuments, and the part restoration of the avenue des Champs-Elysées to its former splendour. He resigned as mayor when he was elected president in 1995. In 2002, he was elected to his second term of office.

Geneviève and Attila

Born just outside Paris around AD 420, Geneviève was a devout Christian. In 451, as the Huns were appoaching Paris, panic spread among the people who prepared to leave the city. But Geneviève galvanised them into organising the town's defences, and Attila and his army were forced back. Geneviève later became the patron saint of Paris.

Top Ten

Above and right: *a fountain and pipes at Centre Georges Pompidou*

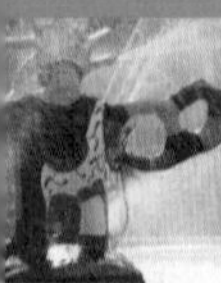

1
Centre Georges Pompidou

Not to everyone's taste, but undeniably eye-catching

This spacious and convivial art centre, in the heart of historic Paris, houses under on roof all forms of modern and contemporary art.

www.centrepompidou.fr

29E3

Place Georges-Pompidou, 75004 Paris

01 44 78 12 33

Centre: Wed–Mon. Modern art museum and exhibitions: 11–9. Library: weekdays 12–10; weekends 11–10. Brancusi workshop 2–6

Restaurant (€€), café and snack bar

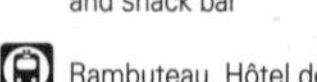

Rambuteau, Hôtel de Ville

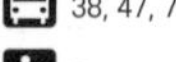

38, 47, 75

Excellent

Free access; museum: moderate (includes Brancusi workshop, children's workshop and level 6)

Audio guides, cash dispenser, shops

With 25,000 visitors a day, the Centre Georges Pompidou is now one of Paris's top sights. Yet at the time it was built, close to the historic Marais which is famous for its elegant architecture, the 'refinery', as Rogers and Piano's post-modern building was nicknamed, deeply shocked French people. In fact, the revolutionary concept of this open-plan 'house of culture for all' ensured its success and brought life back to the district. The centre has had its first major face-lift and been completely refurbished inside; its main asset, the Musée National d'Art Moderne, reached by the external escalator, gained extra exhibition space in the process. The museum is dedicated to the main trends of 20th-century art from 1905 to the present day. Modern art is displayed on level 5. Particularly well represented are Fauvism (Dufy, Derain, Matisse), Cubism (Braque, Picasso, Léger), Dadaism, Surrealism (Dali, Miró), Expressionism (Soutine, Kirchner, Modigliani and to a lesser extent Chagall), various forms of abstract art (Kandinsky, Klee, but also Poliakoff, Dubuffet and the Cobra movement), and pre-1960 American painting. The collections of contemporary art (level 4) include exponents of the new realism (Arman, César), of Pop Art (Warhol), of Minimalist art (Sol Lewitt, Buren) and of monochromes (Manzoni, Klein).

The centre also houses a library, the Institute for Acoustic and Musical Research, the Centre for Industrial Creation, a large exhibition hall, a children's workshop and a reconstruction of Brancusi's workshop.

2
Les Champs-Elysées

For most visitors this prestigious avenue epitomises French elegance, but it is also a dazzling place of entertainment and a luxury shopping mall.

In the late 17th century, Le Nôtre designed a gently rising alleyway as an extension of the Jardin des Tuileries. This later lost its rustic appearance and became a fashionable avenue lined with elegant restaurants and cafés. Nowadays it is the traditional venue for a variety of events such as the Paris Marathon, the arrival of the Tour de France and the march past on 14 July, which celebrates France's national day. But 'les Champs' (the fields) is also a place where people of all ages just relax and feel alive.

The lower section, stretching from the place de la Concorde (with breathtaking views along the whole length of the avenue) to the Rond-Point des Champs-Elysées, is laid out as an English-style park shaded by imposing chestnut trees. On the left are the Grand and Petit Palais, two temples of the arts, while on the right is a monument to the French Resistance hero, Jean Moulin, who was reburied in the Panthéon on 19 December 1964.

The upper section stretches from the Rond-Point, designed by Le Nôtre, to the Arc de Triomphe. This is the 'modern' part of the avenue, with its pavements now revamped and restored to their former comfortable width. Banks, cinemas, airline offices, car showrooms, and large cafés spread out on the pavements, lining the way to the place de l'Etoile. Fashion boutiques cluster along the arcades running between the Champs-Elysées and the parallel rue de Ponthieu. Some shops remain open well into the night and the bustle only quietens down in the early hours of the morning.

www.monum.fr

28B4

Avenue des Champs-Elysées, 75008 Paris

Choice of restaurants (€–€€€)

Concorde, Champs-Elysées-Clemenceau, Franklin-D Roosevelt, George V, Charles-de-Gaulle-Etoile

32, 42, 73

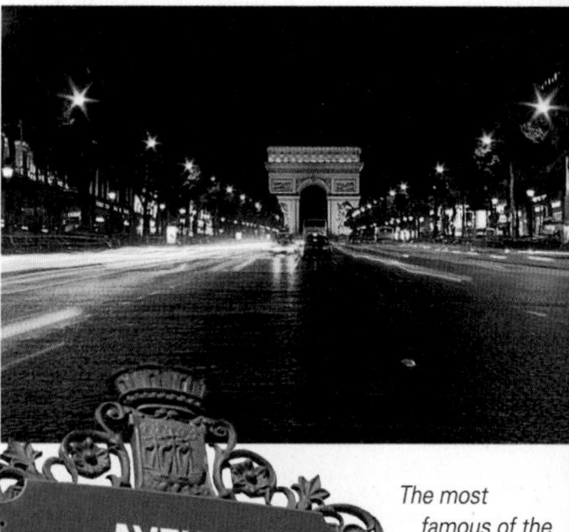

The most famous of the 12 avenues radiating out from the place Charles de Gaulle

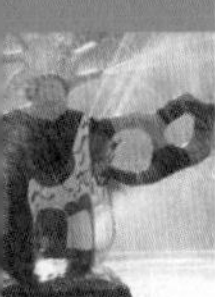

3

La Grande Arche de la Défense

www.grandearche.com

Off map 28A5

1 parvis de la Défense, 92044 Paris-La Défense

01 49 07 27 57 (Grande Arche)

Grande Arche: daily 10–7

Rooftop restaurant, snackbars and cafés in Les Quatre Temps shopping centre (€) and in the CNIT (€ and €€)

La Défense

73, Balabus in summer

Good

Lift Grande Arche: moderate

Video presentation, guided tours, shops

Symbolically guarding the western approach to the city, the Grande Arche is both a recognition of tradition and a bold step towards the future.

From the arch's roof top (110m above ground), accessible by the exterior lift, a marvellous view unfolds in a straight line along an axis to the Arc de Triomphe and, beyond, to the Obelisk at place de la Concorde and to the Louvre, extending the magnificent vista opened up by Le Nôtre. The arch was inaugurated in 1989 for the bicentenary celebrations of the French Revolution and is now a major tourist attraction. The stark simplicity of its architectural outline and the materials used are definitely contemporary, while its sheer size is a marvel of modern technology. The Danish architect, Otto von Spreckelsen, built a perfect hollow concrete cube covered over with glass and white Carrara marble. Steps lead up to the central platform, where the lifts are to be found.

The arch dominates a vast square, known as Le Parvis, decorated with colourful sculptures, including a red 'stabile' by Calde, and flanked by another remarkable building: the CNIT (Centre of New Industries and Technology), shaped like an upside-down-shell, which serves mainly as a conference centre but is also a pleasant meeting place for business people. There are several cafés and a branch of the FNAC, the French equivalent of Virgin stores, stocking a large selection of CDs covering a wide spectrum of musical tastes.

Opposite, there is a huge shopping centre known as Les Quatre Temps, which has some of the best shopping bargains in Paris. Its focal point is the vast hypermarket Auchan.

A striking modern symbol

4
Les Invalides

This is one of Paris's most imposing architectural ensembles, built around two churches and housing several museums.

The Hôtel National des Invalides was commissioned by Louis XIV as a home for wounded soldiers. It is a splendid example of 17th-century architecture, the classical austerity of its 200m-long façade being offset by the baroque features of the Eglise du Dôme, with its gilt dome glittering above the slate roofs of the stone buildings. The huge esplanade filling the gap between the river and the monumental entrance enhances the majesty of the building.

The museums are accessible from the arcaded main courtyard. The Musée de l'Armée is one of the richest museums of its kind in the world. It contains weapons from all over the world, armour and uniforms, mementoes of famous generals, paintings, documents and models. Particularly striking is the comprehensive permanent exhibition devoted to the Second World War.

The Musée des Plans-Reliefs is a fascinating collection of models of fortified French towns, originally started at Louis XIV's request.

On the far side of the courtyard is the entrance to St-Louis-des-Invalides, the soldiers' church, which contains a colourful collection of flags brought back from various campaigns; the organ here dates from the 17th century.

The magnificent Eglise du Dôme, built by Jules Hardouin-Mansart, is a striking contrast: an elegant façade with two tiers of Doric and Corinthian columns and an imposing gilt dome surmounted by a slender lantern. The splendid interior decoration is enhanced by the marble floor. The open circular crypt houses Napoleon's red porphyry tomb.

www.invalides.org

28B3

Esplanade des Invalides, 75007 Paris

01 44 42 37 72

10–5 (6 Apr–Sep). Closed 1 Jan, 1 May, 1 Nov, 25 Dec

Restaurant (€)

Invalides, La Tour Maubourg, Varenne

82, 92 — Good

Moderate

Audio-visual shows, guided tours, shops

Eglise du Dôme beyond the Cour d'Honneur and the soldier's church

5
Le Louvre

This former royal palace, which celebrated its bicentenary in 1993, is today one of the largest museums in the world.

www.louvre.fr

28C3

99 rue de Rivoli 75001 Paris Cedex 01. Main entrance via the pyramid

Recorded information: 01 40 20 51 51; reception desk: 01 40 20 53 17; visitors with disabilities: 0140 20 59 90

Thu–Sun 9–6, Mon and Wed 9AM–9.45PM. Closed 1 Jan, 1 May, 11 Nov and 25 Dec

Palais-Royal/Musée du Louvre

Just one of the 30,000-odd works on show

The Palace

Excavations carried out in 1977 under the Cour Carrée, the courtyard surrounded by the oldest part of the palace, led to the discovery of the original castle built around 1200 by King Philippe-Auguste, which remained a fortress until it was razed to the ground to make way for a Renaissance palace. The tour of the foundations of this medieval Louvre, including the base of the keep, the moat and the outer wall, starts from the main entrance hall under the glass pyramid.

The first palace, built by Pierre Lescot in the style of the Italian Renaissance, was enlarged round the Cour Carrée and along the Seine during the following 200 years.

It is said that Molière performed in front of the court in the splendid Salle des Cariatides where Greek and Roman antiquities are now displayed. Louis XIV enclosed the Cour Carrée with the stately colonnade that faces the Church of St-Germain-l'Auxerrois. Soon afterwards, however, the King left for Versailles and the palace was neglected by the royal family and the court.

Building was resumed by Napoleon, who built part of the north wing and erected the exquisite Arc de Triomphe du Carrousel. During the second half of the 19th century, Napoleon III completed the Louvre along its rue de Rivoli side.

The Museum

The museum was founded in 1793 to house the royal art collections, which were subsequently enriched to the point that a large part of its vast stock could not be displayed. This prompted President Mitterrand to launch a complete renovation of the buildings and to extend the museum over the whole of the Louvre; the project became known as the 'Grand Louvre'. A huge entrance hall was created under a stunning glass pyramid, designed by Ieoh Ming Peï placed in the centre of the Cour Napoleon. This gives access to three main areas

known as Sully, Denon and Richelieu.

The collections are divided into eight departments:

• Egyptian Antiquities include a pink granite *Sphinx from Tanis*, a huge *head of Amenophis IV-Akhenaten* and the famous *Seated Scribe*.

• The most remarkable exhibits in the Oriental Antiquities Department must be the *Assyrian winged bulls*.

• The department of Greek, Etruscan and Roman Antiquities contains numerous masterpieces: do not miss the *Vénus de Milo*, the *Winged Victory* and the Graeco-Roman sculpture in the Salle des Cariatides.

• The painting collections comprise a fine selection from the Italian school (works by Giotto, Fra Angelico, Leonardo da Vinci, Veronese, Titian and Raphael), from the French school (Poussin, Watteau, Georges de la Tour), from the Dutch school (Rembrandt, Rubens and Vermeer) and works by Spanish masters (Murillo, Goya and El Greco).

• French sculpture is particularly well represented and includes fine works by Jean Goujon, Houdon and Pradier.

• *Objets d'art* are now displayed to full advantage in the Richelieu wing; among them are beautiful tapestries and historic items such as Charlemagne's sword.

• The department of Graphic Art, houses drawings, prints and watercolours. The newly created department of Islamic Art will gradually expand over the next few years.

In addition, there is a display of art collections from Africa, Asia, Oceania and the Americas.

The Carrousel du Louvre is a luxury underground shopping precinct with an inverted pyramid in its centre.

Two wildly disparate styles of architecture symbolise the museum's progression into the 20th century

21, 27. 39, 48, 67, 68, 69, 72, 75, 76, 81, 95

Several restaurants (€ and €€) and cafés below the pyramid and in the Carrousel du Louvre

Excellent

Moderate until 3pm, reduced fee after 3 and Sun, free on 1st Sun of the month. To avoid a long wait, buy your ticket in advance: www.louvre.fr

Guided tours, lectures, concerts, film shows, shops. Information: 01 40 20 52 09

6
Notre-Dame

www.cathedraldeparis.com

29E2

Place du Parvis Notre-Dame, 75004 Paris

01 42 34 56 10

This masterpiece of Gothic architecture is one of Paris's most famous landmarks and one of France's most visited religious monuments.

In 1163, the Bishop of Paris, Maurice de Sully, launched the building of the cathedral, which took nearly 200 years to complete. One of the architects involved was Pierre de Montreuil, who also built the nearby Sainte-Chapelle (➤ 73). Later alterations deprived the church of its rood screen and of some of its original stained glass; its statues were mutilated during the Revolution because the Commune thought they were likenesses of the kings of France; the cathedral also lost all its original bells, except the 'gros bourdon', known as Emmanuel, which is traditionally heard on occasions of national importance. Restoration work was carried out in the 19th century by the famous architect Viollet-le-Duc and the area round the cathedral was cleared.

From across the vast square in front of the cathedral you can admire the harmonious proportions and almost perfect symmetry of the façade. The richly decorated portals are surmounted by statues of the kings of Judaea restored by Viollet-le-Duc. Above the central rose window, a colonnade links the elegant twin towers; there is a splendid view from the south tower, if you can face up to the 387-step climb.

The nave is 130m long, 48m wide and 35m high; the side chapels are richly decorated with paintings, sculptures and funeral monuments. Note the beautiful rose window at each end of the transept. The former vestry, on the right of the chancel, houses the Cathedral Treasure, which includes a piece of the Holy Cross.

A classic view of Notre-Dame Cathedral, from pont de l'Archevêché

Cathedral: daily 8–6:45; closed some religious feast days. Treasure: 9:30–11:30 and 1–5:30; closed Sun. Towers: 9:30–7:30 Apr–Sep (9:30–11PM Sat–Sun, Jul–Aug); 10:30–5:30 Oct–Mar

Left Bank (€–€€)

Cité, St Michel

21, 24, 27, 38, 47, 85, 96

Good

Cathedral: free; treasure and towers: inexpensive

7
Orsay, Musée d'

Once a mainline railway station, the Musée d'Orsay has been successfully converted into one of Paris's three major art museums.

Built in 1900, the Gare d'Orsay was narrowly saved from demolition by a daring plan to turn it into a museum dedicated to all forms of art from 1848 to 1914, and intended as the chronological link between the Louvre and the Musée National d'Art Moderne. The Musée d'Orsay was inaugurated by President Mitterrand in 1986.

The main hall, with the station clock, was retained to create a sense of unity between painting, sculpture, architecture, design, photography and the cinema. The collections are spread over three levels:

• The Lower Level deals with the years from 1848 to 1880; small flights of steps lead off the central alleyway to various exhibition areas where major sculptures are displayed, including a group of graceful figures by Carpeaux entitled *La Danse*. On either side is a comprehensive collection of paintings of the same period – works by Ingres, Delacroix, Corot, Courbet and the Realists, as well as the beginning of Impressionism with early works by Monet, Manet, Pissarro etc.

• On the Upper Level is the prestigious Impressionist and post-Impressionist collection, undoubtedly the main attraction of the museum: masterpieces by Manet (*Olympia*), Degas (*Blue Dancers*), Sisley (*Snow in Louveciennes*), Renoir (*Bathers*), Monet (*The Houses of Parliament, Rouen Cathedral*), Cézanne (*The Card Players*), Van Gogh (*The Church at Auvers-sur-Oise*), Gauguin and the school of Pont-Aven, Matisse, Toulouse-Lautrec and many others.

• The Middle Level is dedicated to the period from 1870 to 1914 and includes important works by Rodin (*Balzac*), paintings by the Nabis school, as well as a comprehensive section on art nouveau (Lalique, Gallé, Guimard, Mackintosh and Wright).

www.musee-orsay.fr

28C3

62 rue de Lille (entrance rue de Légion d'Honneur), 75007 Paris

01 40 49 48 48 or 01 40 49 48 00

Tue–Sat 10–6, Sun 9–6; late night: Thu 9:45 (opens 9AM Jul–end-Sep). Closed Mon, 1 Jan, 1 May, 25 Dec

Restaurant (€), café (€)

Solférino

24, 63, 68, 69, 73, 83, 84, 94

Very good

Moderate, free first Sun each month

Guided tours, shops, concerts, film shows

The iron and glass former railway hall

8
Les Quais

 28C3

Quai du Louvre, quai de la Mégisserie (75001), quai de Gesvres, quai de l'Hôtel de Ville, quai des Célestins (75004), quai de la Tournelle, quai de Montebello, quai St-Michel (75005), quai des Grands Augustins, quai de Conti, quai Malaquais (75006), quai Voltaire, quai Anatole-France (75007)

Restaurants and cafés along the way, particularly near place du Châtelet and place de l'Hôtel de Ville on the Right Bank, and around place St-Michel on the Left Bank (€–€€€)

Pont-Neuf, Châtelet, Hôtel de Ville, Pont-Marie, St-Michel, Solférino

 24 follows the Left Bank

 Boat trips along the Seine from pont de l'Alma right round the islands

Street artists at work add to the timeless appeal of a stroll alongside the river

Walk along the banks of the Seine between the pont de la Concorde and the pont de Sully for some of Paris's finest views.

In 1992, the river banks from the pont d'Iéna, where the Tour Eiffel stands, to the pont de Sully, at the tip of the Ile Saint-Louis, were added to Unesco's list of World Heritage sites. Here the townscape has an indefinable charm inspired by the harmonious blend of colours: the pale greys and blues of the water and the sky, the soft green of the trees lining the embankment and the mellow stone colour of the historic buildings. Parisians have been strolling along the embankments for centuries, window-shopping, browsing through the *bouquinistes'* stalls or simply watching the activity on both sides of the river.

The Right Bank

Start from the pont du Carrousel and walk up-river past the imposing façade of the Louvre. From the pont Neuf, enjoy a fine view of the Conciergerie on the Ile de la Cité, or admire the birds and exotic fish on the quai de la Mégisserie. Continue past the Hôtel de Ville towards the lovely pont Marie leading to the peaceful Ile Saint-Louis. Cross over to the Left Bank.

The Left Bank

The familiar green boxes of the *bouquinistes* are here as well! Admire the stunning views of Notre-Dame and its magnificent flying buttresses. The quai Saint-Michel is a favourite haunt of students looking for second-hand books. Further on, stand on the pont des Arts for a romantic view of the historic heart of Paris before walking past the stately façade of the Musée d'Orsay towards the pont de la Concorde.

9
La Tour Eiffel

Paris's most famous landmark has been towering above the city for more than a hundred years, yet its universal appeal remains constant.

The Tour Eiffel was built by the engineer Gustave Eiffel as a temporary attraction for the 1889 World Exhibition. At the time, its 300-m height made it the tallest building in the world and an unprecedented technological achievement. It met with instant success, was celebrated by poets and artists, and its spindly silhouette was soon famous all over the world. In spite of this, it was nearly pulled down when the concession expired in 1909 but was saved because of its invaluable radio aerial, joined in 1957 by television aerials. It was later raised by another 20m to accommodate a meteorological station.

The iron frame weighs 7,000 tonnes, yet the pressure it exerts on the ground is only 4kg per square cm; 40 tonnes of paint are used to repaint it every seven years. To celebrate its one hundredth birthday, it was renovated and halogen lighting was installed making it even more spectacular at night than before.

There are three levels, all accessible by lift, or by stairs – first and second floors only. Information about the tower is available on the first floor (57m above ground); there are also a restaurant, a gift shop and a post office, where letters are post-marked 'Paris Tour Eiffel'.

The second floor (115m above ground) offers fine views of Paris, several boutiques and a restaurant appropriately named 'Jules Verne'.

For a spectacular aerial view of the capital go up to the third floor (276m above ground). There is also a reconstruction of Gustave Eiffel's study and panoramic viewing tables showing 360˚ photos of Paris with the city's landmarks.

There is a good view of the tower (with the statue of General Foch in the foreground) across the Seine from the place du Trocadéro

www.tour-eiffel.fr

28A3

Champ de Mars, 75007

01 44 11 23 23

Daily 9:30AM–11PM (stairs to 6:30) Sep–Jun; 9AM–midnight Jul–Aug

Restaurants (€–€€€)

Bir-Hakeim

42, 69, 72, 82, 87

Good

Lift: 1st–2nd floors inexpensive–moderate, 3rd floor expensive

10
La Villette

www.cite-sciences.fr
www.cite-musique.fr

Off map 29F5

Cité des Sciences et de l'Industrie, parc de la Villette, 30 avenue Corentin Cariou, 75019 Paris; Cité de la Musique, 221 avenue Jean Jaurès, 75019 Paris

Cité des Sciences: 01 40 05 80 00; Cité de la Musique: information bookings 01 44 84 45 45

Cité des Sciences: Tue–Sat 10–6, Sun 10–7; closed 1 May, 25 Dec. Cité de la Musique: Tue–Sat 12–6, Sun 10–6

Restaurants near by (€–€€)

Cité des Sciences: Porte de la Villette; Cité de la Musique: Porte de Pantin

Cité des Sciences: 75, 139, 150, 152, PC; Cité de la Musique: 75, 151, PC

Cité des Sciences: very good; Cité de la Musique, museum: excellent

Cité des Sciences: expensive; Cité de la Musique: free, museum: moderate

Cité des Sciences: exhibitions, lectures, shops; Cité de la Musique: themed tours, workshops, musical tours

La Géode, a huge hemispherical cinema

The Cité des Sciences et de l'Industrie and the Cité de la Musique revitalised the outer district of La Villette, turning it into a new cultural centre.

Situated just inside the boulevard périphérique, between the Porte de la Villette and the Porte de Pantin, the 30-ha parc de la Villette was laid out on the site of Paris's former abattoirs. This ultra-modern park includes two vast cultural complexes, one devoted to science and the other to music, themed gardens scattered with red metal follies and various children's activity areas. A long covered walk joins the main buildings.

Cité des Sciences et de l'Industrie

The abattoirs' former auction hall was transformed into a vast scientific complex surrounded by water in which the public is both spectator and actor. 'Explora' is a permanent exhibition centred on the earth and the universe, life, languages and communication, the use of natural resources and technological and industrial developments. The Cité des Enfants is a fascinating interactive world for children aged 3 to 12. There are also a planetarium, an aquarium, a 3-D cinema, a multimedia library, a research centre, a submarine, a simulation booth (Cinaxe), in which spectators are able to live through the action of a film, and La Géode, a huge sphere equipped with a hemispherical screen that shows films on scientific subjects.

Cité de la Musique

The focal point of the Cité de la Musique is the vast square in front of the Grande Halle where concerts and exhibitions are held. On the left of the square is the new music and dance conservatory, while the triangular building on the right houses concerts halls and a museum (see Musée de la Musique ➤ 63).

What To See

Above: *Institut de France clock detail*

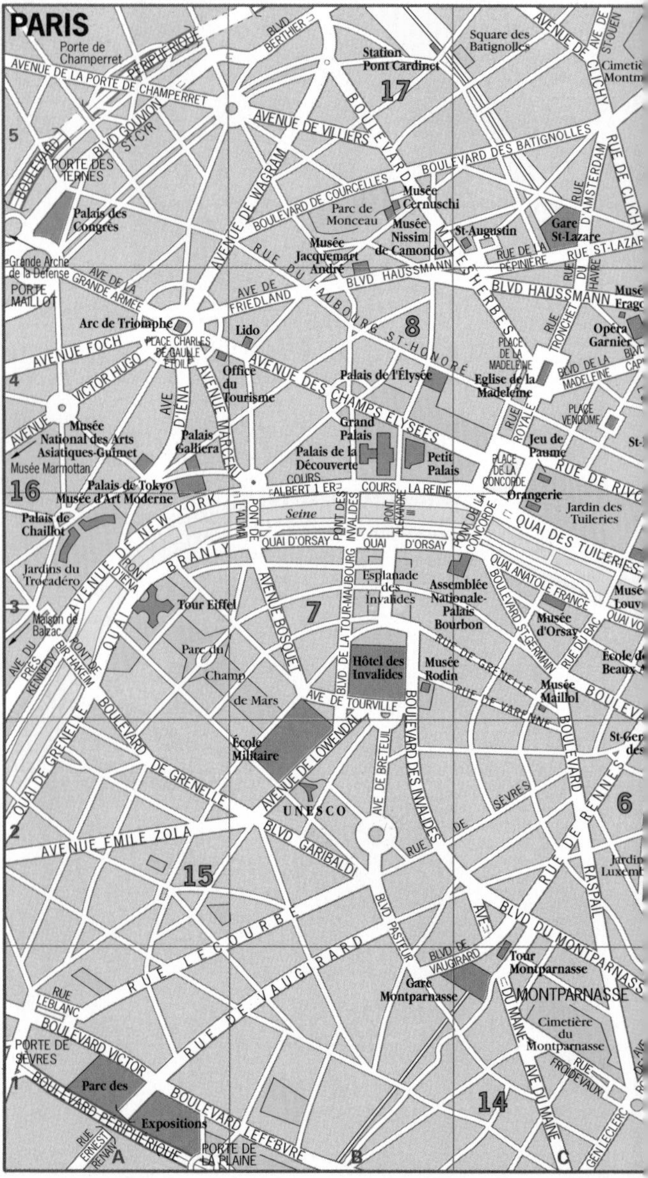

PARIS

Porte de Champerret
Avenue de la Porte de Champerret
Périphérique
Blvd Berthier
Station Pont Cardinet
Square des Batignolles
Avenue de Clichy
Ave de St-Ouen
17
Avenue de Villiers
Boulevard Malesherbes
Boulevard des Batignolles
Rue d'Amsterdam
Rue de Clichy
Blvd Gouvion St-Cyr
Boulevard
Porte des Ternes
Avenue de Wagram
Boulevard de Courcelles
Parc de Monceau
Musée Cernuschi
Musée Nissim de Camondo
St-Augustin
Gare St-Lazare
Palais des Congrès
Musée Jacquemart André
Rue de la Pépinière
Rue St-Lazare
Grande Arche de la Défense
Porte Maillot
Ave de la Grande Armée
Ave de Friedland
Blvd Haussmann
Rue du Havre
Rue du Faubourg St-Honoré
Rue Tronchet
Opéra Garnier
Arc de Triomphe
Place Charles de Gaulle Étoile
Lido
8
Avenue Foch
Avenue Victor Hugo
Office du Tourisme
Avenue des Champs Élysées
Palais de l'Élysée
Place de la Madeleine
Eglise de la Madeleine
Blvd de la Madeleine
Place Vendôme
Ave d'Iéna
Avenue Marceau
Musée National des Arts Asiatiques-Guimet
Palais Galliera
Grand Palais
Palais de la Découverte
Petit Palais
Rue Royale
Jeu de Paume
Place de la Concorde
Rue de Rivoli
Musée Marmottan
Palais de Tokyo Musée d'Art Moderne
16
Cours Albert 1er
Cours la Reine
Orangerie
Jardin des Tuileries
Palais de Chaillot
Avenue de New York
Seine
Pont de l'Alma
Pont des Invalides
Pont Alexandre III
Pont de la Concorde
Quai des Tuileries
Quai d'Orsay
Quai Branly
Jardins du Trocadéro
Pont d'Iéna
Esplanade des Invalides
Assemblée Nationale-Palais Bourbon
Quai Anatole France
Tour Eiffel
Avenue Bosquet
7
Blvd de la Tour-Maubourg
Boulevard St-Germain
Musée d'Orsay
Maison de Balzac
Ave du Président Kennedy
Pont de Bir Hakeim
Quai
Parc du Champ de Mars
Hôtel des Invalides
Musée Rodin
Rue de Grenelle
Rue du Bac
École des Beaux-Arts
Ave de Tourville
Rue de Varenne
Musée Maillol
Boulevard de Grenelle
Quai de Grenelle
École Militaire
Avenue de Lowendal
Ave de Breteuil
Boulevard des Invalides
Boulevard Raspail
UNESCO
Rue de Sèvres
Rue de Rennes
6
Avenue Émile Zola
Blvd Garibaldi
Jardin du Luxembourg
15
Blvd Pasteur
Blvd du Montparnasse
Rue Lecourbe
Rue de Vaugirard
Blvd de Vaugirard
Tour Montparnasse
Gare Montparnasse
Montparnasse
Rue Leblanc
Rue du Maine
Cimetière du Montparnasse
Rue Froidevaux
Porte de Sèvres
Boulevard Victor
Parc des Expositions
Boulevard Lefebvre
Avenue du Maine
14
Boulevard Périphérique
Rue Ernest Renan
Porte de la Plaine
Gen Leclerc
A
B
C
1
2
3
4
5

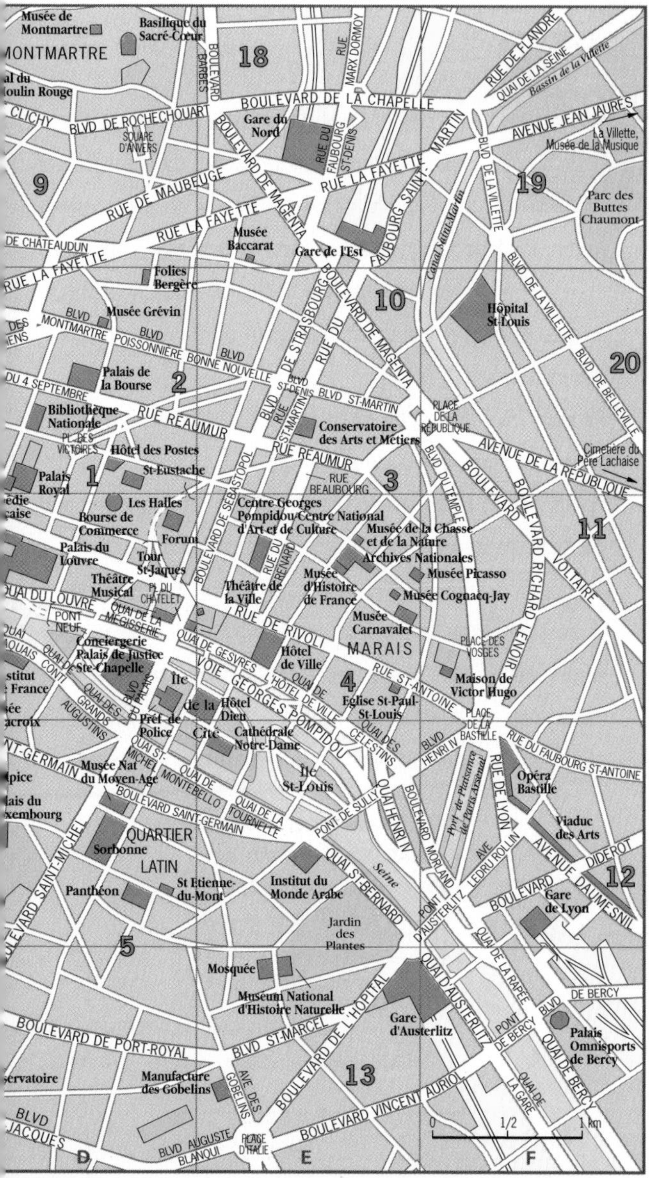

Musée de Montmartre
Basilique du Sacré-Cœur
MONTMARTRE
18
BOULEVARD BARBES
RUE MARX DORMOY
RUE DE FLANDRE
QUAI DE LA SEINE
Bassin de la Villette
Bal du Moulin Rouge
BOULEVARD DE LA CHAPELLE
CLICHY
BLVD DE ROCHECHOUART
SQUARE D'ANVERS
Gare du Nord
RUE DU FAUBOURG ST-DENIS
AVENUE JEAN JAURES
La Villette, Musée de la Musique
BLVD DE LA VILLETTE
9
RUE DE MAUBEUGE
BOULEVARD DE MAGENTA
RUE LA FAYETTE
FAUBOURG SAINT-MARTIN
19
Parc des Buttes Chaumont
Canal Saint-Martin
DE CHATEAUDUN
RUE LA FAYETTE
Musée Baccarat
Gare de l'Est
Folies Bergère
10
Hôpital St-Louis
BOULEVARD DE STRASBOURG
RUE DU
BOULEVARD DE MAGENTA
Musée Grévin
BLVD MONTMARTRE
BLVD POISSONNIÈRE
BLVD BONNE NOUVELLE
20
BLVD DE BELLEVILLE
Palais de la Bourse
2
DU 4 SEPTEMBRE
BLVD ST-DENIS
BLVD ST-MARTIN
PLACE DE LA RÉPUBLIQUE
Bibliothèque Nationale
RUE RÉAUMUR
RUE ST-MARTIN
Conservatoire des Arts et Métiers
PL. DES VICTOIRES
Hôtel des Postes
RUE RÉAUMUR
AVENUE DE LA RÉPUBLIQUE
Cimetière du Père Lachaise
Palais Royal
1
St-Eustache
RUE BEAUBOURG
3
Les Halles
Centre Georges Pompidou/Centre National d'Art et de Culture
BLVD DU TEMPLE
BOULEVARD VOLTAIRE
11
Bourse de Commerce
Forum
Musée de la Chasse et de la Nature
Archives Nationales
BOULEVARD RICHARD LENOIR
Palais du Louvre
Tour St-Jacques
BOULEVARD DE SEBASTOPOL
RUE DU RENARD
Musée Picasso
Théâtre Musical
PL. DU CHÂTELET
Théâtre de la Ville
Musée d'Histoire de France
Musée Cognacq-Jay
QUAI DU LOUVRE
QUAI DE LA MÉGISSERIE
PONT NEUF
RUE DE RIVOLI
Musée Carnavalet
MARAIS
PLACE DES VOSGES
Conciergerie
Palais de Justice
Ste-Chapelle
QUAI DE GESVRES
Hôtel de Ville
VOIE GEORGES POMPIDOU
QUAI DE L'HÔTEL DE VILLE
4
RUE ST-ANTOINE
Maison de Victor Hugo
Institut de France
QUAI DE CONTI
BLVD DU PALAIS
Île de la Cité
Hôtel Dieu
Eglise St-Paul-St-Louis
QUAI DES GRANDS AUGUSTINS
Préf. de Police
Cathédrale Notre-Dame
QUAI DES CÉLESTINS
PLACE DE LA BASTILLE
RUE DU FAUBOURG ST-ANTOINE
BLVD ST-GERMAIN
Musée Nat du Moyen-Age
QUAI ST-MICHEL
QUAI DE MONTEBELLO
Île St-Louis
BLVD HENRI IV
Port de Plaisance de Paris Arsenal
Opéra Bastille
RUE DE LYON
Palais du Luxembourg
BOULEVARD SAINT-GERMAIN
QUAI DE LA TOURNELLE
PONT DE SULLY
QUAI HENRI IV
BOULEVARD MORLAND
Viaduc des Arts
AVE LEDRU ROLLIN
AVENUE DAUMESNIL
DIDEROT
QUARTIER LATIN
Sorbonne
Seine
12
BOULEVARD SAINT-MICHEL
Panthéon
St Etienne-du-Mont
Institut du Monde Arabe
QUAI ST-BERNARD
PONT D'AUSTERLITZ
BOULEVARD
Gare de Lyon
Jardin des Plantes
5
QUAI DE LA RAPÉE
Mosquée
Muséum National d'Histoire Naturelle
QUAI D'AUSTERLITZ
BLVD DE BERCY
Gare d'Austerlitz
PONT DE BERCY
Palais Omnisports de Bercy
BOULEVARD DE PORT-ROYAL
BLVD ST-MARCEL
BOULEVARD DE L'HÔPITAL
QUAI DE BERCY
13
Observatoire
Manufacture des Gobelins
AVE DES GOBELINS
BOULEVARD VINCENT AURIOL
QUAI DE LA GARE
0 1/2 1 km
BLVD ST-JACQUES
BLVD AUGUSTE BLANQUI
PLACE D'ITALIE
D
E
F

Paris

The city of Paris has always played its role of capital of France to the full. It is the place where the French nation's future is decided, where revolutions began in the past and where major political, economic and social changes are traditionally launched. This is as true today as it ever was, in spite of many attempts at decentralisation.

Parisian life reflects the city's leading role in many different ways: the numerous trade exhibitions and international conferences taking place every year testify to its economic and potitical dynamism and healthy competitive spirit. Paris is continually on the move in all fields of human activity: its architectural heritage is constantly expanding and it is proudly setting new trends in the arts, in gastronomy and in fashion. Paris is also a cosmopolitan metropolis where many ethnic groups find the necessary scope to express their differences.

'If you are lucky enough to have lived in Paris as a young man, then wherever you go for the rest of your life, it stays with you, for Paris is a movable feast.'

ERNEST HEMINGWAY
A Movable Feast (1964)

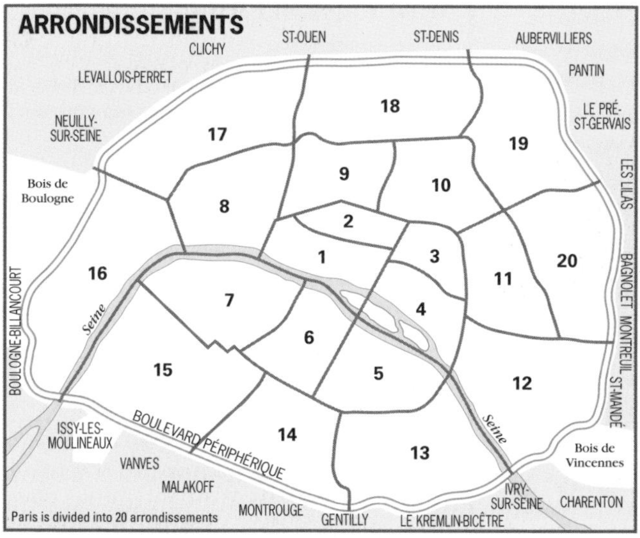

Paris is divided into 20 arrondissements

Exploring Paris

It is tempting for visitors to allow themselves to be whisked off from one major sight to the next without ever getting the feel of the true Paris. You must wander off the beaten track to discover the city's hidden assets, which are often tucked away around unexpected corners.

To get the best out of Paris, you should travel by métro or bus from one main area to the next and then explore the neighbourhood on foot.

Each district has its own characteristics: Montmartre and Montparnasse are associated with artists while the Marais is inhabited by a trendy middle class; the splendid mansions of the Faubourg St-Germain have been taken over by government ministries but St-Germain-des-Prés and the Quartier Latin are still the favourite haunt of intellectuals and students. There are also several colourful ethnic areas: Chinatown in the 13th *arrondissement*, the African district north of the Gare du Nord and the Jewish quarter in the Marais.

Some areas are best avoided at night: around the Gare du Nord, Les Halles and the Grands Boulevards between République and Richelieu-Drouot.

La Marseillaise frieze on the Arc De Triomphe

What to See in Paris

PONT ALEXANDRE III ✪

28B3
Cours La Reine/Quai d'Orsay
Invalides, Champs-Elysées-Clémenceau
63, 83

This is Paris's most ornate bridge, inaugurated for the 1900 World Exhibition and named after the Tsar of Russia to celebrate the Franco-Russian alliance. Its sole arch (107m) spanning the Seine is in line with the Invalides on the Left Bank while, on the Right Bank, the avenue Winston Churchill leads straight to the Champs-Elysées, passing the Grand and Petit Palais. The bridge is decorated with exuberant allegorical sculptures surmounted by gilt horses.

ARC DE TRIOMPHE ✪✪✪

28A4
Place Charles de Gaulle, 75008 Paris
01 55 37 73 77
Oct–Mar: 10AM– 10:30PM; Apr–Sep: 10AM–11PM, closed 1 Jan, 1 May, 25 Dec
Choice of restaurants near by (€–€€€)
Charles de Gaulle-Etoile
73
Very good
Moderate
Video, shops

This stately monument stands in the middle of the circular place Charles de Gaulle, formerly known as the place de l'Etoile because of the 12 avenues that radiate from it. Commissioned by Napoleon, it was completed by France's last reigning monarch and finally dedicated to the memory of an unknown soldier of the Republic who died during World War I.

Looking at the harmonious proportions of its familiar silhouette and its splendid carvings you forget its megalomaniac origins. It stands in line with two other arches – the Arc de Triomphe du Carrousel near the Louvre and the Grande Arche de la Défense. At 50m high, the Arc de Triomphe is twice the height of the former and only half that of the latter.

From the top there is a 360 degree panorama, with, in the foreground, the 12 avenues reaching out like tentacles towards the city beyond.

A ceremony takes place at the Arc de Triomphe every Armistice Day

ARMÉE, MUSÉE DE L' **(➤ 19)**

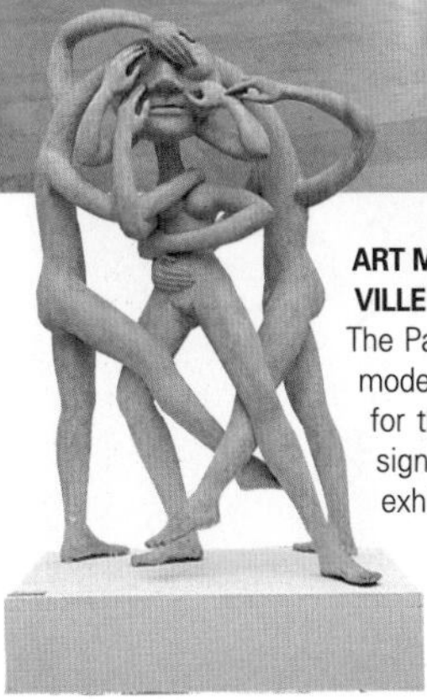

ART MODERNE DE LA VILLE DE PARIS, MUSÉE D'

The Palais de Tokyo housing the modern art collections was built for the 1937 World Exhibition; significantly, one of the main exhibits is a huge work called *La Fée Electricité* , painted by Raoul Dufy for the 'Light pavilion' at the Exhibition. Most of the major artisitic trends of the 20th century are represented; During the restructuring of the museum, part of its collections are exhibited in other museums and local town halls throughout the capital; phone for details or consult the museum's website.

www.mam.paris.fr
28A4
11 avenue du Président Wilson, 75116 Paris
01 53 67 40 00
Closed for restructuring, reopening 2005
Cafe (€)
Iéna, Alma-Marceau
32, 42, 63, 72, 80, 92
Very good
Inexpensive
Guided tours (reservations necessary)

Exciting exhibits at the Musée d'Art Moderne

ARTS ASIATIQUES-GUIMET, MUSÉE NATIONAL DES/PANTHÉON BOUDDHIQUE

The renovated and extended Musée Guimet is now one of the most outstanding museums of Asian art in the world. Its collections, spanning 5,000 years, illustrate all the major civilisations of the Asian continent, with special emphasis on calligraphy, painting, gold plate and textiles. In addition, carefully restored monumental works from Cambodia and Afghanistan are on display for the first time.

www.museeguimet.fr
28A4
Museum: 6 place d'Iéna; Panthéon Bouddhique: 19 avenue d'Iéna, 75116
01 56 52 53 00
Wed–Mon 10–6
Boissiére, Iéna
22, 30, 32, 63, 82
Excellent Moderate

ARTS DÉCORATIFS, MUSÉE DES

Founded in the 19th century in order to display 'Beauty in function', the Museum of decorative arts, housed in the Marsan wing of the Louvre, is gradually reopening its departments after undergoing major restructuring. The Medieval and Renaissance collections include remarkable altarpieces, religious paintings, 16th-century stained glass objects of daily life, as well as fine tapestries exhibited in rotaiton. The reopening of the remaining 17th-, 18th-, 19th- and 20th-century collections is scheduled for 2005.

www.ucad.fr
28C3
107 rue de Rivoli; 75001
01 44 55 57 50
Tue–Fri 11–6, Sat–Sun 10–6
The main Louvre near by
Good Palais-Royal
21, 27, 39, 48, 67, 69, 72, 81
Inexpensive

ARTS ET MÉTIERS-TECHNIQUES, MUSÉE DES NATIONAL

Entirely renovated, this museum is devoted to the artistic aspect of scientific and technical achievements.

29E4 60 rue Réaumur, 75003 Paris 01 53 01 82 00
Tue–Sun 10–6 (Thu to 9.30pm) Moderate

One of the historical figures decorating the Palais-Bourbon, seat of the Assemblée Nationale

ASSEMBLÉE NATIONALE PALAIS-BOURBON ✪

- 28C3
- 33 quai d'Orsay, 75007
- 01 40 63 60 00
- Guided tours only Sat 10AM, 2PM, 3PM; closed bank hols and when Parliament is sitting
- Assemblée Nationale
- 63, 83, 84, 94
- Very good Free
- Shops

The façade of this neo-classical building, housing the lower house of the French parliament, echoes that of the Madeleine across the place de la Concorde. Completed by Louis XV's famous architect Gabriel, the Palais-Bourbon still bears the name of the French royal family to whom it once belonged. Guided tours (identity document required) include the chamber, where members of parliament sit on benches arranged in semicircular tiers, several reception rooms and the library, richly decorated by Delacroix.

BACCARAT, MUSÉE ✪

- 29E5
- 11 place des Etats-Unis, 75016 Paris
- 01 40 22 11 00
- 10–7; closed Sun and Tue
- Château d'Eau
- 32, 38 48
- None Inexpensive
- Guided tours, shops

The prestigious collections of Baccarat crystal are housed in one of the last 19th-century post-houses in Paris. More than one thousand pieces illustrate the evolution of styles and manufacturing techniques since 1764: vases, chandeliers, perfume bottles and various other objects including candelabra ordered by Tsar Nicholas II of Russia. The most fascinating exhibits are probably the unique pieces specially created by Baccarat for various World Exhibitions since 1855.

BALZAC, MAISON DE ✪

www.paris.fr

- Off map 28A3
- 47 rue Raynouard, 75016
- 01 55 74 41 80
- Tue–Sun 10–6; closed public hols
- Passy, La Muette
- 52, 70, 72 None
- Free
- Guided tours, bookshop

This is the house in which Honoré de Balzac lived from 1840 to 1847, while he was writing the series of novels *La Comédie Humaine*. The house contains numerous mementoes of his life and work, such as manuscripts, letters, original drawings and prints and a plaster cast that Rodin used as a study for the monumental statue now standing in Montparnasse. Balzac used the backdoor in the picturesque rue Berton when he needed to avoid the bailiffs!

BASTILLE ✪✪

The place de la Bastille is forever associated with the French Revolution, since it was here that it all began. The dreaded fortress was stormed by the people of Paris on 14 July 1789 and later razed to the ground; its outline can be seen on the paving stones covering the entire square. In the centre stands a 50m-high column erected in memory of the victims of the 1830 and 1848 Revolutions, who were buried beneath the base and whose names are carved on the shaft. The column is surmounted by the gilt winged figure of the *Spirit of Liberty* by Dumont.

The new Paris opera house, one of President Mitterrand's 'Grands projets', was inaugurated for the bicentenary of the 1789 Revolution. It was the subject of bitter controversy from the start as running costs proved too high for an establishment intended as a popular opera house. Designed by the Canadian architect Carlos Ott, the **Opéra National de Paris-Bastille** is a harmonious building with a curved façade in several shades of grey that glitters in the sun and gently glows at night. The acoustics of the main auditorium, which can accommodate 2,700 spectators, are superb and the stage is one of the most sophisticated in the world.

Just south of the opera house, a disused railway viaduct has been converted into a series of workshops and showrooms illustrating a number of traditional crafts known as the **Viaduc des Arts**; the Ateliers du Cuivre et de l'Argent (copper and silver workshops) are particularly interesting and there is a small museum.

29F2

Opéra National de Paris-Bastille

- Place de la Bastille, 75012 Paris
- Recorded information: 01 40 01 19 70
- Listen to the recorded information; closed Sun
- Bar
- Bastille
- 20, 29, 65, 69, 76, 86, 87, 91
- Good · Moderate
- Guided tours, shops

Viaduc des Arts

- 9–129 avenue Daumesnil, 75012 Paris
- Variable; most workshops open Sun
- Near by (€)
- Bastille, Ledru-Rollin, Reuilly-Diderot

Above: *the Bastille monument*

Left: *the Governor of the Bastille being led to the town hall by the revolutionaries*

Food & Drink

In France, eating is an art that reaches its highest expression in Paris, for here the diversity and know-how of traditional regional cuisine are combined with a creative spirit stimulated by a strong cosmopolitan influence. In recent years, a growing awareness of the need for healthier living has prompted the invention of *nouvelle cuisine* and contributed to change the Parisians' eating habits.

Musée du Vin

- 5 square Charles Dickens, 75016 Paris
- 01 45 25 63 26
- Tue–Sun 10–6
- Nice bistro (€)
- Passy
- Good
- Moderate; free for visitors eating in the restaurant
- Maison de Balzac (➤ 34)
- Guided tours, bookshop, gift shop

Opposite: *watching the world go by from pavement cafés is a national pastime; traditional baguettes, bought daily;* tarte au citron, *a popular dessert; expresso coffee – small, dark and strong*

Below: *fresh fish in Le Marais*

Eating Parisian Style

The traditional French breakfast of bread, butter and jam with a large cup of *café au lait* (white coffee) has to a large extent given way to cereals and milk with black coffee, tea or chocolate. The traditional fresh croissants are often a weekend treat, when people breakfast *en famille*.

The majority of working people have lunch out. Cafés and bistros overflow onto the pavements in spring and summer and overworked waiters are continually calling out *un steak frites* (steak and chips) at the tops of their voices, as Parisians order their favourite lunchtime dish. Some of the trendiest places to have lunch are *bars à huîtres* (oyster bars, serving a variety of seafood) and cyber cafés where you can have a snack and a drink while surfing the Internet!

Dinner at home around 8PM is the first relaxing meal of the day, enjoyed with family or friends; it starts with hors-d'oeuvre, finishes with cheese or a sweet and may include a freshly prepared dish bought from a local *traiteur* (delicatessen), accompanied by a glass of wine.

Shopping for Food

Parisians are still very fond of their local street markets where they can buy fresh vegetables and fruit as well as cheese, charcuterie, fish and meat. One traditional item which is still going strong is the *baguette*, the light and crisp bread that is better in Paris than anywhere else in France!

Eating Out

Eating out is one of the Parisians' favourite forms of entertainment as conviviality is as important as the food itself. Friday night and Saturday night are the most popular evenings, while families with children tend to go out for Sunday lunch. Parisian cuisine includes a wide choice of regional and traditional dishes, although the tendency nowadays is to lighten sauces. Typical Parisian dishes are *soupe à l'oignon gratinée* (onion soup *au gratin*) and *pieds de cochon* (grilled pig's trotters), traditionally eaten near Les Halles when this was the chief food market in Paris. Oysters and seafood in general are also very popular, judging by the numerous take-away seafood stalls outside restaurants in the city centre.

Wine is a must with any good meal, preceded by an aperitif, which may consist of port, whisky or champagne. A *digestif* (brandy, Cointreau or any other liqueur) is served with coffee at the end of the meal.

Musée du Vin

Anyone interested in wine should visit this museum, appropriately housed in the old cellars of Passy Abbey. It illustrates the history of wine in France and the main wine-producing areas, and has a collection of tools, bottles, and wax figures. An added inducement is the opportunity for some wine-tasting.

The Galerie Vivienne, a charming arcade linked to the Bibliothèque Nationale de France

www.bnf.fr
29D4
Richelieu: 58 rue de Richelieu, 75002 Paris; François Mitterrand: quai François Mauriac, 75013 Paris
Richelieu: 01 53 79 59 59 rguided tours: 01 53 79 86 87; François Mitterrand: 01 53 79 59 59
Richelieu: Galeries and Crypt: Tue–Sat 10–7, Sun 12–7. Cabinet des Médailles: daily 1–5; Sun 12–6. François Mitterrand: visits of the building on Tue–Sat 2, Sun 3 by appointment only.
Richelieu: restaurant in Galerie Vivienne (€)
Richelieu: Bourse, Palais-Royal-Musée du Louvre; François Mitterrand: Quai de la Gare
Richelieu: 29, 39, 48; François Mitterrand: 62, 89
Very good
Richelieu: moderate; François Mitterrand: free

BIBLIOTHÈQUE NATIONALE DE FRANCE

The national library is seen by the French as a symbol of their culture. Until 1996, the BN, as Parisians call it, was housed in Cardinal Mazarin's former palace situated at the back of the Palais-Royal, extended many times and now stretching from the rue de Richelieu to the rue Vivienne. However, with around 13 million books and as many prints and photographs, it had long been overcrowded. The building of a new library along the river in the 13th arrondissement was President Mitterrand's last 'Grand Projet'. The BNF, as it is now called, occupies two sites known as 'Richelieu' and 'François Mitterrand'.

The new library houses the huge stock of printed books and documents and is intended to serve as a public library and a research centre equipped with the most modern means of data transmission. Four corner towers looking like open books surround an imposing base with a central garden where the reading rooms are situated.

The Richelieu building houses manuscripts, prints and medals and holds exhibitions in the Galerie Mansart (Galerie de Photographie), the Galerie Mazarine (which has a magnificent painted ceiling) and the Crypte. The Cabinet des Médailles et des Antiques displays coins and medals from antiquity to the present day as well as *objets d'art*, cameos and bronzes from the former royal collections.

Two charming arcades linked to the library, the Galerie Vivienne and the Galerie Colbert, offer an unexpected insight into Parisian social life in the 19th century.

CARNAVALET, MUSÉE ✪✪

This museum retraces the history of Paris from antiquity to the present day, and is worth visiting for the building alone: a beautiful Renaissance mansion, one of the oldest in Le Marais, remodelled in the 17th century. The Hôtel Carnavalet was the residence of diarist, Madame de Sévigné, who depicted Parisian society at the time of Louis XIV with a great deal of humour. Note the 16th-century lions guarding the entrance and Louis XIV's statue by Coysevox in the centre of the courtyard. In 1989, the museum was linked to the nearby Hôtel Le Peletier de St Fargeau, which dates from the late 17th century. The Hôtel Carnavalet deals with the period from the origins of the city to 1789, with mementoes of Madame de Sévigné and splendid Louis XV and Louis XVI furniture. The Hôtel Le Peletier de St Fargeau houses collections from 1789 to the present day. The Revolution is extensively illustrated, while the 19th and 20th centuries are represented by a number of reconstructions such as Marcel Proust's bedroom and the art nouveau reception room of the Café de Paris.

29E3
23 rue de Sévigné, 75003 Paris
01 44 59 58 58
Tue–Sun 10–6; closed some public hols
Restaurants and cafés near by in rue des Francs-Bourgeois (€–€€€)
Saint-Paul
29, 96
Some weehlchair access; tel: 01 44 59 58 31
Free, except for some temporary exhibitions
Guided tours, shops

The courtyard of the Musée Carnavalet

CENTRE GEORGES POMPIDOU (► 16, TOP TEN)

CERNUSCHI, MUSÉE ✪

The banker and art collector Henri Cernuschi bequeathed his elegant private mansion to the city of Paris at the end of the 19th century. Situated on the edge of the parc Monceau, the building houses Cernuschi's superb collection of ancient Chinese art on the ground floor (terra-cottas, bronzes, jades and ceramics) and contemporary traditional Chinese paintings on the first floor.

28B5
7 avenue Velasquez, 75008 Paris
01 45 63 50 75
Closed for restructuring until 2005
Villiers  30, 94
Good Inexpensive

Magnificent bronzes, pools and fountains front the Palais de Chaillot

www.mnhn.fr
www.musee-marine.fr
28A3
Place du Trocadéro, 75116 Paris
Musée de l'Homme: 01 44 05 72 72; Musée de la Marine: 01 53 65 69 69
Musée de l'Homme: Mon, Wed–Fri 9:45–5:15,Sat–Sun 10–6:30; closed bank hols. Musée de la Marine: Wed–Mon 10–6; closed 1 Jan, 1 May, 25 Dec
Trocadéro
22, 30, 32, 63, 72, 82
Musée de l'Homme: none; Musée de la Marine: good
Both museums: moderate
Both museums have a bookshop; guided tours in Musée de la Marine

CHAILLOT, PALAIS DE

This imposing architectural complex on top of a hill overlooking the river and facing the Tour Eiffel across the pont d'Iéna offers magnificent views and houses two interesting museums.

Designed for the 1937 World Exhibition, the building consists of two separate pavilions with curved wings, on either side of a vast terrace decorated with monumental statues. Just below, the tiered Jardins du Trocadéro extend to the edge of the river. The ornamental fountain is particularly impressive at night when the powerful spray of water shines under the spotlights.

The Musée de l'Homme, devoted to Man as a species, is being restructured over five years. Meanwhile, three exhibitions give a foretaste of what the new museum will be like: La Nuit des Temps (the human adventure), Six milliards d'hommes (the growth of the world's population) and Tous parents, tous différents (the similarities and diversity of mankind).

The Musée de la Marine is devoted to French maritime history from the 18th century onwards. The extensive collections show the development of navigational skills and include beautiful models of 18th-century sailing ships; they also provide an insight into the modern navy and retrace the history of maritime transport and great expeditions across the world.

The east wing was seriously damaged by fire in 1997 and the two museums it contained are now closed. The Musée des Monuments Français will reopen once building work has finished, whereas the Musée du Cinéma Henri Langlois will probably move to new premises in the former American Center in Bercy.

CHAMPS-ELYSÉES, LES (➤ 17, TOP TEN)

CHASE ET DE LA NATURE, MUSÉE DE LA (➤ 56)

Did you know ?

The eight bridges linking the island to the river banks were destroyed and rebuilt many times. Some of them, however, have retained their medieval names: the Pont au Change was the place where foreigners exchanged their currency before entering Paris while the name of the Pont au Double refers to the toll levied on crossing the bridge.

CITÉ, ILE DE LA ✪✪✪

The Ile de la Cité is not only the historic centre of Paris, it is also a place of exceptional natural beauty and an architectural gem.

The Celtic tribe the Parisii settled on the largest island in an area known as Lutetia, which under the Romans expanded onto the Left Bank of the Seine. Nevertheless, the island (the Cité), which the king of the Franks chose as his capital in 508, remained for 1,000 years the seat of royal, judicial and religious power. During the Middle Ages, the Ile de la Cité was an important intellectual centre as its cathedral schools attracted students from all over Europe. Even after the kings of France left the royal palace for larger premises on the right bank, the Cité lost none of its symbolic importance and remains to this day the 'guardian' of 2,000 years of history.

The appearance of the Cité has, of course, changed considerably over the years; in the 19th century, the centre of the island was cleared and the vast square in front of Notre-Dame Cathedral created. At the other end of the island, the Conciergerie (➤ 44) and Sainte-Chapelle (➤ 73) are the only remaining parts of the medieval royal palace, now incorporated in the huge Palais de Justice.

- 29E2
- Ile de la Cité, 75001 and 75004 Paris
- Restaurants and cafés (€–€€) on the island and on the Right and Left banks
- Cité, Pont Neuf, St-Michel, Châtelet, Hôtel de Ville
- 21, 24, 27, 38, 47, 58, 70, 85, 96

A view of Ile de la Cité and pont Neuf

A Walk Along the Seine & On the Islands

This relatively compact area offers stately historic buildings, breathtaking views, provincial charm and the liveliness of a great city.

Start from the place du Châtelet on the Right Bank.

The monumental fountain was commissioned by Napoleon on his return from Egypt.

Walk along the quai de Gesvres, then across the pont Notre-Dame.

The flower market on the place Louis Lépine is a refreshing sight. On Sunday, flowers are replaced by birds.

Walk east along the embankment, turn right into rue des Ursins then left and left again.

The narrow streets of the medieval cathedral precinct have some old houses. At the tip of the island is an underground memorial to the victims of Nazi concentration camps.

Cross over to the Ile Saint-Louis and turn left, following the quai de Bourbon.

Enjoy the peaceful atmosphere of this sought-after residential area (➤ 72).

Turn right into rue des Deux Ponts and cross over to the Left Bank. Walk west to the square Viviani then cross rue St-Jacques into rue St-Séverin.

This is one of the oldest parts of the Quartier Latin. The Gothic Church of St-Séverin has a magnificent interior.

From the place St-Michel, cross back on to the Ile de la Cité.

Sainte-Chapelle (➤ 73) is very close. The place Dauphine at the western end of the island is another haven of peace. Admire the view from the pont Neuf, Paris's oldest bridge.

Cross over to the Right Bank and the pont Neuf métro station.

Distance
4km

Time
2–4 hours depending on church visits

Start point
Place du Châtelet
29D3
Châtelet or 21, 38, 85, 96

End point
Pont Neuf
29D3
Pont Neuf or 21, 58, 67, 70

Lunch
Le Vieux Bistrot
14 rue du Cloître-Notre-Dame, 75004 Paris
01 43 54 18 95

Left: *Pont Neuf*
Below: *Place du Châtelet salutes Napoleon's Egyptian campaign*

Macabre associations always attract crowds, and La Conciergerie, Paris's oldest prison, is no exception

29E3
Hôtel Donon, 8 rue Elzévir, 75003 Paris
01 40 27 07 21
10–6; closed Mon and public hols
Near by (€–€€)
Saint-Paul 29, 96
None Free
Guided tours, bookshop

COGNACQ-JAY, MUSÉE

The collections of 18th-century European art bequeathed to the city of Paris by Ernest Cognacq and his wife Louise Jay, founders of the Samaritaine department stores, are displayed in one of the beautiful mansions of Le Marais. The refinement of the Enlightenment period is illustrated by the works of French artists Watteau, Chardin, Fragonard and La Tour, and also by Tiepolo, Guardi and Reynolds. The Rembrandt adds a welcome contrasting note. Various *objets d'art*, including Saxe and Sèvres porcelain, are exhibited in glass cabinets.

28D3
2 boulevard du Palais, 75001 Paris
01 53 40 60 97
Daily 9:30–6; closed 1 Jan, 1 May, 25 Dec
Cité, Châtelet
21, 24, 27, 38, 58, 85, 81, 85, 96, Balabus
None
Moderate
Guided tours, bookshop

LA CONCIERGERIE

For most people, the name 'Conciergerie' suggests crowds of innocent prisoners waiting to be taken to the guillotine. Nowadays, its familiar round towers covered with conical slate roofs and the square clock tower, which housed the first public clock in Paris, are one of the most picturesque sights of the Ile de la Cité. The Conciergerie is the last remaining authentic part of a 14th-century royal complex, administered by a 'concierge' or governor. The twin towers marked the main entrance to the palace. In the late 14th century, the Conciergerie was turned into a prison but it only acquired a sinister connotation during the Revolution, when it held a number of famous prisoners, including Queen Marie-Antoinette, Madame du Barry and the poet André Chénier, as well as Danton and Robespierre.

The visit includes the original guards' room, a magnificent great hall with Gothic vaulting and kitchens with monumental fireplaces. There is also a reconstruction of Marie-Antoinette's cell.

CONCORDE, PLACE DE LA ✪✪✪

This is undoubtedly the most impressive square in Paris: its stately elegance, its size and its magnificent views are simply breathtaking. Built in the mid-18th century to celebrate Louis XV 'the beloved', it was designed by Gabriel who erected two classical pavilions on either side of the rue Royale; its octagonal shape is emphasised by eight allegorical statues representing major French cities.

The pink granite obelisk from Luxor, offered to the French nation by the viceroy of Egypt in 1836, is at the centre of the square, flanked by two graceful fountains. Two magnificent vistas open up: one towards the Champs-Elysées and Le Louvre beyond the beautiful gates of the Jardin des Tuileries, the other towards the Madeleine at the end of the rue Royale and the Assemblée Nationale across the pont de la Concorde.

28C4
75008 Paris
Concorde
42, 73, 84, 94

Decorative architecture and statuary (left and above) grace place de la Concorde

EUGÈNE DELACROIX, MUSÉE NATIONAL ✪

The old-world charm of the tiny rue de Furstenberg, hidden behind the Church of St-Germain-des-Prés, is the perfect setting for a museum devoted to one of the major French Romantic painters. Delacroix lived and worked here until the end of his life and, besides a few paintings, the place is full of mementoes of the artist, letters, sketches...and his palette. There is also a bookshop. It is well worth taking time to explore the picturesque neighbourhood and the open market in rue de Buci.

www.musee-delacroix.fr
29D3
6 rue de Furstenberg, 75006 Paris
01 44 41 86 50
9:30–5; closed Tue and public holidays
St-Germain-des-Prés
39, 48, 63, 95
None Inexpensive

FAUBOURG ST-GERMAIN ✪✪

28C3
75007 Paris
For the museums' opening times, see the relevant entries
Cafés and restaurants near by in boulevard St-Germain (€–€€)
Varenne, Rue du Bac
69, 83, 84, 94

This 'suburb' is today one of the most elegant districts of central Paris.

Its name came from the nearby Abbaye de St-Germain-des-Prés to which it belonged in medieval times. University students loved to stroll through fields and meadows stretching down to the river west of the abbey and the area remained in its natural state until the 18th century, when it became fashionable for the aristocracy and the wealthy middle class to have mansions built there by the famous architects of the time. Today, a few streets have retained some of their past elegance even though most of the mansions have now been taken over by ministries and foreign embassies.

The rue de Varenne (a distortion of *garenne*, the French word for warren, which confirms the area's rural origins!), is lined with the famous Hôtel Matignon, built in 1721 and now the Prime Minister's residence, and the Hôtel Biron, better known as the Musée Rodin (➤ 70). The parallel rue de Grenelle is equally interesting for its wealth of authentic architecture, including the Hôtel de Villars, which is now the town hall of the 7th *arrondissement*. Further along the street, on the opposite side, there is an interesting museum (No 59) devoted to the sculptor Maillol (➤ 55) and, next to it, the beautiful Fontaine des Quatre Saisons (Fountain of the Four Seasons).

Typical Parisian apartments, four to six storeys high, in Faubourg-St-Germain. Uniformly painted in shades of white and grey, the mansions date from the 17th and 18th centuries

Did you know ?

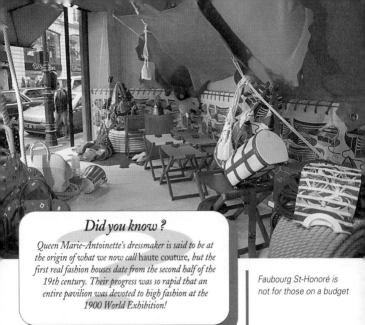

Queen Marie-Antoinette's dressmaker is said to be at the origin of what we now call haute couture, *but the first real fashion houses date from the second half of the 19th century. Their progress was so rapid that an entire pavilion was devoted to high fashion at the 1900 World Exhibition!*

Faubourg St-Honoré is not for those on a budget

FAUBOURG ST-HONORÉ ✪✪

This other 'suburb', this time on the Right Bank, is centred on the very long street of the same name, running parallel to the Champs-Elysées and famous for its *haute couture* establishments and luxury boutiques as well as for the Palais de l'Elysée, the official residence of the French president.

Leading fashion houses have been established in the area for over a hundred years: Louis Féraud, Christian Lacroix and Lanvin are still in the rue du Faubourg St-Honoré, but the majority are now in the avenue Montaigne across the Champs-Elysées. Opposite the British Embassy, No 54 opens into a couple of courtyards surrounded by boutiques selling beautiful furniture, *objets d'art*, paintings etc. Many modern art galleries line the perpendicular avenue Matignon, while the avenue Gabriel, which runs along the Champs-Elysées gardens past the American Embassy, makes a peaceful stroll through this select area.

28B4
75008 Paris
St-Philippe-du-Roule, Madeleine
52
A stamp market takes place near the Rond-Point des Champs-Elysées on Thu, Sat and Sun 9–7

GALLIÉRA, MUSÉE ✪

This museum of fashion is appropriately housed in a neo-Renaissance mansion dating from the late 19th century, the Palais Galliéra. Its rich collections of urban fashion, are shown in temporary exhibitions from the 18th century to the present and are continually being extended with donations from prestigious fashion houses (Dior, Yves St-Laurent) and well-known personalities. In addition to the costumes (several thousands in all), there are etchings and photographs connected with fashion.

Off map 28A4
Palais Galliéra, 10 avenue Pierre Ier de Serbie, 75016 Paris
01 56 52 86 00
10–6; closed Mon
Iéna — 32, 63, 72, 92
None — Moderate
Children's workshops

GOBELINS, MANUFACTURE NATIONALE DES ✪

The former royal tapestry factory, founded by Colbert in 1664 to make beautiful tapestries for the royal household, is still going strong. Priceless works of art, based on paintings by artists such as Le Brun and Boucher and, more recently, Lurçat and Picasso, have been produced in the workshops over the last three centuries. Techniques have hardly changed since the 17th century and looms are either upright (*haute lice* method) or horizontal (*basse lice* method). The 17th-century buildings also house the Savonnerie carpet factory, founded in 1604, and the Beauvais tapestry factory, founded at the same time as the Gobelins.

- 29E1
- 42 avenue des Gobelins, 75013 Paris
- 01 44 54 19 33/ 01 44 08 52 00
- Tue, Wed, Thu guided tours only at 2 and 2:45; closed public hols
- Les Gobelins
- 27, 47, 83, 91
- None
- Moderate

LA GRANDE ARCHE DE LA DÉFENSE (➤ 18, TOP TEN)

GRAND PALAIS ✪✪

Built at the same time as the Pont Alexandre III for the 1900 World Exhibition, this enormous steel and glass structure, concealed behind stone walls, is typical of the *belle époque* style: Ionic columns line the imposing façade and colossal bronze statues decorate the four corners.

Major international art exhibitions – Tutankhamun, Renoir, Gauguin and Picasso, to name but a few – are traditionally held in the Galeries Nationales, on the Champs-Elysées side of the building.

The west part of the Grand Palais houses the Palais de la Découverte, inaugurated in 1937 to bring science within the grasp of the general public and keep them informed of the latest scientific developments. There are interactive experiments, documentary films and a planetarium. Recent additions are the Electrostatic exhibition and the Sun room.

- 28B4
- Galeries Nationales: avenue du Général Eisenhower, 75008 Paris; Palais de la Découverte, avenue Franklin-D-Roosevelt, 75008 Paris
- Galeries Nationales: 01 44 13 17 17; Palais Découverte: 01 56 43 20 21
- Galeries Nationales: variable; Palais Découverte: 9:30–6, Sun 10–7; closed Mon
- Café-bar (€)
- Champs-Elysées-Clemenceau
- 28, 42, 49, 72, 73, 80, 83
- Galeries Nationales: excellent; Palais: none
- Galeries Nationales: variable; Palais Découverte: moderate

Elaborate statues adorn the Grand Palais

The Passage des Panoramas shopping arcade in boulevard Montmartre

GRANDS BOULEVARDS

These busy arteries, stretching from the place de la République to the Madeleine and lined with cinemas, theatres, cafés and shops, have today fallen victim to their long tradition of popular entertainment, choked by traffic jams and disfigured by aggressive neon signs, cheap snack bars and general neglect.

The 'boulevards' were laid out as a tree-lined promenade in the 17th century, when some of the city's medieval fortifications were demolished; two ceremonial arches, the Porte St-Martin and the Porte St-Denis, replaced the town gates.

The popularity of the boulevards peaked during the 19th century, with popular attractions in the east (theatre, dancing, circus and busking) and a more refined choice of entertainment in the west, especially after the building of the opera house. Several shopping arcades were also opened, including the Passage des Panoramas in boulevard Montmartre, opposite **Musée Grévin**, the famous waxworks museum, and at the end of the century, one of the first cinemas was inaugurated in boulevard St-Denis by the Lumière brothers.

Today, the boulevards still attract crowds of cinema- and theatre-goers but their general shabby appearance also encourages a rowdy element, particularly between the Porte St-Martin and the rue de Richelieu. Fortunately, complete renovation is underway.

Grands Boulevards

28C4

From east to west: boulevards St-Martin, St-Denis, de Bonne Nouvelle, Poissonnière, Montmartre, des Italiens, des Capucines and de la Madeleine

République, Strasbourg-St-Denis, Bonne Nouvelle, Rue Montmartre, Richelieu-Drouot, Opéra, Madeleine

Musée Grévin

29D4

10 boulevard Montmartre, 75009 Paris

01 47 70 85 05

Mon–Fri 10–6.30; Sat–Sun 10–7

Near by along the boulevards (€–€€)

Rue Montmartre

20, 48, 74, 85

None Expensive

Shop

In the Know

If you only have a short time to visit Paris, or would like to get a real flavour of the city, here are some ideas:

10 Ways To Be A Local

Stand on the place Charles-de-Gaulle during the rush hour to get the feel of the Parisian pace of life.
Go into a crowded café at lunchtime and rub shoulders with hard-working Parisians.
Go to 'Les Champs' (Champs-Elysées) on Saturday night and meet Parisians enjoying themselves.
Soak in the atmosphere of old Paris along the Canal St-Martin.
Buy a baguette and some cheese in the rue Mouffetard for an outdoor lunch in the nearby square des Arènes de Lutèce.
Sample the village atmosphere in Le Marais on Sunday afternoon, together with thousands of Parisians.
Talk to the *bouquinistes* along the Seine, usually only too willing to comment on local news and people.
Mingle with Parisian youth along boulevard St-Germain.
Learn how to bargain at the Marché aux Puces, Porte de Clignancourt.
Don't talk to a Parisian about local driving.

10 Good Places To Have Lunch

Le Caveau du Palais (€€) ✉ 17 place Dauphine, 1st, ☎ 01 43 26 04 28; view of the lovely place Dauphine.
Brasserie de l'Ile Saint-Louis (€€) ✉ 55 quai de Bourbon, 4th, ☎ 01 43 54 02 59; *choucroute garnie.*
Le Polidor (€) ✉ 41 rue Monsieur-le-Prince, 6th, ☎ 01 43 26 95 34; French cuisine in the heart of the Latin Quarter.
La Victoire Suprême du Coeur (€€) ✉ 41 rue des Bourdonnais, 1st, ☎ 01 40 41 93 95; international vegetarian cuisine.
Georges (€€–€€€) ✉ Centre Pompidou (6th floor), 4th ☎ 01 44 78 47 99; fabulous views of Paris.
Le Toupary (€€) ✉ Samaritaine, 5th floor, 2 quai du Louvre, 1st, ☎ 01 40 41 29 29; panoramic view.
Bofinger (€€) ✉ 5 rue de la Bastille, 4th, ☎ 01 42 72 87 82; *belle époque* setting.
Restaurant du Palais-Royal (€€) ✉ 43 rue de Valois, 1st, ☎ 01 40 20 00 27; overlooking the Jardin du Palais-Royal.
A Priori Thé (€) ✉ 35–7 Galerie Vivienne, 2nd, ☎ 01 42 97 48 75; old-world surroundings.
Altitude 95 (€–€€) ✉ Tour Eiffel 1st floor, Champs de Mars, 7th, ☎ 01 45 55 20 04; brasserie with original airship décor.

10 Top Activities

Walking (pedestrian areas): footpath along the river; quartier Montorgueil north of Les Halles.
Cycle tours: Paris à Vélo, c'est Sympa! 22 rue Alphonse Baudin, 11th, 01 48 87 60 01.
Rowing on the lake in Bois de Boulogne.
Horse riding: Société d'Equitation de Paris, 01 45 01 20 06.
Theme parks: Disneyland Paris (➤ 81), Parc Astérix (➤ 85).
Parc Floral de Paris Bois de Vincennes, 12th; flowers, medicinal plants etc.
Aquaboulevard 4–6 rue Louis-Armand, 15th, 01 40 60 10 00; fun with water.
Hot-air ballooning: Montgolfières Aventures, 01 40 47 61 04.
Roller skating rallies: 01 44 54 07 44; held every Sun.
Leisure park: Base de Plein Air, St-Quentin-en-Yvelines, 01 30 62 20 12, RER C.

10 Bird's-Eye Views

- Tour Eiffel (➤ 25)
- Sacré-Coeur (➤ 70)
- Tour Montparnasse (➤ 62)
- Grande Arche de la Défense (➤ 18)
- Towers of Notre-Dame (➤ 22)
- Arc de Triomphe (➤ 32)
- Dôme of Les Invalides (➤ 19)
- Centre Georges Pompidou (6th floor, ➤ 16)
- Palais de Chaillot (➤ 40)
- Institut du Monde Arabe (➤ 54)

10 Famous and Picturesque Cafés

- Café de la Paix, 12 boulevard des Capucines, Opéra
- Fouquet's, 99 Champs-Elysées, George V
- Café Marly, Le Louvre, Palais-Royal
- Café de Flore, 172 boulevard St-Germain, St-Germain-des-Prés
- Les Deux Magots, 6 place St-Germain-des-Prés, St-Germain-des-Prés
- Le Procope, 13 rue de l'Ancienne-Comédie, Odéon
- Café de la Mairie, 8 place St-Sulpice, St-Sulpice
- Café Martini, 11 rue du Pas de la Mule, Chemin-Vert
- La Closerie des Lilas, 171 boulevard du Montparnasse, Vavin
- Le Sancerre, 35 rue des Abbesses, Abbesses

Forum des Halles

29D3
Rue Pierre Lescot, rue Rambuteau, rue Berger, 75001 Paris
In the complex (€)
Les Halles
29, 38, 47
Lifts to all levels

LES HALLES 

Paris's legendary food market has long gone from the centre of the capital, but the name is here to stay, tinged for many Parisians with a certain nostalgia, for when the 19th-century steel and glass 'pavillons de Baltard' were removed in 1969 and the noisy activity of the market suddenly stopped, the character of this popular district changed beyond recognition. A vast gaping hole was left between one of the most beautiful churches in Paris and a lovely Renaissance fountain. A commercial and cultural complex was built underground with a central patio surrounded by glass-roofed galleries that barely reach ground level. Above ground, a garden was laid over the remaining space, with a children's area and shaded walks and yet more graceful steel and glass structures.

The underground complex, spread over several levels, comprises shops, including a group of young fashion designers (Poste Berger, level –1), restaurants, an auditorium, a gymnasium and a swimming pool, as well as a tropical greenhouse.

A huge stone head leaning against a hand decorates the semicircular paved area in front of the Eglise St-Eustache. The latter was built over a period of a hundred years, in a blend of late Gothic, Renaissance and neo-classical styles. From the church, a path leads across the gardens to the square des Innocents and the beautiful Renaissance fountain, built and carved in the mid-16th century by Pierre Lescot and Jean Goujon, who also worked on the Louvre.

HISTOIRE NATURELLE, MUSÉE NATIONAL D'

(➤ 68)

HOMME, MUSÉE DE L'

(➤ 40)

Eglise St-Eustache, with the incongruous giant head and hand sculpture

Place de l'Hôtel de Ville, formerly called place de Grève (grève *is French for shore)*

Above: *the town hall clock*

HÔTEL DE VILLE

The town hall of the city of Paris has been standing on this site since the 14th century. Destroyed by fire during the Paris Commune in 1871, it was rebuilt almost straight away in neo-Renaissance style. On the exterior are 136 statues representing famous historic figures.

Near by stands the 52m-high Tour St-Jacques, the only remaining part of a demolished church. In 1648, Pascal used the tower to verify his experiments on the weight of air. Later, a meteorological station was set up at the top and the tower became the property of the city of Paris.

On the east side of the town hall, the Eglise St-Gervais-St-Protais is a splendid example of a successful blend of Flamboyant Gothic and classical styles.

29E3
Place de l'Hôtel de Ville, 75004 Paris
01 42 76 54 04
Guided tour by appointment only
Hôtel de Ville
38, 47, 58, 67, 70, 72, 74, 75, 96,
Good
Free

INSTITUT DE FRANCE

The imposing classical building facing the Louvre across the river was commissioned by Cardinal Mazarin, as a school for provincial children, and designed by Le Vau; it is surmounted by a magnificent dome and houses the Institut de France, an institution created in 1795 to unite under one roof five prestigious academies, including the famous (and oldest) Académie Française founded in 1635 by Richelieu. It also houses the Bibliothèque Mazarine, Mazarin's own collection of rare editions.

29D3
23 quai de Conti, 75006 Paris
01 44 41 44 35
Sat, Sun guided tours by appointment only
Pont Neuf, Louvre, Odéon
24, 27, 39, 48, 58, 70, 95
None
Inexpensive

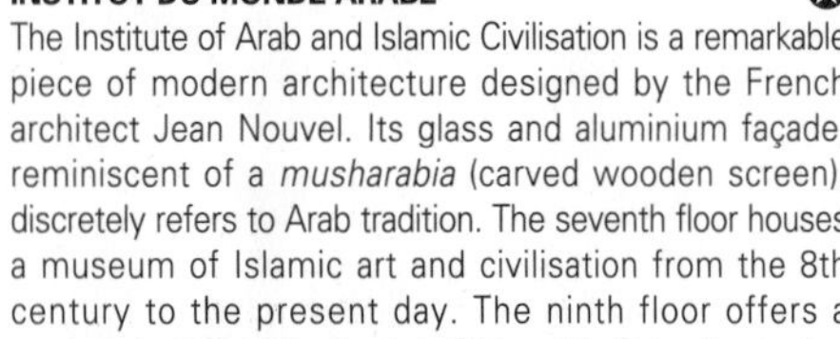

INSTITUT DU MONDE ARABE ✪

The Institute of Arab and Islamic Civilisation is a remarkable piece of modern architecture designed by the French architect Jean Nouvel. Its glass and aluminium façade, reminiscent of a *musharabia* (carved wooden screen), discretely refers to Arab tradition. The seventh floor houses a museum of Islamic art and civilisation from the 8th century to the present day. The ninth floor offers a panoramic view of the Ile de la Cité and Ile St-Louis near by.

- 29E2
- 1 rue des Fossés St-Bernard, 75005 Paris
- 01 40 51 38 38
- 10–6; closed Mon, 1 May
- Restaurant (€–€€)
- Jussieu
- 24, 63, 67, 86, 87, 89
- Good · Inexpensive
- Guided tours, shops

LES INVALIDES (➤ 19, TOP TEN)

JACQUEMART-ANDRÉ, MUSÉE ✪✪

This elegant 19th-century mansion, recently refurbished, houses the remarkable collections of European art bequeathed by the wealthy widow of a banker to the Institut de France. French 18th-century art includes paintings by Boucher, Chardin, Greuze and Watteau, as well as sculptures by Houdon and Pigalle, furniture, Beauvais tapestries and *objets d'art*. There are also 17th-century Dutch and Flemish masterpieces and an exceptionally fine collection of Italian Renaissance art including works by Mantegna, Donatello, Botticelli and Uccello.

- 28B5
- 158 boulevard Haussmann, 75008 Paris
- 01 42 62 11 59
- 10–6
- Tearoom (£)
- Miromesnil, St-Philippe-du-Roule
- 22, 28, 43, 52, 80, 83, 84, 93
- None · Moderate

JEU DE PAUME ✪

One of two pavilions built in the late 19th century at the entrance of the Jardin des Tuileries, the Jeu de Paume, on the rue de Rivoli side, was intended for the practice of a game similar to tennis. It later housed the national collection of Impressionist paintings until it was transferred to the Musée d'Orsay. Reopened in June 2004 after refurbishment, the Jeu de Paume is now exclusively devoted to the art of photography, holding thematic and monographic exhibitions from the 19th century to the 21st century.

- 28C4
- 1 place de la Concorde, 75001 Paris
- 01 47 03 12 52
- Wed–Fri 12–7, Sat–Sun 10–7, Tue 12–9:30
- Café (€) · Concorde
- 24, 42, 52, 72, 73, 84, 94
- Very good · Moderate
- Shop

Opposite page: *Eglise de la Madeleine, not instantly recognisable as a church*

Right: *home of Edouard Jacquemart and Nélie André's European art collection; the former owners' private apartments are also on show*

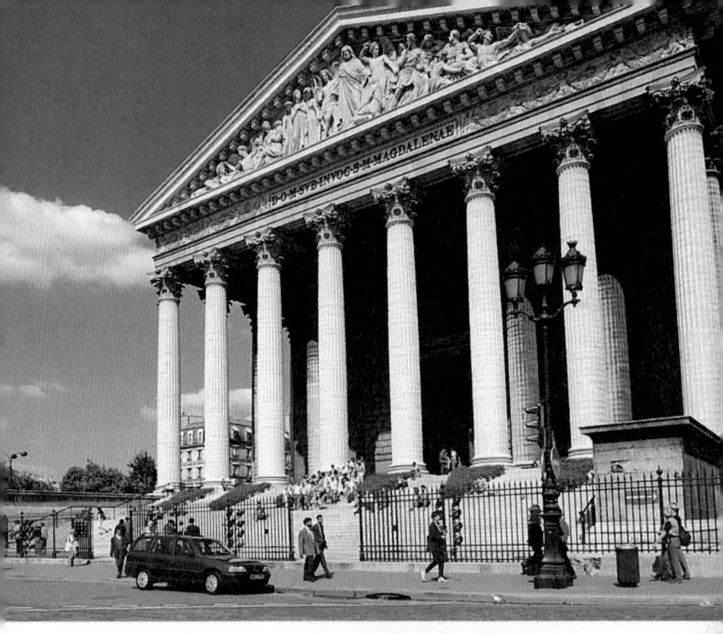

LE LOUVRE (➤ 20–1, TOP TEN)

MADELEINE, EGLISE DE LA ✪✪

Work started on this imposing neo-classical building in 1764, shortly after the completion of the place de la Concorde, but troubled times lay ahead and the partly constructed building was abandoned until 1806, when Napoleon decided to erect a temple to the glory of his 'Great Army'. He ran out of time to complete his ambitious project. It was then decided that the edifice would be a church after all and it was consecrated in 1845. The result is an impressive Graeco-Roman temple completely surrounded by tall Corinthian columns. Steps lead up to the entrance, which is surmounted by a monumental pediment. The interior is decorated with sculptures by Rude and Pradier; the magnificent organ was made by Cavaillé-Coll in 1846 and several well-known composers, including Camille Saint-Saëns, held the post of organist.

- 28C4
- Place de la Madeleine, 75008 Paris
- 01 44 51 69 00
- 7:30–7, Sun 7:30–1:30 and 3:30–7; bank hols variable
- Madeleine
- 24, 42, 52, 84, 94
- None
- Free
- Shops

MAILLOL, MUSÉE ✪✪

This atttractive museum, situated in the rue de Grenelle next to a beautiful 18th-century fountain, is interesting on two accounts: it displays a great many works by the French painter and sculptor Aristide Maillol (1861–1944) as well as a private collection of works by Ingres, Cézanne, Dufy, Matisse, Bonnard, Degas, Picasso, Gauguin, Rodin, Kandinsky, Poliakoff etc.

Maillol's obsessive theme was the nude, upon which he conferred an allegorical meaning; he produced smooth rounded figures, some of which can be seen in the Jardin des Tuileries.

- 28C3
- 59–61 rue de Grenelle, 75007 Paris
- 01 42 22 59 58
- 11–6; closed Tue and bank hols
- Cafeteria (€)
- Rue du Bac
- 63, 68, 83, 84
- Good
- Moderate
- Shop

LE MARAIS ✪✪✪

The sedate old-world atmosphere of this historic enclave at the heart of the city, its architectural beauty and cultural diversity are unique.

As its name suggests, Le Marais was once an area of marshland on the Right Bank of the Seine. In the 13th century, the area was drained and cultivated by monks and the Knights Templars. However, it was the construction of the place des Vosges at the beginning of the 17th century and the subsequent rapid urbanisation of the district that produced a wealth of beautiful domestic architecture and gave Le Marais its unique character. When fashions changed in the late 18th century, the district gradually became derelict and had to wait until the 1970s to be rediscovered and renovated.

Today Le Marais, which extends from the Hôtel de Ville to the place de la Bastille, offers visitors narrow picturesque streets, cafés and bistros, elegant mansions, tiny boutiques and a lively population that includes an important Jewish community. It is also one of the favourite haunts of the gay community.

Around every corner is another delightful mansion. These houses are no longer privately owned: some have been turned into museums, sometimes with striking results (Musée Picasso, ➤ 67). One of the most imposing, the Hôtel de Soubise, houses the **Musée de l'Histoire de France**, where historic documents are displayed amidst a profusion of Louis XV decoration. An unusual museum dedicated to hunting and nature (**Musée de la Chasse et de la Nature**) is housed in the Hôtel de Guénégaud des Brosses, built by François Mansart. Here hunting arms dating from prehistory until the 19th century are on display, plus paintings and decorative arts on the subject of hunting.

MARINE, MUSÉE DE LA (➤ 40)

Capturing the mansions, fountains and plane trees of the place des Vosges

Musée de l'Histoire de France

- 29E3
- Hôtel de Soubise, 60 rue des Francs-Bourgeois, 75003 Paris
- 01 40 27 60 96
- Telephone in advance for opening times: restructuring taking place until spring 2005; temporary exhibitions
- Hôtel de Ville
- 29, 75, 96 | None
- Inexpensive | Shop

Musée de la Chasse et de la Nature

- 29E3
- Hôtel de Guénégaud des Brosses, 60 rue des Archives, 75003 Paris
- 01 53 01 92 40
- 11–6; closed Mon and bank hols
- Hôtel de Ville
- 29, 75
- None | Moderate
- Bookshop

A Walk Through Le Marais

Picturesque streets and carefully restored architectural gems make this an enjoyable walk.

Walk north from place de l'Hôtel de Ville along rue des Archives.

The Eglise des Billettes, on your right, has the last remaining medieval cloister in Paris.

Turn right into rue Ste-Croix de la Bretonnerie, then third left and first right.

Rue des Rosiers, at the heart of the Jewish quarter, is lined with a colourful array of traditional shops and restaurants.

Turn left into rue Pavée then left again.

Rue des Francs-Bourgeois is the liveliest street in the Marais, with unusual boutiques selling clothes, antiques and trinkets.

Turn right into rue du Temple.

The Musée d'Art et d'Histoire du Judaïsme, illustrates the history of Jewish communities from the Middle Ages to the 20th century.

Turn right into rue des Haudirettes and continue to the tiny place de Thorigny. The Musée Picasso (➤ 67) is on the left. Turn right, down rue Elzévir, past the Musée Cognacq-Jay (➤ 44) then left up the rue Payenne and right down rue Sévigné.

This is a delightfully peaceful area. Have a look inside the courtyard of the Hôtel Carnavalet (➤ 39).

Walk east to the end of rue des Francs-Bourgeois.

Soak in the unique atmosphere of the place des Vosges (➤ 75). Come out from the southern end.

Turn right in the rue St-Antoine. The walk ends in front of Eglise St-Paul-St-Louis.

Distance
3.8km

Time
2–4 hours depending on museum visits

Start point
Place de l'Hôtel de Ville
29E3
Hôtel de Ville

End point
Eglise St-Paul-St-Louis
29E3
St Paul

Lunch
Café Martini
11 rue du Pas-de-la-Mule, 4th
01 42 77 05 04

Fashionable though the area may be, long-established shops and businesses still survive in Le Marais

MARMOTTAN-MONET, MUSÉE

Off map 28A4
2 rue Louis Boilly, 75016 Paris
01 42 24 07 02
10–5:30; closed Mon, 1 May, 25 Dec
Cafés and restaurants (€–€€) in nearby place de la Muette
La Muette
22, 32, 52, 63
Good
Moderate
Shops

Although situated off the beaten track, this gallery is a must for anyone interested in the Impressionist movement and in Monet in particular.

The museum was named after Paul Marmottan, who bequeathed his house and his private collections of Renaissance and 18th- and 19th-century art to the Institut de France. These were later enriched by several bequests, including 100 paintings by Monet donated by his son: detailed studies of Monet's garden in Giverny, particularly a group of *nymphéas* (water lilies) paintings, provide insights into the artist's approach (see also Musée de l'Orangerie, ➤ 64) and there are paintings of Rouen Cathedral (done in different light conditions according to the time of day) and of the River Thames in London. Most important of all, perhaps, is a relatively early work, called *Impression, Soleil levant* (1872), which created a sensation at the time and gave its name to the Impressionist movement.

There are also interesting works by Monet's contemporaries, Renoir, Pissarro, Sisley, Morisot and Gauguin.

MONNAIE DE PARIS, MUSÉE DE LA

Off map
11 quai de Conti
01 40 46 55 35
Tue–Fri 11–5.30, Sat–Sun 12–5.30
Odéon, Pont-Neuf
24, 27, 39, 48, 58, 70, 95
None
Inexpensive

This museum devoted to the history of French currency is housed in the Hôtel des Monnaies (the Mint), a fine 18th-century building standing on the left bank, next to the Institut de France. Coins, medals, paintings, sculptures, historic documents, ancient tools and machinery illustrate the evolution of minting in France from around 300BC to the present. Note in particular the Ulhorn press dating from 1807. There are audiovisual presentations and a tour specially tailored to children.

MONTMARTRE

29D5
75018 Paris
Several (€–€€€)
Abbesses, Anvers, Lamarck-Caulaincourt
Montmartrobus

Musée de Montmartre
12 rue Cortot, 75018 Paris
01 46 06 61 11
10–12.30, 1.30–6; closed Mon, 1 Jan, 1 May, 25 Dec
None Inexpensive
Exhibitions, bookshop

This unassuming village overlooking Paris became a myth during the 19th century, when it was taken over by artists and writers attracted by its picturesque surroundings and Bohemian way of life. La 'Butte' (the mound) managed to retain its village atmosphere and now that the area has become a major tourist attraction, an undefinable nostalgia lingers on, perpetuating Montmartre's magic appeal.

In its heyday, the district was the favourite haunt and home of many famous artists. They met in cafés and in cabarets such as the Moulin-Rouge (1889), whose singers and dancers acquired world-wide fame through Toulouse-Lautrec's paintings and posters. Halfway up the hill, a wooden construction (13 place Emile-Goudeau) known as the Bateau-Lavoir, where, amongst others, Picasso,

Braque and Juan Gris had their studios, was the modest birthplace of Cubism; destroyed by fire in 1970, it has since been rebuilt. At the top of the hill stands the village square, place du Tertre, close to the Sacré-Coeur basilica (➤ 70). The **Musée de Montmartre** has works and memorabilia by the artists who lived here, and the narrow cobbled streets of the 'Butte' still have some amazing sights to offer, including a vineyard in the picturesque rue des Saules and two windmills in the twisting rue Lepic.

Today's artists follow in the footsteps of the famous 19th- and early 20th-century painters who made Montmartre their home

LE CONSULAT

MENU
A
1 PLAT
CAFÉ
BAR

A Walk Through Montmartre

A walk through Montmartre is more like a pilgrimage. Allow 3 hours and time for the unexpected such as having your portrait done in place du Tertre!

Start from the square d'Anvers and walk north along rue de Stienkerque.

Facing you are the impressive steps leading to the Sacré-Coeur basilica. On the left, a funicular makes the climb easier.

Walk west along rue Tardieu to place des Abbesses.

This is the focal point of social life in Montmartre. Le Sancerre near by (if you can get in), is the most popular bar in the area. The métro entrance is in typical art nouveau style.

Continue northwest and turn right into rue Ravignan leading to place Emile-Goudeau.

The tiny square is one of the most authentic spots in Montmartre. The wooden Bateau-Lavoir, immortalised by Picasso, Braque and Gris, stood at No 13.

Continue up the winding street to rue Lepic then turn right towards the intersection of rue des Saules and rue St-Rustique.

The Auberge de la Bonne Franquette was the favourite haunt of the Impressionists, of Toulouse-Lautrec and Utrillo.

Rue Poulbot on the right leads to place du Calvaire (view), right round to place du Tertre.

The whole square is congested with easels and would-be artists. Go round the right side of the 12th-century Eglise St-Pierre to the Sacré-Coeur basilica (➤ 70).

Walk back to rue des Saules and follow it down to the other side of the hill.

At the corner of rue St-Vincent, watch out for the Montmartre vineyard and the Au Lapin Agile nightclub, the rendezvous of young artists and writers in the early 1900s.

Rue St-Vincent on the left leads to rue Caulaincourt where the walk ends.

Distance
2.2km

Time
3–4 hours

Start point
Square d'Anvers
29D5
Anvers

End point
Rue Caulaincourt
Off map 29D5
Lamarck-Caulaincourt

Lunch
Au Clair de la Lune
9 rue Poulbot
01 42 58 97 03

Opposite page:
Montmartre by night

Left: *rue de la Gaîté, Montparnasse*
Right: *the Musée de la Musique*

MONTPARNASSE ✪✪

Fashions change quickly in artistic circles and, soon after the turn of the century, young artists and writers left Montmartre to settle on the Left Bank, in an area which had been known as Montparnasse since medieval times. Modigliani, Chagall, Léger and many others found a home and a studio in La Ruche, the counterpart of the Bateau-Lavoir in Montmartre (➤ 59). They were later joined by Russian political refugees, musicians and, between the wars, American writers of the 'lost generation', among them Hemingway. They met in cafés along the boulevard Montparnasse, which have since become household names: La Closerie des Lilas, La Rotonde, Le Select, La Coupole and Le Dôme.

Since the 1960s the district has been systematically modernised and a new business complex built south of the boulevard. The 200m-high **Tour Montparnasse** stands in front of one of the busiest stations in Paris. The tower's 56th and 59th floors are open to the public and offer a restaurant and panoramic views. To the south-west, the circular place de Catalogne, surrounded by rows of glass columns, was designed by Ricardo Bofill.

- 28C1
- 75014 Paris
- Montparnasse-Bienvenüe, Vavin

Tour Montparnasse

- rue de l'Arrivée, 75015 Paris
- 01 45 38 52 56
- 9:30AM–10:30PM (11:30PM in summer)
- Le Ciel de Paris (€€)
- Good Moderate

MOYEN-AGE, MUSÉE NATIONAL DU ✪✪

This splendid museum of medieval art, also known as the Musée de Cluny, is housed in a 15th-century Gothic mansion – one of the last remaining examples of medieval domestic architecture in Paris.

The building stands at the heart of the Quartier Latin, on the site of Gallo-Roman baths dating from the 3rd century AD. The ruins are surrounded by a public garden. Inside the main courtyard, the elegant stair tower and corner turrets are particularly noteworthy.

The museum illustrates all the arts and crafts of the medieval period, the most famous exhibit being a set of tapestries known as 'La Dame à la Licorne', made in a Brussels workshop at the end of the 15th century. There is also an exceptionally fine collection of sculptures, including the heads of the kings of Judaea that decorated the façade of Notre-Dame Cathedral and were knocked down during the Revolution.

www.musee-moyenage.fr

- 29D2
- 6 place Paul Painlevé, 75005 Paris
- 01 53 73 78 00; 01 53 73 78 16
- 9:15–5:45; closed Tue, 1 Jan, 1 May, 25 Dec
- In boulevard St-Michel near by (€–€€)
- Cluny-La Sorbonne
- 21, 27, 38, 63, 85, 86, 87
- None
- Inexpensive
- Guided tours, shops, concerts

MUSIQUE, MUSÉE DE LA ✪✪

Housed within the vast Cité de la Musique (➤ 26), the museum presents a permanent exhibition consisting of some 900 musical instruments (out of a stock of around 4,500) dating from the Renaissance to the present day as well as a whole range of works of art and *objets d'art* inspired in some way by music. Temporary exhibitions are also organised in order to highlight the museum's collections, regular concerts and lectures and various cultural events take place in the 230-seat auditorium.

- Off map 29F5
- 221 avenue Jean-Jaurès, 75019 Paris
- 01 44 84 44 84
- Tue–Sat 12–6, Sun 10–6; closed Mon
- Porte de Pantin
- 75, 151, PC
- Very good; Moderate
- Guided tours, shops

NISSIM DE CAMONDO, MUSÉE ✪✪

This museum offers a delightful journey back into the 18th century.

In 1935, Count Moïse de Camondo bequeathed his private residence on the edge of the parc Monceau to the French nation in memory of his son Nissim, killed in action in 1917. The interior is arranged as an authentic 18th-century private home, including wall panelling, Aubusson and Savonnerie tapestries, paintings by Vigée-Lebrun and Hubert Robert, sculptures by Houdon and Sèvres and Chantilly porcelain.

- 28B5
- 63 rue de Monceau, 75008 Paris
- 01 53 89 06 50
- 10–5; closed Mon, Tue, 1 Jan, 14 Jul, 25 Dec
- Villiers
- 84, 94
- None
- Inexpensive
- Guided tours

NOTRE-DAME (➤ 22, TOP TEN)

Above: *the Opéra Garnier, epitome of late 19th-century ostentation*

OPÉRA GARNIER

- 28C4
- Place de l'Opéra, 75009 Paris
- 01 41 10 08 10
- 10–4:30; closed 1 Jan, 1 May and matinee performances
- Opéra
- 20, 21, 22, 27, 29, 42, 52, 53, 56, 68, 81, 95
- None
- Moderate
- Guided tours at noon, shops

A night at the opera to see *Giselle* or *Sleeping Beauty* is one of the great moments of a visit to Paris, not only for the quality of the productions but also for the sheer splendour of what is still referred to as *the* opera, in spite of the fact that there are now two opera houses in Paris!

The Palais Garnier (named after its architect) was built in 1875 in neo-classical style, but the decoration is unmistakably late 19th century and includes a group of statues called *La Danse* by Carpeaux, a copy of the original now held in the Musée d'Orsay. Inside, the grand staircase and the foyer are magnificent. In the main hall, restored to its original splendour, visitors can now fully appreciate the ceiling decorated by Chagall.

The museum contains paintings, watercolours and pastels illustrating the history of opera and ballet from the 18th century to the present day, mainly through portraits of famous singers, dancers and composers.

ORANGERIE, MUSÉE NATIONAL DE L'

- 28C3
- Place de la Concorde, Jardin des Tuileries, 75001 Paris
- 01 42 61 30 82 (fax)
- Closed for restructuring
- Concorde
- 24, 42, 52, 72, 73, 84, 94
- Very good
- Moderate
- Guided tours, shops

The Orangerie houses the Walter-Guillaume Collection, consisting mainly of Impressionist and 20th-century paintings, and a set of monumental paintings offered by Monet to his country, representing the famous Nymphéas (water lilies, see also Musée Marmottan ➤ 58) in the artist's garden at Giverny. During the restructuring of the museum, a late-16th-century fortified wall, erected to protect the new Tuileries Palace commissioned by Catherine de Médicis, was discovered on the site. Reopening is scheduled for the beginning of 2006.

ORSAY, MUSÉE D' (➤ 23, TOP TEN)

PALAIS-ROYAL ✪✪

This is more than just another historic building, it is a pleasant, relatively peaceful area with the Jardin du Palais-Royal in its centre. Here, cultural institutions occupy a prominent place, next to charming arcades and picturesque old streets. The palace built by Richelieu and bequeathed to the king on the cardinal's death now houses the ministry of culture and two important constitutional bodies, but the gardens are accessible through archways situated all round. Enclosed by arcading on three sides and an elegant double colonnade along the fourth, they are a haven of peace, where Parisians working in the area love to window-shop during their lunch hour along the row of quaint little boutiques hidden under the arcades.

An 18th-century addition to the original building houses the Comédie-Française, France's National Theatre, where all the classics are performed. From the place André Malraux in front, the Opéra Garnier can be seen at the top of the avenue de l'Opéra.

To the east of the Palais-Royal, off the rue Croix des Petits Champs, the Galerie Véro-Dodat is one of several elegant arcades in the area. Further up the street, the place des Victoires, designed by Mansart in the 17th century, is worth a detour for its classical architecture and for its fashion boutiques.

- 29D4
- Place du Palais-Royal, 75001 Paris
- Jardin: 8AM–11PM (midnight in summer)
- In the gardens (€€)
- Palais-Royal
- Jardin: free access

The peaceful arcades of the Palais-Royal (left) and (above) innovative sculpture in the main courtyard

29D2
Place du Panthéon, 75005 Paris
01 44 32 18 00
Apr–Sep 10–6:30; Oct–Mar 10–6; closed 1 Jan, 1 May, 25 Dec
Cardinal-Lemoine
84, 89
None
Moderate
Shops

PANTHÉON

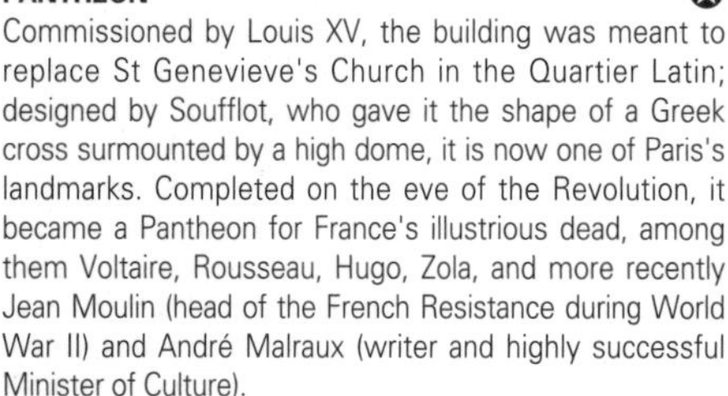

Commissioned by Louis XV, the building was meant to replace St Genevieve's Church in the Quartier Latin; designed by Soufflot, who gave it the shape of a Greek cross surmounted by a high dome, it is now one of Paris's landmarks. Completed on the eve of the Revolution, it became a Pantheon for France's illustrious dead, among them Voltaire, Rousseau, Hugo, Zola, and more recently Jean Moulin (head of the French Resistance during World War II) and André Malraux (writer and highly successful Minister of Culture).

The domed Panthéon, imposing enough from a distance, but rather austere within

www.fragonard.com
28C4
9 rue Scribe, 75009 Paris; 39 boulevard des Capucines, 75002 Paris
Free

PARFUM, MUSÉE DU

The history of perfume from the time of the ancient Egyptians to the present is the fascinating subject of this museum, housed within the Fragonard perfumery, in two different places, both near the opera house.

29E2
21 boulevard Morland, 75004 Paris
01 42 76 33 97
Tue–Sat 10:30–6:30, Sun 11–7; closed Mon
Sully-Morland 67, 86, 87
 Good Free

PAVILLON DE L'ARSENAL

The late 19th-century iron and glass building houses an information centre devoted to Paris's urban planning and architecture throughout its troubled history. The permanent exhibition 'Paris, visite guidée' (Paris, a city in the making) shows the constant evolution of the cityscape by means of a dynamic, chronological display covering the ground, walls and ceiling of the main hall, with models, films, interactive terminals...a fascinating experience!

PÈRE-LACHAISE, CIMETIÈRE DU ✪

Situated on the eastern edge of the city, the Cimetière du Père-Lachaise is Paris's most famous cemetery. The rising ground and abundant vegetation give the place a romantic atmosphere in spite of the great number of unsightly funeral monuments. Many famous people are buried here, including Musset, Chopin, Molière, Oscar Wilde, Delacroix, Balzac, even the unhappy lovers Héloïse and Abélard. In the south-east corner stands the Mur des Fédérés where the last 'communards' were shot in 1871.

- Off map 29F4
- Boulevard de Ménilmontant, 75020 Paris
- 01 55 25 82 10
- Mon–Fri 8–6, Sat 8:30–6, Sun 9–6 (5:30 in winter)
- Père-Lachaise
- Free
- Guided tours (in English) Sat 3 in summer

PICASSO, MUSÉE ✪✪✪

This is one of the most comprehensive museums devoted to the great 20th-century Spanish artist who lived and died in France. The collection was brought together after Picasso's death and consists of works donated to the State by his family in lieu of death duties, and his private collection – together totalling more than 200 paintings, sculptures, prints, drawings and ceramics.

The Hôtel Salé, situated at the heart of the historic Marais, was chosen to house this important collection. Like many other mansions in the area, it had been neglected and underwent extensive renovation to turn it into a museum. The interior decoration is very discreet, focusing attention on the beautiful stone staircase with its elegant wrought-iron banister.

Displayed in chronological order, the works illustrate the different phases of Picasso's artistic creation and the various techniques he used, from the blue period tainted with a certain pessimism (*Autoportrait bleu*), through the more optimistic pink period, to the successive Cubist periods. The tour of the museum is a fascinating journey in the company of one of the most forceful creative minds of this century. Picasso's private collection includes works by Renoir, Cézanne, Rousseau, Braque etc.

www.musee-picasso.fr
- 29F3
- Hôtel Salé, 5 rue de Thorigny, 75003 Paris
- 01 42 71 25 21
- Apr–Sep 9:30–6 (5:30 Oct–Mar); closed Tue, 1 Jan, 25 Dec
- St-Paul, Chemin Vert
- 29, 69, 75, 76, 93
- Very good
- Moderate
- Guided tours, shop

Above: *Picasso's* Femmes à Leur Toilette *(1938), from the museum*

29E2
57 rue Cuvier, 75005 Paris
01 40 79 30 00
Gardens: 7:30–sunset. Museum: 10–5; closed Tue. Zoo: 9–6
Cafeteria (€)
Jussieu
Good
Gardens: free; museum and zoo: moderate
Lectures, exhibitions, workshops for children, shop

Jardin des Plantes

PLANTES, JARDIN DES

The botanical gardens owe their name to the 'royal garden of medicinal plants' created in the 17th century and extended by Buffon in the 18th century. Today they form the experimental gardens of the Musée National d'Histoire Naturelle (Natural History Museum) and make an ideal spot for a leisurely stroll; children love the ménagerie (zoo). There are also hothouses, an alpine garden and several exhibition halls, the most fascinating being the Grande Galerie de l'Evolution, illustrating the evolution of life on earth and Man's influence on it. Here, the display of endangered and extinct species is particularly interesting. Also featured are the scientists closely associated with evolution and the latest discoveries in the field of genetics.

LES QUAIS (➤ 24, TOP TEN)

29D2

Sorbonne
47 rue des Ecoles and place de la Sorbonne (church), 75005 Paris
01 40 46 20 15
By appointment
Cluny-La Sorbonne
None   Moderate

St-Etienne-du-Mont
Place Ste. Geneviève, 75005 Paris
9–7:30; closed lunchtime and Mon in Jul & Aug

QUARTIER LATIN

This lively district remains to this day the undisputed kingdom of Parisian students. Situated on the Left Bank between the Carrefour de l'Odéon and the Jardin des Plantes, it was known in medieval times as the 'Montagne Ste-Geneviève' after the patron saint of Paris, and was later given the name of 'Quartier Latin' because Latin was spoken at the university until the late 18th century.

The **Sorbonne**, the most famous French university college, was founded in 1257; the present building dates from the late 19th century when well-known artists such as Puvis de Chavannes decorated the interior. The adjacent 17th-century church is a model of Jesuit style.

The **Church of St-Etienne-du-Mont**, dating from the late 15th century, combines Gothic Flamboyant and Renaissance styles.

A Walk Through the Quartier Latin & St-Germain-des-Prés

These lively Left Bank districts are the favourite haunt of Parisian youth.

Start at the crossroads of boulevard St-Germain and boulevard St-Michel.

Soak in the Left Bank atmosphere as you walk up the 'Boul Mich', a nickname used by generations of students. The small cafés on place de la Sorbonne are packed with students.

Take the next street on the left to reach the Church of St-Etienne-du-Mont (► 68).

It is well worth going inside to admire the Gothic chancel, Renaissance nave and magnificent rood screen.

Behind the church, follow rue Descartes to the right.

Beyond the charming place de la Contrescarpe lies the rue Mouffetard, known as 'la Mouffe', with its untidy shops and picturesque signs.

Go through the Passage des Postes (No 104) and turn right into rue Lhomond which leads back to boulevard St-Michel.

Stroll through the Jardin du Luxembourg past the beautiful Fontaine de Médicis. Come out by the west gate.

Walk down rue Bonaparte past place St-Sulpice and its superb fountain to boulevard St-Germain.

Near by are the picturesque rue de Furstenberg, rue Cardinale, rue de l'Echaudé and rue de Buci, with its lively market.

Rue St-André-des-Arts leads to the square of the same name with its quaint Fontaine Wallace. The walk ends here.

Distance
5km

Time
3–4 hours depending on stops

Start point
Crossroads of boulevard St-Germain and boulevard St-Michel
29D2
Cluny-La Sorbonne

End point
Place St-André-des-Arts
29D2
St-Michel

Lunch
Brasserie Lipp
151 boulevard St-Germain, 6th
01 45 48 53 91

Daily exercise in place St-Sulpice

RODIN, MUSÉE ✪✪✪

One of the lovely mansions in the elegant Faubourg St-Germain, built by Gabriel in 1728, houses a unique collection of works by the sculptor Auguste Rodin (1840–1917). Rodin spent the last few years of his life in the Hôtel Biron as a guest of the French nation; when he died the collection of his works reverted to the State and the mansion was turned into a museum.

His forceful and highly original style brought him many disappointments and failures: his *Man with a Broken Nose* (now in the museum) was refused at the 1864 Salon and Rodin had to wait for another 15 years before his talent was fully acknowledged through his *St John the Baptist*. His major works are displayed inside the museum (*The Kiss, Man Walking*) and in the peaceful gardens (*The Thinker, The Burghers of Calais, The Gates of Hell*).

www.musee-rodin.fr
- 28B3
- 77 rue de Varenne, 75007 Paris
- 01 44 18 61 10
- 9:30–4:45 (5:45 in summer, park 6:45); closed Mon, 1 Jan, 25 Dec
- Cafeteria (€)
- Varenne
- 69, 82, 87, 92
- Good
- Inexpensive
- Guided tours, shops

One of Rodin's most famous pieces, The Thinker

SACRÉ-COEUR, BASILIQUE DU ✪✪

The white domes and campaniles of this neo-Byzantine basilica stand out against the Parisian skyline, high above the rooftops of the capital. Its construction at the top of Montmartre was undertaken as a sign of national reconciliation and hope after the bitter defeat suffered by France in the 1870 war against Prussia. Funds were raised by public subscription and work started in 1875, but the basilica took nearly 45 years to build and was inaugurated only in 1919, at the end of another war!

The view over Paris from the terrace in front of the building is breathtaking; an impressive number of steps leads down to the place St-Pierre; from the dome, an even more stunning panoramic view stretches for 50km around the city. The interior of the basilica is profusely decorated with mosaics.

www.sacre-coeur-montmartre.com
- 29D5
- Place du Parvis du Sacré-Coeur, 75018 Paris
- 01 53 41 89 00
- Basilica: 7AM–11PM; dome and crypt: 9–6 (7 in summer)
- Abbesses (from here walk along rue Yvonne Le Tac, then take funicular or walk up steps)
- 30, 54, 80, 85, Montmartrobus
- Very good; access from the back of the basilica
- Basilica: free; dome and crypt: inexpensive
- Shops

Sacré-Coeur, among the city's most famous landmarks: the dome is the second highest point after La Tour Eiffel

ST-GERMAIN-DES-PRÉS

✪✪

The oldest church in Paris stands at the heart of the lively Left Bank district of St-Germain-des-Prés. The Benedictine Abbey of St-Germain-des-Prés, founded in the 6th century, was throughout the Middle Ages so powerful a religious and cultural centre that it became a town within the town. It was completely destroyed during the Revolution; only the church was spared. In spite of many alterations, the church is a fine example of Romanesque style: the tower dates from the 11th century as does the nave; note that the carved capitals on the pillars are copies of the originals kept in the Musée National du Moyen-Age (➤ 62). The chancel and ambulatory date from the 12th century.

Facing the church is the Café des Deux Magots which, like its neighbour the Café de Flore, was the favourite haunt of intellectuals, in particular Sartre and Simone de Beauvoir, immediately after World War II.

It is well worth exploring the old streets on the north and east sides of the church and strolling along boulevard St-Germain. The area between boulevard St-Germain and the river and between the rue du Bac and the rue de Seine is full of antique shops and art galleries.

- 28C3
- Place St-Germain-des-Prés, 75006 Paris
- 01 55 42 81 33
- 8–7
- Cafés and restaurants near by (€–€€)
- St-Germain-des-Prés
- Free

Despite unsympathetic 19th-century restoration, the interior of the Church of St-Germain-des-Prés has retained its Romanesque beauty

29E2
75004 Paris
In rue St-Louis-en-l'Ile (€€)
Pont Marie
67, 86, 87

SAINT-LOUIS, ILE

The peaceful atmosphere of this island is apparent as soon as you walk along its shaded embankment, lined with elegant private mansions that stand as silent witnesses of a bygone era. The island was formed at the beginning of the 17th century, when two small islands were united and joined to the mainland by a couple of bridges linked by the rue des Deux Ponts, which still exists; at the same time, private residences were built along the embankment and the straight narrow streets. The whole project was completed in a remarkably short time between 1627 and 1664. Since then, time seems to have stood still on the Ile Saint-Louis, which to this day retains its provincial character.

A few architectural gems can be seen along quai de Bourbon and quai d'Anjou, which offer fine views of the Right Bank. From the western tip of the island you can see Notre-Dame and the Ile de la Cité. Concerts are regularly given in the classical Church of St-Louis-en-l'Ile, richly decorated inside.

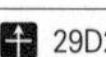

29D2
Place St-Sulpice, 75006 Paris
01 46 33 21 78
7:30–7:30
St-Sulpice
Free

ST-SULPICE, ÉGLISE

The church and square of St-Sulpice form a harmonious architectural ensemble, mostly dating from the 18th century except for part of the church and the central fountain.

The original church, founded by the Abbey of St-Germain-des-Prés, was rebuilt and extended in the 17th century but was not completed until the mid-18th century. The Italian-style façade, designed by Servandoni, is surmounted by two slightly different towers crowned by balustrades and is in marked contrast to the rest of the building. Among the wealth of interior decoration are several statues by Bouchardon and outstanding murals by Delacroix (first chapel on the right) as well as a splendid organ by Cavaillé-Coll, traditionally played by the best organists in France.

Servandoni had also submitted plans for the square in front of the church, but they were abandoned and a monumental fountain designed by Visconti was eventually placed in its centre in 1844.

In place St-Sulpice, the Fontaine des Quatre Points Cardinaux features the busts of four respected churchmen. Although their figures face the four cardinal points of the compass, none of the men ever became cardinals!

Even without the support of flying buttresses, the soaring Gothic masterpiece of Sainte-Chapelle has stood the test of time

SAINTE-CHAPELLE ✪✪✪

The full splendour of this magnificent Gothic chapel can only be appreciated from inside, as Sainte-Chapelle is unfortunately closely surrounded by the Palais de Justice buildings. Commissioned by Saint-Louis to house the Crown of Thorns and a fragment of the true Cross, it was built in less than three years by Pierre de Montreuil (who also worked on Notre-Dame) and consecrated in 1248.

The building consists of two chapels, the lower one intended as a parish church for the palace staff and the upper one reserved for the royal family. The latter is a striking example of technical prowess: walls have been replaced by 15m-high stained-glass panels linked by slender pillars which also support the vaulting. The stained-glass windows, which cover an area of more than 600sq m, are mainly original and illustrate scenes from the Old and New Testaments.

29D3
4 boulevard du Palais, 75001 Paris
01 53 40 60 97
10–5 (9:30–6 Apr–Sep); closed 1 Jan, 1 May, 1 Nov
Cité
96
None
Moderate
Shop

LA TOUR EIFFEL (➤ 25, TOP TEN)

- 28C3
- Rue de Rivoli, 75001 Paris
- Apr–Sep: 7:30AM–8PM; Oct–Mar: 7:30AM–7PM
- Cafeterias (€)
- Tuileries (access from rue de Rivoli); Palais-Royal (access from the Louvre)
- 24, 68, 72, 73, 84, 94
- Free

TUILERIES, JARDIN DES 

This formal French-style garden was laid out by Le Nôtre in the 17th century, and was even then a popular public garden. The practice of hiring chairs goes back to the 18th century. The garden deteriorated over the years through extensive use and the increasing effects of pollution, but has now been entirely renovated as part of the Grand Louvre project. The stately central alleyway stretches in a straight line from the flower beds near the Arc de Triomphe du Carrousel to the place de la Concorde, where an octagonal ornamental pool is surrounded by various statues (the seasons, rivers) and flanked by terraces. On either side of the alleyway are groups of allegorical statues. There is a lovely view of the river and the gardens with the Louvre in the background from the Terrasse du Bord de l'Eau running along the riverbank.

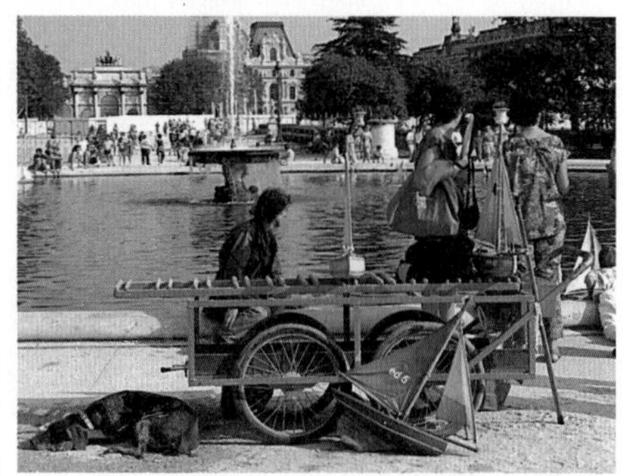

The Tuileries, a popular place for whiling away a few hours, whether it be sailing model boats, strolling or sunbathing

- 28C4
- 75001 Paris
- Opéra
- 72

VENDÔME, PLACE 

This square illustrates Louis XIV's style at its best, classical and elegant without being too emphatic. It was designed by Jules Hardouin-Mansart at the end of the 17th century and an equestrian statue of the King was placed in its centre. However, the statue was destroyed during the Revolution and in 1810 Napoleon had a tall bronze-clad column erected in its place, somewhat spoiling the architectural harmony created by the combination of arcades, pilasters and rows of dormer windows interrupted by the occasional pediment. In 1849, Frédéric Chopin died in No 12. Today the square is the headquarters of Paris's top jewellers.

A rather comical game of musical chairs went on for over 60 years to decide who should stand at the top of the column: Napoleon dressed as Caesar was replaced by Henri IV then by a huge *fleur de lys* before Napoleon reappeared...in less pompous attire, but not for long. A copy of the original statue commissioned by Napoleon III started another round; in 1871 the Commune took it down in anger but the Third Republic had it reinstated as a demonstration of tolerance...'much ado about nothing!'

Flat out in the place des Vosges: too much sightseeing?

VICTOR HUGO, MAISON DE (SEE BELOW)

LA VILLETTE (➤ 26, TOP TEN)

VOSGES, PLACE DES ✪✪✪

Totally unspoilt, this is Paris's oldest square and perhaps the loveliest for its moderate size, its discreet charm, its delightful brick and stone architecture and its peaceful central garden.

We owe this brilliant piece of town planning to 'Good King Henri' (Henri IV) whose initiative launched the development of Le Marais. The square is lined with identical pavilions over continuous arcading, dormer windows breaking up the monotony of the dark slate roofs; in the centre of the south and north sides stand two higher pavilions, known respectively as the Pavillon du Roi and Pavillon de la Reine. The square changed names during the Revolution and was finally called 'place des Vosges' in 1800 in honour of the first *département* to pay its taxes!

No 6, where Victor Hugo (1805–85) lived for 16 years, is now a museum (**Maison de Victor Hugo**), containing family mementoes, furniture, portraits, drawings by the writer himself as well as reconstructions of the various homes Hugo lived in.

29F3
75004 Paris
St-Paul, Bastille, Chemin Vert
20, 65, 69, 76

Maison de Victor Hugo
6 place des Vosges
01 42 72 10 16
10–6, closed Mon and holidays
Restaurants near by
Bastille
None
Free
Musée Carnavalet, place de la Bastille

St-Nom-La-Bretèche-Fôret-de-Marly SNCF
Gabriel Péri (Asnières-Gennevilliers)
C1 Pontoise
C3 Argenteuil
RER
Saint-Denis Université 13
4 Porte de Clignancourt
RER D1 Orry La Ville Coye
Stade de Fr... Saint-Denis
Versailles Rive Droite SNCF
SNCF Bécon-Les-Bruyères
13
Mairie de Clichy
Mairie de Saint Ouen
Simplon
Asnières-sur-Seine
Garibaldi
A1 St-Germain-en-Laye
A3 Cergy-le-Haut
A5 Poissy
RER
Porte de Clichy
Porte de St Ouen
Jules Joffrin
Marcadet-Poissonniers
Lamarck
Château Rouge
Grande Arche de La Défense 1
3 Pont de Levallois-Bécon
Clichy-Levallois
Brochant
Guy Môquet
Abbesses
Anvers (Sacré Cœur)
Anatole France
La Fourche
Blanche
Pigalle
Barbès-Rochechouart
Esplanade de La Défense
Place de Clichy
St Georges
Pont-Cardinet
Cadet
Gare du No...
Louise Michel
Notre-Dame-de-Lorette
Le Peletier
Pont de Neuilly (Avenue de Madrid)
Poissonnière
Porte de Champerret
Liège
Trinité (d'Estienne d'Orves)
Péreire-Levalois
Péreire (Maréchal Juin)
Rome
Richelieu-Drouot
Grands Boulevards
Bonne... Nouvell...
Les Sablons (Jardin d'Acclimatation)
Wagram
E1
Chaussée d'Antin (La Fayette)
Malesherbes
Haussmann St-Lazare
Villiers
14
Monceau
St-Lazare
Porte Maillot
Courcelles
Opéra
Neuilly-Porte Maillot (Palais des Congres)
Ternes
Europe
Havre-Caumartin
Quatre Septembre
Bourse
Sentier
Argentine
Auber
Charles de Gaulle Étoile 6
Châtelet Les Halle...
Victor Hugo
Miromesnil
Saint Augustin
Pyramides
2 Porte Dauphine (Maréchal de Lattre de Tassigny)
Avenue Foch
George V
St Philippe-du Roule
Madeleine
Tuileries
Louvre-Rivo...
Alma-Marceau
Franklin D. Roosevelt
Champs-Élysées-Clemenceau
Concorde
Palais Royal Musée du Louvre
Kléber
Boissière
Invalides
SEINE
Pont-Neu... (La Monnai...)
Iéna
Avenue Henri Martin
Rue de la Pompe
Trocadéro
Pont de l'Alma
Assemblée Nationale
Solférino
Musée d'Orsay
Rue du Bac
St-Michel
Boulainvilliers
La Muette
Passy
Champ de Mars-Tour Eiffel
Varenne
Bir-Hakeim (Grenelle)
La Tour Maubourg
Sèvres-Babylone
Mabillon
Ranelagh
Vaneau
Avenue du Président Kennedy
Jasmin
Dupleix
Ecole Militaire
St François Xavier
Rennes
St Germa... des Prés
Michel Ange-Auteuil
La Motte-Picquet Grenelle
Duroc
Notre-Dame-des Champs
St Sulpice
10 Porte d'Auteuil
Javel
Charles Michels
Eglise d'Auteuil
Ségur
St Placide
Javel André Citroën
Avenue Emile Zola
Boulogne Jean Jaurès
Cambronne
Falguière
Vavin
Michel Ange-Molitor
Chardon-Lagache
Mirabeau
Pasteur
Commerce
Montparnasse-Bienvenüe
Edgar Quinet
10 Boulogne Pont de St Cloud (Rhin et Danube)
Sèvres-Lecourbe
Exelmans
Boulevard Victor
Volontaires
Gaîté
Félix Faure
Porte de St-Cloud
T2 Issy Val de Seine
Boucicaut
Vaugirard (Adolphe Chérioux)
Pernéty
Marcel Sembat
Lourmel
Convention
Plaisance
Billancourt
Jacques-Henri Lartigue
Pont de Sèvres 9
Balard 8
Porte de Versailles
Porte de Va...
Grande Arche de La Défense T2
Brimborion
Meudon sur-Seine
Les Moulineaux
Corentin Celton
Malakoff Plateau de V...
RER
C5 Versailles Rive Gauche (Palais de Versailles)
C7 St-Quentin-en-Yvelines
12 Mairie d'Issy
Châtillon-Montrouge 13

U.D.N.7c

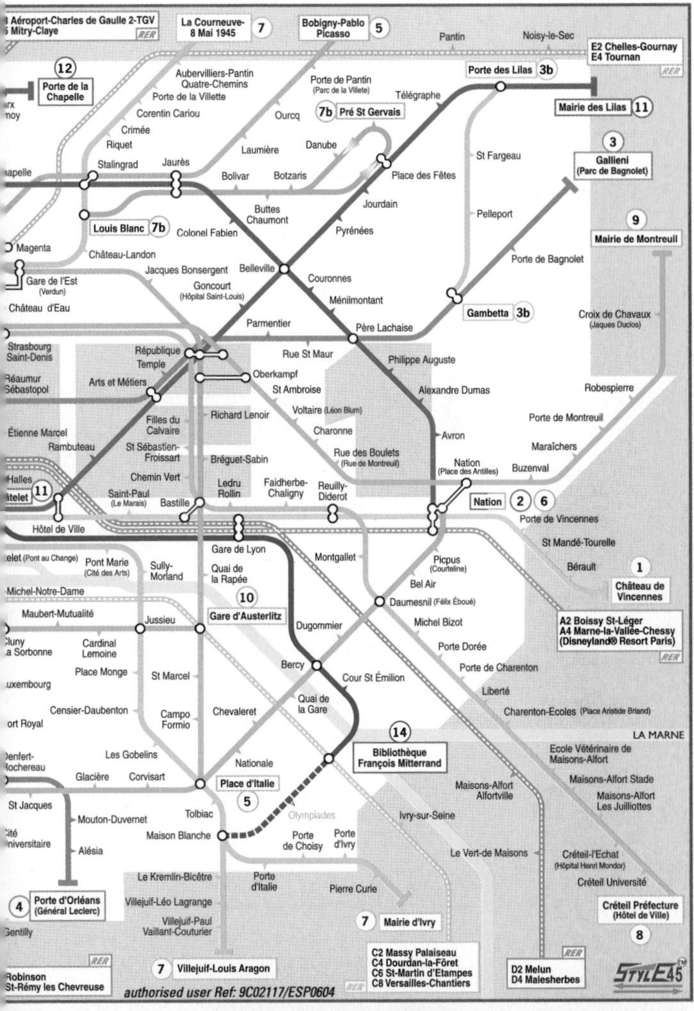

B Aéroport-Charles de Gaulle 2-TGV
5 Mitry-Claye
RER
La Courneuve-8 Mai 1945 7
Bobigny-Pablo Picasso 5
Pantin
Noisy-le-Sec
E2 Chelles-Gournay
E4 Tournan
RER
12
Porte de la Chapelle
Aubervilliers-Pantin Quatre-Chemins
Porte de la Villette
Corentin Cariou
Crimée
Riquet
Porte de Pantin (Parc de la Villete)
Ourcq
7b Pré St Gervais
Télégraphe
Porte des Lilas 3b
Mairie des Lilas 11
Laumière
Danube
3
Gallieni (Parc de Bagnolet)
Stalingrad
Jaurès
Bolivar
Botzaris
Place des Fêtes
St Fargeau
Jourdain
Buttes Chaumont
Louis Blanc 7b
Colonel Fabien
Pyrénées
Pelleport
9
Mairie de Montreuil
Magenta
Château-Landon
Porte de Bagnolet
Gare de l'Est (Verdun)
Jacques Bonsergent
Belleville
Goncourt (Hôpital Saint-Louis)
Couronnes
Château d'Eau
Ménilmontant
Gambetta 3b
Croix de Chavaux (Jaques Duclos)
Parmentier
Père Lachaise
Strasbourg Saint-Denis
République
Temple
Rue St Maur
Philippe Auguste
Réaumur Sébastopol
Arts et Métiers
Oberkampf
St Ambroise
Alexandre Dumas
Robespierre
Filles du Calvaire
Richard Lenoir
Voltaire (Léon Blum)
Étienne Marcel
Charonne
Porte de Montreuil
Rambuteau
St Sébastien-Froissart
Avron
Maraîchers
Bréguet-Sabin
Rue des Boulets (Rue de Montreuil)
Halles
Chemin Vert
Nation (Place des Antilles)
Buzenval
Châtelet 11
Ledru Rollin
Faidherbe-Chaligny
Reuilly-Diderot
Saint-Paul (Le Marais)
Bastille
Nation 2 6
Porte de Vincennes
Hôtel de Ville
St Mandé-Tourelle
Gare de Lyon
Châtelet (Pont au Change)
Pont Marie (Cité des Arts)
Sully-Morland
Quai de la Rapée
Montgallet
Picpus (Courteline)
Bérault
1
Château de Vincennes
Bel Air
St-Michel-Notre-Dame
10
Daumesnil (Félix Éboué)
Maubert-Mutualité
Gare d'Austerlitz
A2 Boissy St-Léger
A4 Marne-la-Vallée-Chessy (Disneyland® Resort Paris)
RER
Jussieu
Dugommier
Michel Bizot
Cluny La Sorbonne
Cardinal Lemoine
Porte Dorée
Bercy
Place Monge
St Marcel
Porte de Charenton
Luxembourg
Cour St Émilion
Liberté
Quai de la Gare
Censier-Daubenton
Campo Formio
Chevaleret
Charenton-Ecoles (Place Aristide Briand)
Port Royal
14
LA MARNE
Denfert-Rochereau
Les Gobelins
Bibliothèque François Mitterrand
Ecole Vétérinaire de Maisons-Alfort
Nationale
Glacière
Corvisart
Place d'Italie 5
Maisons-Alfort Stade
Maisons-Alfort Alfortville
Maisons-Alfort Les Juilliottes
St Jacques
Mouton-Duvernet
Tolbiac
Olympiades
Ivry-sur-Seine
Cité Universitaire
Maison Blanche
Porte de Choisy
Porte d'Ivry
Alésia
Le Vert-de Maisons
Créteil-l'Echat (Hôpital Henri Mondor)
Le Kremlin-Bicêtre
Porte d'Italie
Pierre Curie
Créteil Université
4 Porte d'Orléans (Général Leclerc)
Villejuif-Léo Lagrange
Créteil Préfecture (Hôtel de Ville)
Villejuif-Paul Vaillant-Couturier
7 Mairie d'Ivry
8
Gentilly
RER
Robinson
St-Rémy les Chevreuse
7 Villejuif-Louis Aragon
C2 Massy Palaiseau
C4 Dourdan-la-Fôret
C6 St-Martin d'Etampes
C8 Versailles-Chantiers
RER
D2 Melun
D4 Malesherbes
RER
STYLE45 ™
authorised user Ref: 9C02117/ESP0604

Ile de France

'Ile de France', as the Paris region is called, means the heart of France; and this is exactly what it has always been and still is, the very core of the country, a prosperous and dynamic region, inhabited by one French person in five, with Paris in its centre. Roads, motorways and international railway lines converge on this central region, which has become one of Europe's main cross-roads, with two major international airports.

Besides its tremendous vitality, the Ile de France offers visitors attractive natural assets, a rich cultural heritage and a gentle way of life. The countryside is domestic rather than spectacular, graced by picturesque villages, country inns, manor houses, historic castles, abbeys, cathedrals and beautiful parks and gardens.

'Here is the island shaded by poplars and Rousseau's grave...the castle by the still waters of the lake and the lawn which stretches like a savannah beneath the line of shadowy hills.'

GÉRARD DE NERVAL,
Sylvie (new edition 1946,
first published 1854)

Château de Dampierre

A Drive in the Painters' Footsteps

Distance
89km

Time
8–9 hours

Start point
Porte de Clichy

End point
Porte de la Chapelle

Lunch
Maison de Van Gogh
✉ Place de la Mairie 95430 Auvers-sur-Oise
☎ 01 30 36 60 60

Musée Pissarro
✉ 17 rue du Château, 95300 Pontoise
☎ 01 30 32 06 75
🕐 Wed–Sun 2–6; closed bank hols

Maison de Van Gogh
✉ Place de la Mairie 95430 Auvers-sur-Oise
🕐 10–6; closed Mon

Château d'Auvers-sur-Oise
✉ Rue de Léry
☎ 01 34 48 48 50
🕐 Tue–Sun 10:30–4:30 (6, Apr–Oct); last admission 1½ hours before closing
? Audio-visual show recreating life at the time of the Impressionists

Abbaye de Royaumont
✉ 95270 Asnières-sur-Oise
☎ 01 30 35 59 00
🕐 10–6 Mar–Oct; 10–5:30 Nov–Feb

This drive takes you along the valley of the River Oise in the footsteps of the Impressionist painters who immortalised the little town of Auvers-sur-Oise.

Start from Porte de Clichy and drive north to Cergy-Pontoise (A15) and leave at exit 9 to Pontoise.

Camille Pissarro worked in Pontoise between 1872 and 1884; housed in a large house overlooking the river, the Musée Camille Pissarro contains works by the artist and some of his contemporaries.

Continue northeast along the D4 to Auvers-sur-Oise.

Several Impressionist painters settled here in the 1870s encouraged by Doctor Gachet, himself an amateur painter: Corot, Cézanne, Renoir and above all Van Gogh, whose painting of the village church has acquired world-wide fame. He died in the local inn, known as the Auberge Ravoux, and is buried in the cemetery, next to his brother Theo.

Cross the river and drive north along the D922 to L'Isle-Adam.

From the old bridge, there are lovely views of the river and its pleasure boats; on the way out towards Beaumont, have a look at the 18th-century Chinese folly, known as the Pavillon Cassan.

Follow the D922 to Viarmes and turn left on the D909 to the Abbaye de Royaumont.

Founded by St-Louis in 1228, this is the best preserved Cistercian abbey in the Ile de France.

Turn back. The D909 joins the N1 which takes you back to Porte de la Chapelle and the boulevard périphérique.

What to See in the Ile de France

CHANTILLY, CHÂTEAU DE ✪✪

Surrounded by a lake and beautiful gardens designed by Le Nôtre, the Château de Chantilly is one of the most attractive castles in the Paris region. It houses the Musée Condé, named after one of its most distinguished owners, Le Grand Condé. The 16th-century Petit Château contains the 'Princes' apartments' and a library full of precious illuminated manuscripts including *Les Très Riches Heures du Duc de Berry*, dating from the 15th century; the Grand Château, destroyed during the Revolution and rebuilt in Renaissance style at the end of the 19th century, houses a magnificent collection of paintings by Raphael, Clouet, Ingres, Corot, Delacroix, as well as porcelain and jewellery.

Facing the famous racecourse, the impressive 18th-century stables have been turned into a museum, the Musée Vivant du Cheval, illustrating the various crafts, jobs and sports connected with horses.

40km north of Paris. BP 70243, 60631 Chantilly Cedex
Château and Musée Conde: 03 44 62 62 62; Musée Vivant du Cheval: 03 44 57 40 40
Chateau: Mar–Oct 10–6, Nov–Feb 10:30–12:45, 2–5; closed Tue. Musée du Cheval: Mar–Oct 10:30–6:30; Nov–Feb 2–6
Near the station (€)
Gare du Nord to Chantilly-Gouvieux
Moderate

Did you know ?

In 1671, while Louis XIV was visiting Chantilly at the invitation of Le Grand Condé, the most famous French chef, Vatel, killed himself because the fish he had ordered for the royal meal did not arrive on time!

Chantilly – everything you could wish for in a château

DISNEYLAND RESORT PARIS ✪✪

The famous theme parks imported from the USA are now fully integrated into the French way of life and attracts an increasing number of families from all over Europe. They offer fantasy, humour, *joie de vivre*, excitement and the latest technological devices to ensure that your visit is a memorable one. Besides Disneyland Park and Walt Disney Studios, there is a whole range of 'typically' American hotels to tempt you to stay on for a day or two.

30km east of Paris. BP100 77777 Marne-la-Vallée
UK: 08705 03 03 03; in France: 01 60 30 60 53
Varies with the season
Inside the park (€–€€€)
RER A Marne-la-Vallée/Chessy
Good Moderate

ECOUEN, CHÂTEAU D' ✪✪

19km north of Paris. 95440 Ecouen
01 34 38 38 50
9:45–12:30 and 2–5:15; closed Tue and holidays
In the château (€)
Gare du Nord to Ecouen-Ezanville, then 269 bus
Very good
Inexpensive
Guided tours, shops

This elegant Renaissance castle dating from the first half of the 16th century is reminiscent of the famous castles of the Loire Valley; its painted fireplaces are especially noteworthy. It houses the Musée National de la Renaissance, whose collections of paintings, sculptures, enamels, tapestries, embroideries, ceramics, furniture, jewellery and stained glass illustrate the diversity of Renaissance art. Particularly fine is the 75m-long tapestry depicting David and Bathsheba's love story, made in a Brussels workshop at the beginning of the 16th century.

FONTAINEBLEAU, CHÂTEAU DE ✪✪✪

65km southeast of Paris. 77300 Fontainebleau
01 60 71 50 70
9:30–5 (6PM Jun–Sep). Closed Tue, 1 Jan, 1 May, 25 Dec
In the town nearby (€–€€€)
Gare de Lyon to Fontainebleau-Avon and A or B
Very good Moderate
Guided tour, shops

As the name suggests, a fountain or spring, now in the Jardin Anglais, is at the origin of this splendid royal residence, which started out as a hunting pavilion at the heart of a vast forest. It was François I who made Fontainebleau into the beautiful palace it is today, although it was later remodelled by successive monarchs.

The imposing horseshoe staircase decorating the main façade was the scene of Napoleon I's moving farewell to his faithful guard in 1814 (see the Musée Napoléon I). Beyond this building lies the Etang des Carpes (carp pool) with a lovely pavilion in its centre, and further on the formal French gardens redesigned by Le Nôtre. The oldest part of the palace, including the keep of the medieval castle, surrounds the Cour Ovale.

The richly decorated State Apartments contain a remarkable collection of paintings, furniture and *objets d'art*, in addition to the fine coffered ceiling of the Salle de Bal and the frescoes in the Galerie François I.

Fontainbleau, a favourite retreat of royalty from the 16th century

A Drive In & Around the Forêt de Fontainebleau

The forest of Fontainebleau extends over a vast area along the left bank of the Seine, to the southeast of the capital.

Start at the Porte d'Orléans and follow the A6 motorway towards Evry and Lyon. Leave at the Fontainebleau exit and continue on the N37 for 7km; turn right to Barbizon.

This village gave its name to a group of landscape painters who settled there in the mid-19th century, among them Jean-François Millet. They were joined later by some of the future Impressionists: Renoir, Sisley and Monet.

The **Auberge Ganne**, which they decorated with their paintings, is now a museum.

Leave Barbizon towards Fontainebleau.

Take time to visit the castle (► 82), or at least the park, and to stroll around the town.

Drive southeast along the D58 for 4km bearing left at the Y-junction. Turn right onto the Route Ronde (D301).

This scenic route takes you through the forest and offers many possibilities for walking and cycling.

Turn left on the D409 to Milly-la-Forêt.

This small town nestling round an imposing covered market is a traditional centre for growing medicinal plants. The Cyclop (1km north) is a monumental modern sculpture which took 20 years to complete.

Follow the D372 for 3.5km and bear left for Courances.

The **Château de Courances** looks delightful, set like a jewel in a magnificent park designed by Le Nôtre, with pools, canals and small waterfalls.

Return to the main road and continue for 5km, then rejoin the motorway back to Paris.

Distance
143km

Time
7–9 hours depending on length of visits

Start/end point
Porte d'Orléans

Lunch
Le Caveau des Ducs
✉ 24 rue de Ferrare, 77300 Fontainebleau
☎ 01 64 22 05 05

Auberge Ganne
✉ 92 Grande Rue, 77630 Barbizon
☎ 01 60 66 22 27
🕐 Apr–Sep 10–12:30 and 2–6 (5 in winter), weekends 10–6 (5 in winter); closed Tue
Moderate

Château de Courances
✉ 91240 Milly-la-Forêt
☎ 01 64 98 41 18
🕐 Apr–Oct: Sat, Sun and bank hols 2–6:30
Moderate
? Guided tours

Barbizon's main street

25km west of Paris. 25 route du Mesnil, 78990 Elancourt
01 30 16 16 30
Apr–early Nov 10–6 (7 in Jul and Aug); last admission 1 hour before closing
Two restaurants (€–€€)
Gare Montparnasse
Good Moderate
Audio-visual show, outdoor activities

FRANCE MINIATURE 

This open-air museum comprises a huge three dimensional map of France on which 166 miniature historic monuments have been arranged into a harmonious whole, partly re-creating the atmosphere inherent to each place; for instance the Château de Chenonceau reflected in the calm waters of the Loire suggests the peaceful atmosphere of the Loire Valley. There are models of the Tour Eiffel, the Sacré Coeur, the solitary Mont-St-Michel, the pont du Gard and Gallo-Roman arenas, as well as many beautiful castles, all made to a scale of 1:30. Here and there, a typical French village focuses on ordinary daily life.

14km west of Paris. Avenue du Château, 92500 Rueil-Malmaison
01 41 29 05 55
10–12:30, 1:30–5:15 (5:45 in summer); closed Tue, 1 Jan, 25 Dec. Bois-Préau closed for renovation
RER Rueil-Malmaison
Good
Inexpensive
Guided tours, shop

MALMAISON, CHÂTEAU DE

The memory of Napoleon and his beloved Josephine lingers on around 'La Malmaison' and the nearby Château de Bois-Préau.

Josephine bought the 17th-century castle in 1799 and had the wings and the veranda added. The couple spent several happy years in Malmaison, and after their divorce Josephine continued to live in it up until her death in 1814. In the summer of 1815, Napoleon went to La Malmaison once more before sailing for St-Helena. The castle then passed through many hands before it was bought by a banker, restored and donated to the State in 1904. It contains various collections of 18th- and 19th-century paintings (David, Greuze etc), porcelain and furniture.

The Château de Bois-Préau was offered to France by a wealthy American, Edward Tuck, and now forms an annexe to the collections in La Malmaison.

Château de Malmaison with one of the garden statues

PARC ASTÉRIX

This Gallic version of a made-in-USA theme park is based on the comic adventures of a friendly little Gaul named Astérix and his companions, who are determined to resist the Roman invaders. The story became famous worldwide through a series of more than 50 strip cartoons by Goscinny and Uderzo, which have since been translated into many languages.

Inside the park, visitors are invited to share Astérix's adventures as they wander through the Gauls' Village, the Roman City and Ancient Greece, travel on the impressive roller-coaster of the Great Lake and journey back and forth in time along the rue de Paris!

30km north of Paris. BP 8, 60128 Plailly
03 44 62 34 04
Variable
Several choices (€–€€)
RER B3 from Châtelet or Gare du Nord to Roissy-Charles-de-Gaulle 1 then Courriers Ile-de-France every half hour
Excellent Moderate
Gift shops, picnic areas, pushchair rental

SAINT-CLOUD, PARC DE

This beautiful park, situated on the outskirts of Paris, extends over a vast hilly area overlooking the Seine. The castle designed by Jules-Hardouin Mansart for 'Monsieur', Louis XIV's brother, was destroyed by fire in 1870 and razed to the ground in 1891. It had been Bonaparte's favourite official residence when he was consul of the Republic.

The park was designed by Le Nôtre, who took advantage of the steep terrain to build a magnificent 'grande cascade', in which water flows gracefully from one pool to the next over a distance of 90m. At the top the site of the former castle is now a terrace offering lovely views of the capital. Near by is the Jardin du Trocadéro, an English-style garden with an ornamental pool and an aviary. There are many shaded alleyways offering delightful walks through the 460-ha park.

11km west of Paris. 92210 Saint-Cloud
01 41 12 02 90
7:30AM–8:50PM (7:50PM Nov–Feb, 9:50 May–Aug)
Cafés (€)
Pont de Saint-Cloud
Free

Fun for all the family at Parc Astérisk

SAINT-DENIS, BASILIQUE

✪✪✪

- 9km north of Paris. 1 rue de la Légion d'Honneur, 93200 Saint-Denis
- 01 48 09 83 54
- Winter: 10–5:15 (Sun 12–5:15); summer: 10–6:15 (Sun 12–6:15). Closed 1 Jan, 1 May, 25 Dec
- Saint-Denis Basilique
- None
- Moderate
- Guided tours

So many great architects and artists have contributed to make the Basilique St-Denis what it is today that the building is in itself a museum of French architecture and sculpture of the medieval and Renaissance periods.

An abbey was built on the site where St-Denis died following his martyrdom in Montmartre. Designed in the early 12th century by Abbot Suger, the nave and transept of the abbey church were completed in the 13th century by none other than Pierre de Montreuil, who also worked on Notre-Dame. It was for centuries the burial place of the kings and queens of France as well as of illustrious Frenchmen such as Du Guesclin. There is a wealth of recumbent figures and funeral monuments dating from the 12th to the 16th centuries, most of them the work of great artists: Beauneveu (Charles V, 14th century), Philibert Delorme (François I, 16th century), Germain Pilon (Catherine de Médicis, 16th century), Jean Bullant and Il Primaticcio (16th century). The basilica underwent restoration by Gabriel in the 18th century and again by Viollet-le-Duc in the 19th century.

SAINT-GERMAIN-EN-LAYE

✪✪

- 23km west of Paris.

Château de Saint-Germain-en-Laye

- BP 3030, 78103 Saint-Germain-en-Laye Cedex
- 01 39 10 13 00
- 9–5:15; closed Tue, some bank hols
- RER Saint-Germain-en-Laye
- Very good
- Inexpensive
- Guided tours, shops

The historic city of Saint-Germain-en-Laye clusters round its royal castle, once the favourite residence of Louis XIV. François I commissioned the present Château Vieux (Old Castle) and retained Saint-Louis's chapel and the 14th-century square keep, now surmounted by a campanile. Le Nôtre later designed the gardens and the magnificent 2,400m-long Grande Terrasse. The Sun King stayed in Saint-Germain for many years and during that time private mansions were built around the castle for members of his court. When the court moved to Versailles in 1682, the castle was somewhat neglected but it was eventually restored by Napoleon III and turned into the Musée des Antiquités Nationales, which houses interesting archaeological collections illustrating life in France from earliest times to the Middle Ages.

The Grand Terrace of the Château de Saint-Germain-en-Laye

SCEAUX, CHÂTEAU DE ✪✪

Very little remains of this castle, built for Colbert: the main entrance decorated with sculptures by Coysevox, the Orangerie to the left, the old stables opposite and the Pavillon de l'Aurore tucked away on the right. But the splendid park has been preserved: it is one of the most 'romantic' ever designed by Le Nôtre, with its tall trees reflected in the secluded octagonal pool, its peaceful Grand Canal and its impressive Grandes Cascades.

The castle, rebuilt in the 19th century, houses the Musée de l'Ile de France illustrating ancient regional arts and crafts and the history of castles in the Paris Region.

- 10km south of Paris. Château de Sceaux, 92330 Sceaux
- 01 41 87 29 50
- Park: daily 8–sunset. Museum: 10–5 (6 in summer); closed Tue, 1 Jan, Easter, 1 May, 1 Nov, 11 Nov, 25 Dec
- Cafeteria (€)
- RER B Bourg-La-Reine
- Good
- Park: free. Museum: inexpensive
- Guided tours

A fine Sèvres urn at the porcelain museum

SÈVRES, MUSÉE NATIONAL DE LA CÉRAMIQUE DE ✪

The name of this Paris suburb was made famous by the porcelain factory transferred here in 1756 from its previous location in Vincennes. The unique 'Sèvres blue' ware, also known as 'lapis blue', became its trademark. The Musée National de la Céramique was founded at the beginning of the 19th century to house various collections of Sèvres and Saxe porcelain, Italian Renaissance ceramics, antique terracotta objects, glazed earthenware from the Far East and ceramics from elsewhere.

- 11km southwest of Paris. Place de la Manufacture, 92310 Sèvres
- 01 41 14 04 20
- 10–5; closed Tue, 1 Jan, Easter Mon, Whit Mon, 1 Nov, 25 Dec
- Métro: Pont de Sèvres
- Good
- Inexpensive
- Guided tours

VAUX-LE-VICOMTE, CHÂTEAU DE ✪✪✪

This architectural gem, a 'little Versailles' built before Versailles was even designed, cost its owner, Nicolas Fouquet, his freedom and eventually his life – although much appreciated by the king for his competence in financial matters, he had dared to outdo his master! Fouquet, who had excellent taste, had commissioned the best artists of his time: Le Vau for the building, Le Brun for the decoration and Le Nôtre for the gardens. Louis XIV was invited to a dazzling reception given for the inauguration of the castle in 1661. The King did not take kindly to being outshone: Fouquet was arrested and spent the rest of his life in prison, while Louis XIV commissioned the same artists to build him an even more splendid castle, Versailles.

The castle stands on a terrace overlooking magnificent gardens featuring canals, pools and fountains; walking to the end of the terrace allows an overall view of the gardens and the castle. In the stables is a museum (Musée des Equipages) devoted to horse-drawn carriages.

- 51km southeast of Paris. Domaine de Vaux-le-Vicomte, 77950 Maincy
- 01 64 14 41 90
- Mid-Mar to mid-Nov: Mon–Fri 10–1, 2–6, Sat, Sun 10–6. Candlelit visits: mid–May to mid–Oct Thu, Sat 8PM–midnight
- Cafeteria (€)
- Gare de Lyon to Melun then taxi
- None
- Expensive
- Shops

www.chateauversailles.fr

- 20km southwest of Paris. 78000 Versailles
- 01 30 83 78 00
- Château: 9–5:30 (6:30 in summer); closed Mon, some bank hols. Trianons: noon–5:30 (6:30 in summer); Parc: 7–5:30 (up to 9:30PM depending on the season) ceremonies
- Cafeteria (€) and restaurant (€€)
- Gare St-Lazare to Versailles Rive Droite
- Good
- Moderate
- Guided tours, shops

VERSAILLES, CHÂTEAU DE

The physical expression of a king's superego, Versailles turned out to be one of the most splendid castles in the world through the genius of the artists who built and decorated it. What began as a modest hunting lodge became the seat of government and political centre of France for over a hundred years. A town grew up around the castle to accommodate the court. Several thousand men worked on the castle for 50 years, thousands of trees were transplanted, and 3,000 people could live in it.

The castle is huge (680m long) and it is impossible to see everything in the course of one visit. Aim for the first floor where the State Apartments are, including the famous Galerie des Glaces, as well as the Official Apartments and the Private Apartments of the royal couple, situated on either side of the marble courtyard. The north wing contains the two-storey Chapelle St-Louis built by Mansart and the Opéra, added later, by Gabriel.

The focal point of the park is the Bassin d'Apollon, a

Versailles: the south wing (left) and the Apollo Basin (above)

Below: *Château de Vincennes*

magnificent ornamental pool with a bronze sculpture in its centre representing Apollo's chariot coming out of the water. Two smaller castles, Le Grand Trianon and Le Petit Trianon, are also worth a visit, and Le Hameau, Marie-Antoinette's retreat, offers a delightful contrast.

VINCENNES, CHÂTEAU DE ✪✪

This austere castle, situated on the eastern outskirts of Paris, was a royal residence from the Middle Ages to the mid-17th century. Inside the defensive wall, there are in fact two castles: the 50m-high keep (currently undergoing repair) built in the 14th century, which later held political prisoners, philosophers, soldiers, ministers and churchmen; and the two classical pavilions built by Le Vau for Cardinal Mazarin in 1652, Le Pavillon de la Reine, where Anne d'Autriche, mother of Louis XIV lived, and Le Pavillon du Roi, where Mazarin died in 1661. The Chapelle Royale, started by Saint-Louis and completed by François I, stands in the main courtyard.

6km east of Paris. Avenue de Paris, 94300 Vincennes
01 48 08 31 20
10–noon, 1–5 (6 in summer); closed 1 Jan, 1 May, 1 Nov, 11 Nov, 25 Dec
Métro: Porte de Vincennes
None
Inexpensive
Guided tours, shops

A Drive Through the Vallée de Chevreuse

This drive will take you through the wooded Vallée de Chevreuse to Rambouillet, its castle and its park.

From the Porte de Saint-Cloud, follow signs for Chartres/Orléans. After 17km, leave for Saclay and take the N306 towards Chevreuse.

The little town of Chevreuse is dominated by the ruins of its medieval castle, which houses the Maison du Parc Naturel Régional de la Haute Vallée de Chevreuse (Natural Regional Park Information Centre).

From Chevreuse, drive southwest on the D906 to Rambouillet.

The 14th-century fortress is now an official residence of the presidents of the Republic. In the park, criss-crossed by canals, look for the Laiterie de la Reine (Marie-Antoinette's dairy).

Drive back on the D906 for 10km and turn left on the D91 towards Dampierre.

The 16th-century stone and brick Château de Dampierre was remodelled by Jules Hardouin-Mansart for Colbert's son-in-law and still belongs to the de Luynes family.

Continue on the D91 across the River Yvette, negotiating the picturesque '17 bends' to the ruined Abbaye de Port-Royal-des-Champs (parking on left-hand side of the road).

During the 17th century, this former Cistercian abbey was at the centre of a religious battle between Jesuits and Jansenists. The Musée National des Granges de Port-Royal is in the park.

Continue along the D91 to Versailles and return to the Porte de Saint-Cloud by the Route de Paris (D10).

Above: *statue in the parkland of Château de Rambouillet*

Distance
93km

Time
7–9 hours depending on visits

Start/end point
Porte de Saint-Cloud

Lunch
Cheval Rouge
✉ 78 rue Général de Gaulle, 78120 Rambouillet
☎ 01 30 88 80 61

Maison du Parc, Chevreuse
www.parc-naturel.chevreuse.org
☎ 01 30 52 09 09
🕐 Weekdays 10–12 and 2–6

Château de Rambouillet
☎ 01 34 83 00 25

Château de Dampierre
☎ 01 30 52 53 24

Musée National des Granges de Port-Royal
☎ 01 30 43 73 05

Where To...

Above: *at the Jardin des Tuileries*

Paris

Prices
Prices for a three-course meal vary from around 15 euros to over 200 euros; the average price for each restaurant listed is shown by the pound symbol:

€ = budget (up to €30)
€€ = moderate (€30–75)
€€€ = expensive to luxury (over €75)

Nowhere is the saying 'Variety is the spice of life' truer than in Paris, for the city with a well-deserved reputation of being the gastronomic capital of the West has such a wide choice of eating establishments that selecting one can prove a hard task, even for Parisians. In Paris, the reality behind the word 'restaurant' is particularly complex since you can eat a three-course meal for as little as 10 euros in one of the local bistros, their red and white chequer-board tablecloths having become emblems of Parisian life, or for more than 200 euros in one of the temples of *haute cuisine*.

In between, there is an amazing array of cafés serving the inevitable *steak-frites* and *jambon-beurre* sandwiches, of *brasseries* with splendid late 19th-century settings, of chain restaurants marrying constant quality with a definite French touch, of wine bars and seafood places, of regional restaurants proudly reminding gourmets that French gastronomy is not the prerogative of Parisian chefs, and of cosmopolitan restaurants specialising in African, Lebanese or Vietnamese cuisine – to name but a few – and in Tex-Mex fare, increasingly popular with young French crowds.

Bistros are traditionally versatile and a great favourite of Parisians and visitors alike. Up to now, their ambitions had remained modest. However, in recent years, a new generation of bistros has emerged on the Paris scene: the famous chefs of several exclusive restaurants have opened up-market bistros serving *haute cuisine* in less formal surroundings and at more affordable prices. Needless to say that these new bistros are very much in fashion: such is the case of La Régalade (► 97) and l'Epi Dupin (► 96), both on the Left Bank, where young chefs Yves Camdeborde and François Pasteau regale enthusiastic customers.

Right Bank Restaurants

L'Alsace (€€)
Alsatian specialities and seafood; terrace in summer.
✉ 39 avenue des Champs-Elysées, 75008 Paris ☎ 01 53 93 97 00 ⌚ 24 hours 🚇 Franklin-D Roosevelt

Les Amognes (€€)
Bistro serving imaginative cuisine in a relaxed atmosphere.
✉ 243 rue du Faubourg St-Antoine, 75011 Paris ☎ 01 43 72 73 05 ⌚ Lunch, dinner; closed Sat and Mon lunch, Sun and 10–31 Aug 🚇 Faidherbe Chaligy

Bar à Huîtres (€–€€)
Fashionable seafood brasserie.
✉ 33 boulevard Beaumarchais, 75003 Paris ☎ 01 48 87 98 92 ⌚ Lunch, dinner, open until 2AM 🚇 Bastille

Beauvilliers (€€–€€€)
Gourmet cuisine served in an elegant Napoleon III setting; terrace in summer.
✉ 52 rue Lamarck, 75018 Paris ☎ 01 42 54 54 42 ⌚ Lunch, dinner; closed Mon lunch, Sun 🚇 Lamarck Caulaincourt

Bistro de Gala (€€)
In the 'Grands Boulevards' area, serving traditional French cuisine.
45 rue du Faubourg Montmartre, 75009 Paris 01 40 22 90 50 Lunch, dinner; closed Sat lunch, Sun and 2 weeks in Aug Le Peletier

Blue Elephant (€€)
Thai cuisine in appropriate setting near Bastille. Try the *chiang rai.*
43 rue de la Roquette, 75011 Paris 01 47 00 42 00 Lunch, dinner; closed Sat lunch Voltaire

Bon (€€)
Trendy restaurant; some vegetarian dishes.
25 rue de la Pompe, 75016 Paris 01 40 72 70 00 Lunch, dinner La Muette

Brasserie Flo (€–€€)
1900-style Alsatian inn specialising in *choucroute* (sauerkraut) and seafood.
7 Cour des Petites Ecuries, 75010 Paris 01 47 70 13 59 Lunch, dinner Château d'Eau

La Butte Chaillot (€€)
Refined cuisine served in a striking contemporary setting.
110 bis avenue Kléber, 75016 Paris 01 47 27 88 88 Lunch, dinner; closed Sat lunch and 2 weeks Aug Trocadéro

Caveau François Villon (€)
Charming bistro located in 15th-century cellars. Live music is played at night.
64 rue de l'Arbre Sec, 75001 Paris 01 42 36 10 92 Lunch, dinner; closed Mon and Sat lunch, Sun Louvre-Rivoli

Chez Clément Élysées (€)
Home style cooking.
123 avenue des Champs-Élysées, 75008 Paris 01 40 73 87 00 Lunch, dinner Charles de Gaulle-Étoile

Chez Madame Vong (€)
Chinese and Vietnamese cuisine.
10 rue de la Grande Truanderie, 75001 Paris 01 42 97 49 07 Lunch, dinner; closed Sat and Sun lunch Les Halles

Le Dôme du Marais (€€)
Imaginative cuisine based on fresh seasonal produce; historic surroundings.
53 bis rue des Francs-Bourgeois, 75004 Paris 01 42 74 54 17 Lunch, dinner; closed Sun Hôtel de Ville

Le Dos de la Baleine (€)
Typical marais restaurant with undressed-stone walls; innovative cuisine.
40 rue des Blancs-Manteaux, 75004 Paris 01 42 72 38 98 Lunch, dinner; closed Sat lunch and Mon Rambuteau

L'Etrier (€–€€)
Traditional French cuisine; good value. Reserve a table in advance.
154 rue Lamarck, 75018 Paris 01 42 29 14 01 Lunch, dinner; closed Mon, Sun and Aug Guy Môquet

Grand Véfour (€€€)
Haute cuisine, surroundings of 18th-century décor; beautiful view of the Jardin du Palais-Royal.
17 rue de Beaujolais, 75001 Paris 01 42 96 56 27 Lunch, dinner; closed Fri night, Sat, Sun and Aug Palais-Royal

How to Get The Best Value for Money
Whenever possible, choose one of the fixed *menus* rather than *à la carte*. Also note that *menus* are cheaper at lunchtime and that, unless otherwise specified, service is included in the prices quoted. Wines are generally expensive but house wines are often worth trying and are more reasonably priced.

Les Halles Tradition
In the days when the Paris food market was situated where the Forum des Halles now stands, there were many restaurants in the vicinity, such as Au Pied de Cochon, which served pig's trotters and onion soup to workers kept busy throughout the night. It later became fashionable for people out on the town to end up in one of those places in the early hours of the morning.

Les Grandes Marches (€–€€)
Seafood brasserie overlooking place de la Bastille.
6 place de la Bastille, 75012 Paris 01 43 42 90 32 Lunch, dinner Bastille

Le Jardin (€€€)
Mediterranean-style *haute cuisine*; speciality: lobster roasted with spices.
Hôtel Royal Monceau, 37 avenue Hoche, 75008 Paris 01 42 99 98 70 Lunch, dinner; closed Sat, Sun and bank hols Charles de Gaulle-Etoile

Jipangue (€–€€)
Excellent Japanese cuisine.
96 rue La Boétie, 75008 Paris 01 45 63 77 00 Lunch, dinner; closed Sat lunch and Sun St-Philipe-du-Roule

Lucas Carton (€€€)
Haute cuisine with authentic late 19th-century décor by Majorelle; good roast duck.
9 place de la Madeleine, 75008 Paris 01 42 65 22 90 Lunch, dinner; closed Sat lunch, Sun, Aug and Christmas Madeleine

Nos Ancêtres les Gaulois (€€)
Convivial atmosphere; menu includes as much wine as you can drink.
39 rue St-Louis-en-l'Ile, 75004 Paris 01 46 33 66 07 Dinner only, lunch on Sun Pont-Marie

Pavillon Puebla (€€–€€€)
In the lovely parc des Buttes Chaumont; elegant Napoleon III décor; speciality: lobster *à la catalane*.
Parc des Buttes Chaumont (entrance on the corner of avenue Bolivar and rue Botzaris), 75019 Paris 01 42 08 92 62 Lunch, dinner; closed Sun, Mon Buttes Chaumont

Le Piano des saisons (€)
Attractive new restaurant; seafood cuisine from south-west France.
11 rue Treilhard, 75008 Paris 01 45 61 09 46 Lunch, dinner; closed Sat–Sun Miromesnil; St-Augustin

Piccolo Teatro (€)
Refreshing and inspired vegetarian dishes. Try the excellent soups.
6 rue des Ecouffes, 75004 Paris 01 42 72 17 79 Lunch, dinner; closed Mon, Christmas St-Paul

Au Pied de Cochon (€€)
Traditional 'Les Halles' restaurant; try the pig's trotters and onion soup.
6 rue Coquillère, 75001 Paris 01 40 13 77 00 24 hours Châtelet Les Halles

La Poule au Pot (€€)
A bistro maintaining the traditions of Les Halles.
9 rue Vauvilliers, 75001 Paris 01 42 36 32 96 Dinner; open until 6AM; closed Mon Louvre Rivoli

Le Rouge Gorge (€€)
Charming wine bar with lots of atmosphere.
8 rue St-Paul, 75004 Paris 01 48 04 75 89 Lunch, dinner; closed Sun dinner St-Paul

Stresa (€€)
Trendy Italian restaurant; booking advisable.
7 rue de Chambiges, 75008 Paris 01 47 23 51 62 Lunch, dinner; closed Sat dinner, Sun, Aug and Christmas Alma-Marceau

Terminus Nord (€€)
A 1920s-style brasserie near the Gare du Nord; speciality: duck's *foie gras* with apple and raisins, seafood.
23 rue de Dunkerque, 75010 Paris 01 42 85 05 15 Lunch, dinner Gare du Nord

Timgad (€€€)
Spectacular Moorish interior, innovative, exciting food and attentive service at one of France's best known Arab restaurants.
21 rue Brunel, 75017 01 45 74 23 70 Daily Argentine

Train Bleu (€€)
Brasserie with late 19th-century décor illustrating the journey from Paris to the Mediterranean.
Place Louis Armand, Gare de Lyon, 75012 Paris 01 43 43 09 06 Lunch, dinner Gare de Lyon

Le Viaduc Café (€€)
Trendy bistro in the new Viaduc des Arts complex of workshops near Bastille.
43 avenue Daumesnil, 75012 Paris 01 44 74 70 70 Lunch, dinner Bastille

Le Vieux Bistrot (€€)
Facing the north side of Notre-Dame; traditional French cooking.
14 rue du Cloître-Notre-Dame, 75004 Paris 01 43 54 18 95 Lunch, dinner Cité

Wally el Saharien (€€)
This restaurant serves North African specialities with mountains of couscous.
36 rue Rodier, 75009 Paris 01 42 85 51 90 Closed Mon, Sun Anvers

Left Bank Restaurants

Le Bamboche (€€)
Typical fish dishes from Provence.
15 rue de Babylone, 75007 Paris 01 45 49 14 40 Lunch, dinner; closed Sat lunch and Sun Sèvres-Babylone

Bistrot du 7e (€)
Charming bistro near les Invalides, excellent value for money.
56 boulevard de la Tour-Maubourg, 75007 Paris 01 45 51 93 08 Lunch, dinner; closed for lunch Sat–Sun Invalides, La Tour-Maubourg

Les Bookinistes (€€)
Fashionable restaurant along the embankment; up-and-coming young chef has made *nouvelle cuisine* into an art.
53 quai des Grands-Augustins, 75006 Paris 01 43 25 45 94 Lunch, dinner; closed Sat lunch, Sun Saint-Michel

Brasserie Balzar (€€)
Popular smart brasserie close to the Sorbonne, serving good French dishes.
49 rue des Écoles, 75005 Paris 01 43 54 13 67 Daily Cluny-La Sorbonne

Brasserie Lipp (€€)
Founded in 1880, this restaurant is always popular with the famous.
151 boulevard St-Germain, 75006 01 45 48 53 91 Daily St-Germain-des-Prés

Le Ciel de Paris (€€–€€€)
On the 56th floor of the Tour

Fast Food and Brunch
When the first McDonald's opened in Paris, most people thought it would be a flop! Well, fast food has become part of the French way of life and now the mecca of gastronomy has adopted another Anglo-Saxon habit – the brunch. More and more bistros in central Paris now specialise in this 'new' kind of meal, definitely 'in'.

French and Cosmopolitan Cuisine
Most restaurants selected here serve traditional French regional cuisine or what is loosely called *nouvelle cuisine*, as Paris's top chefs innovate in an effort to adapt to changing tastes and eating habits. There is a new emphasis on fish and seafood and it is now possible to enjoy a gastronomic meal without meat! There is also a strong tradition of world cuisine, essentially Italian, North African, Vietnamese, and Japanese.

Montparnasse; live music from 9PM.
Tour Montparnasse, 33 avenue du Maine, 75015 Paris 01 40 64 77 64 Lunch, dinner Montparnasse-Bienvenüe

D'Chez Eux (€€)
Bistro specialising in *cassoulet* (haricot-bean stew with Toulouse sausages). Terrace.
2 avenue Lowendal, 75007 Paris 01 47 05 52 55 Lunch, dinner; closed Sun and first 3 weeks of Aug Ecole Militaire

Côté Seine (€–€€)
Along the embankment between Notre-Dame and the pont Neuf. Good value for money; book ahead.
45 quai des Grands-Augustins, 75006 Paris 01 43 54 49 73 Dinner Saint-Michel

La Coupole (€€)
Famous brasserie from the 1920s with art deco setting; excellent seafood. Reasonable late-night menu (after 11PM).
102 boulevard du Montparnasse, 75014 Paris 01 43 20 14 20 Daily 8:30AM–1PM Vavin

La Criée (€)
For lovers of seafood at affordable prices!
15 rue Lagrange, 75005 Paris 01 43 54 23 57 Lunch, dinner Maubert–Mutualité

La Dinée (€€)
Imaginative cuisine with an emphasis on fish; young chef already hailed by gourmets.
85 rue Leblanc, 75015 Paris 01 45 54 20 49 Lunch, dinner; closed Sat, Sun and 2 weeks in Aug Javel

Le Divellec (€€€)
One of the top seafood restaurants in Paris complete with nautical décor, and very good service.
107 rue de l'Université, 75007 Paris 01 45 51 91 96 Lunch, dinner; closed Sat, Sun, Christmas Invalides

Le Dôme (€€–€€€)
Brasserie specialising in all types of seafood. Especially good is the *bouillabaisse* from Provence.
108 boulevard du Montparnasse, 75014 Paris 01 43 35 25 81 Lunch, dinner Vavin

L'Epi Dupin (€)
Sought-after, reasonably priced restaurant with regular change of menu; book well in advance. Best ingredients from Rungis market. Terrace.
11 rue Dupin, 75006 Paris 01 42 22 64 56 Lunch, dinner; closed Sat, Sun, Mon lunch and 3 weeks in Aug Sèvres-Babylone

La Frégate (€–€€)
Next to the Musée d'Orsay and facing the Louvre; good value traditional French cuisine.
35 quai Voltaire, 75007 Paris 01 42 61 23 77 Lunch, dinner Rue de Bac

Jacques Cagna (€€€)
High-class traditional French cuisine in 17th-century residence with wood panelling and beams; Dutch paintings to match.
14 rue des Grands-Augustins, 75006 Paris 01 43 26 49 39 Lunch, dinner; closed Sat, Mon lunch, Sun, 1–21 Aug and Christmas Saint-Michel

Mavrommatis (€–€€)
Refined traditional Greek cuisine; alfresco dining on the terrace in summer.
42 rue Daubenton, 75005 Paris 01 43 31 17 17 Lunch, dinner; closed Mon Censier-Daubenton

Mon Vieil Ami (€€)
Recently opened restaurant; trendy rustic décor; delicious, reasonably priced dishes.
69 rue Saint-Louis-en-l'Ile, 75004 Paris 01 40 46 01 35 Lunch, dinner; closed Mon and Tue lunch Pont-Marie

La Parcheminerie (€–€€)
Charming bistro in picturesque pedestrian street of the Latin Quarter.
31 rue de la Parcheminerie, 75005 Paris 01 46 33 65 12 Lunch, dinner; closed Sun and Mon Saint-Michel; Cluny-la-Sorbonne

Le Procope (€–€€)
An 18th-century literary café known to Voltaire and Benjamin Franklin, now a historic monument.
13 rue de l'Ancienne Comédie, 75006 Paris 01 40 46 79 00 Lunch, dinner Odéon

La Régalade (€–€€)
Haute cuisine at relatively low prices in unassuming setting; book well in advance.
49 avenue Jean Moulin, 75014 Paris 01 45 45 68 58 Lunch, dinner; closed Sat Sun and Mon lunch Alesia

Le Reminet (€–€€)
Refined bistro-style fare; terrace in summer. Extraordinarily good desserts. Friendly service.
3 rue des Grands-Degrés, 75005 Paris 01 44 07 04 24 Lunch, dinner, closed Mon, Tue, 1–21 Jan and 15–31 Aug St-Michel

Susan's Place (€)
Convivial Tex Mex restaurant also serving vegetarian dishes.
51 rue des Écoles, 75005 Paris 01 43 54 23 22 Lunch, dinner; closed Sun lunch, Mon Maubert-Mutualité

Thoumieux (€–€€)
High-class brasserie specialising in home-made duck *cassoulet*.
79 rue Saint-Dominique, 75007 Paris 01 47 05 49 75 Lunch, dinner Invalides

La Tour d'Argent (€€€)
Haute cuisine served in exceptional surroundings with remarkable view of Notre-Dame and the river; speciality: *canard* (duck) *Tour d'Argent*.
15–17 quai de la Tournelle, 75005 Paris 01 43 54 23 31 Lunch, dinner; closed Mon, Tue lunch Pont-Marie

La Truffière (€€)
Very refined cuisine served in pleasant surroundings. The menu makes good use of truffles, as the name suggests.
4 rue Blainville, 75005 Paris 01 46 33 29 82 Lunch, dinner; closed Mon, 1–20 Aug Place Monge

Ze Kitchen Galerie (€€)
Trendy restaurant popular with the local crowd; innovative cuisine served in original surroundings.
4 rue des Grands-Augustins, 75006 Paris, 01 44 32 00 32 Lunch, dinner; closed Sat lunch and Sun Saint-Michel

Where to Eat
Restaurants usually serve meals from midday to 2PM and from 7.30 to 10.30PM. *Brasseries* (the word means breweries) are restaurants where one can often eat at any time of the day and that often have *choucroute* on their menu, served with a glass of draught beer. Bistros are usually more modest (although some of them are very fashionable) and convivial, boasting quick, friendly service.

Ile de France

Prices
The same price rating as for Paris has been applied to restaurants in nearby towns; however, you can expect to get much better value for money outside the capital; it is also important to remember that service finishes earlier in the evening than in Paris, usually around 9:30.

Chantilly

Gare du Nord to Chantilly-Gouvieux

Château de la Tour (€€)
Refined cuisine and wood-panelled décor; terrace in summer.
Chemin de la Chaussée, 60270 Gouvieux (1km from Chantilly) 03 44 62 38 38 Lunch, dinner

Condé Ste Libiaire (3km from Disneyland)

RER A Marne-la-Vallée/Chessy

La Vallée de la Marne (€-€€)
Peaceful setting; dining-room overlooks the garden on the banks of the River Marne. Fresh local produce.
2 quai de la Marne, 77450 Condé-Ste Libiaire 01 60 04 31 01 Lunch, dinner; closed Mon dinner, Tue

Fontainebleau

Gare de Lyon to Fontainebleau-Avon then A or B

L'Atrium (€–€€)
Pizzeria in the town centre; with attractive year-round terrace dining.
20 rue France, 77300 Fontainebleau 01 64 22 18 36 Lunch, dinner

Le Caveau des Ducs (€€)
Elegant restaurant in vaulted cellars; terrace in summer.
24 rue Ferrare, 77300 Fontainebleau 01 64 22 05 05 Lunch, dinner

Le Montijo (€€)
Brasserie in luxury hotel facing the Château; terrace in summer.
Grand Hôtel de l'Aigle Noir, 27 place Napoléon Bonaparte, 77300 Fontainebleau 01 60 74 60 00 Lunch, dinner

Drive In and Around the Forêt de Fontainebleau

Barbizon

L'Angélus (€€)
Convivial gastronomic restaurant with a terrace in summer.
31 rue Grande, 77630 Barbizon 01 60 66 44 30 Lunch, dinner; closed Tue

Hostellerie du Bas-Préau (€€–€€€)
Haute cuisine meals served in the garden. Queen Elizabeth II and Emperor Hiro Hito have both stayed here.
22 rue Grande, 77630 Barbizon 01 60 66 40 05 Lunch, dinner

Bourron-Marlotte (9km south of Fontainebleau)

Les Prémices (€€)
Within the Fontainebleau forest; dishes are served on the terrace in summer.
12 bis rue Blaise de Montesquiou. 77780 Bourron-Marlotte 01 64 78 33 00 Lunch, dinner; closed Sun dinner, Mon and first two weeks in August

Rueil-Malmaison

RER Rueil-Malmaison

Le Fruit Défendu (€€)
Picturesque inn along the Seine; traditional French cuisine.
80 boulevard Belle-rive, 92500 Rueil-Malmaison 01 47 49 60 60 Lunch, dinner; closed Sun dinner, Mon

Saint-Cloud

Gare Saint-Lazare to Saint-Cloud

Quai Ouest (€€)
This 'Floating warehouse' serving appetising fish and poultry dishes is the place to go when the sun is out.
1200 quai Marcel Dassault, 92210 Saint-Cloud 01 46 02 35 54 Lunch, dinner

Saint-Denis

Métro Saint-Denis-Basilique

Campanile Saint-Denis Basilique (€)
One of a chain of inn-style modern hotels serving reliably good cuisine.
14 rue Jean-Jaurès, 93200 Saint-Denis 01 48 20 74 31 Lunch, dinner

Saint-Germain-en-Laye

RER Saint-Germain-en-Laye

Cazaudehore-La Forestière (€€€)
Sophisticated garden setting for refined summer meals; the menu even includes frogs' legs!
1 avenue du Président Kennedy, 78100 Saint-Germain-en-Laye 01 30 61 64 64 Lunch, dinner; closed Mon except hols

Ermitage des Loges (€€)
Reasonably priced, cuisine with an emphasis on fish and seafood. Summer eating is in the garden.
11 avenue des Loges, 78100 Saint-Germain-en-Laye 01 39 21 50 90 Lunch, dinner

Feuillantine (€)
You will find tasty cuisine at moderate prices in this elegant commuterland setting close to the impressive château.
10 rue Louviers, 78100 Saint-Germain-en-Laye 01 34 51 04 24 Lunch, dinner

10km from Vaux-Le-Vicomte

Gare de Lyon to Melun

La Mare au Diable (€€)
Lovely old house with beams (see panel); terrace for summer meals.
RN6, 77550 Melun-Sénart 01 64 10 20 90 Lunch, dinner; closed Sun dinner, Mon

Versailles

Gare Saint-Lazare to Versailles Rive-Droite; RER C to Versailles Rive Gauche

Le Boeuf à la Mode (€)
Old-fashioned brasserie with sunny terrace serving excellent duck and vegetable spaghettis.
4 rue au Pain, 78000 Versailles 01 39 50 31 99 Lunch, dinner

La Cuisine Bourgeoise (€€)
Tasty refined cuisine served in cosy surroundings; perfect place to stop on a day out to Versailles.
10 boulevard du Roi, 78000 Versailles 01 39 53 11 38 Lunch, dinner; closed Sat lunch, Sun, Mon and 3 weeks in Aug

Le Potager du Roy (€–€€)
Extremely good-value bistro. Traditional dishes served in elegant surroundings.
1 rue du Maréchal-Joffre, 78000 Versailles 01 39 50 35 34 Lunch, dinner; closed Sun dinner and Mon

Drive through the Vallée De Chevreuse

Rambouillet

Le Cheval Rouge (€–€€)
Restaurant in the heart of the old town; traditional cuisine served in convivial setting; pleasant winter garden.
78 rue du Général-de-Gaulle, 78120 Rambouillet, 01 30 88 80 61 Lunch, dinner; closed Tue evening and Wed

La Mare au Diable
Memories of George Sand linger on in this 15th-century manor house, named after one of her most famous 'rural' novels; it was here that the young romantic Aurore Dupin met her future husband and later decided on her pen-name.

Paris

Prices
Prices indicated below are per room:
€ = **budget (under €100)**
€€ = **moderate (€100–€200)**
€€€ = **expensive to luxury (over €200)**

Note that luxury hotels such as the Ritz or the Crillon can charge over 700 euros for a double room. Payment can be made by credit cards in most hotels except in some budget hotels.

Hôtel de l'Abbaye (€€€)
A roaring log fire and a delightful inner garden ensure comfort whatever the season.
www.hotel-abbaye.com
10 rue Cassette, 75006 Paris
01 45 44 38 11 All year
Saint-Sulpice

Hôtel d'Angleterre Saint-Germain-des-Prés (€€–€€€)
The largest rooms of this quiet luxury hotel overlook the secluded garden.
44 rue Jacob, 75006 Paris
01 42 60 34 72 All year
St-Germain-des-Prés

Hôtel Caron de Beaumarchais (€€)
Recently restored 18th-century town house in the Marais; refined period decoration and air conditioning in all rooms.
www.carondebeaumarchais.com 12 rue Vieille-du-Temple, 75004 Paris 01 42 72 34 12 All year Hôtel de Ville

Hôtel Esmeralda (€)
Some rooms in this old-fashioned yet cosy hotel offer delightful views of Notre-Dame. Beware no lift!
4 rue Saint-Julien-le-Pauvre, 75005 Paris 01 43 54 19 20 All year Saint-Michel

Hôtel Franklin-Roosevelt (€€€)
Bright comfortable bedrooms with striking murals and functional bathrooms; warm welcome.
www.groupfrontenac.com/introFRF.Rtm 18 rue Clément Marot, 75008 Paris 01 53 57 49 50 All year
Franklin-D Roosevelt

Hôtel Galileo (€€)
Modern refined hotel near the Champs-Elysées with air conditioning and well-appointed bedrooms, a few with verandas.
www.hotel-ile-saintlouis.com
54 rue Galilée, 75008 Paris
01 47 20 66 06 All year
George V

Hôtel du Jeu de Paume (€€€)
Exclusive hotel on the Ile Saint-Louis, housed in converted Jeu de Paume (inside tennis court), with striking galleries and mezzanines.
www.hoteljeudepaume.com
54 rue Saint-Louis-en-l'Ile, 75004 Paris 01 43 26 14 18 All year Pont-Marie

Hôtel du Lys (€)
Simple hotel at the heart of the Quartier Latin; no lift but modern bathrooms, warm welcome and reasonable prices; book well in advance.
23 rue Serpente, 75006 Paris
01 43 26 97 57 All year
Saint-Michel, Odéon

Hôtel Montalembert (€€€)
Luxury hotel, with discreet yet original decoration, sound-proofing and air conditioning; a quality hotel at top prices.
www.montalembert.com
3 rue de Montalembert, 75007 Paris 01 45 49 68 68 All year Rue du Bac

Hôtel de Nevers (€)
Simple but charming, in a former convent building; private roof terraces for top-floor rooms.
83 rue du Bac, 75007 Paris
01 45 44 61 30 All year
Rue du Bac

Hôtel du Panthéon (€€)
An elegant hotel conveniently situated in the university district, with well-appointed air-conditioned bedrooms.
www.hoteldupantheon.com
✉ 19 place du Panthéon, 75005 Paris ☎ 01 43 54 32 95 ⌚ All year Ⓜ Cardinal-Lemoine

Hôtel Place des Vosges (€)
Picturesque quiet hotel just off the place des Vosges.
✉ 12 rue de Birague, 75004 Paris ☎ 01 42 72 60 46 ⌚ All year Ⓜ Saint-Paul, Bastille

Hôtel Le Régent (€€)
Air conditioning and bright well-appointed bedrooms in this cleverly restored 18th-century house in St-Germain-des-Prés.
✉ 61 rue Dauphine, 75006 Paris ☎ 01 46 34 59 80 ⌚ All year Ⓜ Odéon

Hôtel Relais du Louvre (€€)
Warm colours, antique furniture and modern comfort, a stone's throw from the Louvre.
www.relaisdulouvre.com
✉ 19 rue des Prêtres Saint-Germain-l'Auxerrois, 75001 Paris ☎ 01 40 41 96 42 ⌚ All year Ⓜ Louvre-Rivoli

Résidence les Gobelins (€)
A haven of peace near the lively rue Mouffetard; warm welcome.
www.hotelgobelins.com
✉ 9 rue des Gobelins, 75013 Paris ☎ 01 47 07 26 90 ⌚ All year Ⓜ Les Gobelins

Hôtel Les Rives de Notre-Dame (€€€)
Elegant and comfortable, with sound-proofed bedrooms overlooking the quai Saint-Michel and the Ile de la Cité.
www.rivesdenotredame.com
✉ 15 quai Saint-Michel, 75005 Paris ☎ 01 43 54 81 16 ⌚ All year Ⓜ Saint-Michel

Hôtel Ritz Paris (€€€)
Sometimes called the palace of kings and the king of palaces, the Ritz shares with the Crillon the top of the list of Paris's luxury hotels. Overlooking the place Vendôme, it boasts a beautiful swimming pool and luxury fitness centre; prices are accordingly very high.
www.ritzparis.com
✉ 15 place Vendôme, 75001 Paris ☎ 01 43 16 30 70 ⌚ All year Ⓜ Opéra

Select Hôtel (€€)
Fully modernised hotel in the heart of the Latin Quarter, close to the Luxembourg gardens; cosy atmosphere; glass-roofed patio.
www.selecthotel.fr ✉ 1 place de la Sorbonne, 75005 Paris ☎ 01 46 34 14 80 ⌚ All year Ⓜ Cluny-la-Sorbonne; Odéon

Tim Hôtel Montmartre (€€)
In the old part of Montmartre, with lovely views; attention to detail makes it a comfortable if simple place to stay.
www.timhotel.com
✉ 11 rue Ravignan, 75018 Paris ☎ 01 42 55 74 79 ⌚ All year Ⓜ Abbesses

Hôtel Le Tourville (€€–€€€)
Refined decoration for this modern hotel in the elegant 7th *arrondissement*, close to Les Invalides.
www.tourville.com
✉ 16 avenue de Tourville, 75007 Paris ☎ 01 47 05 62 62 ⌚ All year Ⓜ Ecole Militaire

Historic Hotels
The Hôtel d'Angleterre was the seat of the British Embassy in the 18th century, at the time of American Independence; more recently, it was one of the temporary homes of Ernest Hemingway.
The Jeu de Paume, recently converted into a hotel, was built in the early 17th century as part of the development of the Ile Saint-Louis. It was the first one of its kind in Paris.
The exclusive Hôtel Ritz has had many famous guests, including the Duke of Windsor and Ernest Hemingway.

Ile de France

Country Hotels
The hotels listed in this section have been selected as much for their picturesque, even outstanding setting and surroundings as for their high level of comfort. The price range is the same as that of Paris hotels but these country hotels offer much better value for money.

Chantilly

Gare du Nord to Chantilly-Gouvieux

Château de Montvillargenne (€€–€€€)

Large mansion in vast own grounds; covered swimming pool, sauna, sports facilities. **www.chateaudemontvillargenne.com 1 avenue François Mathet, 60270 Gouvieux 03 44 62 37 37 All year**

Château de la Tour (€€)

Late 19th-century mansion, with swimming pool, terrace and large park.
www.chateaudelatour.fr Chemin de la Chaussée, 60270 Gouvieux 03 44 62 38 38 All year

Le Relais d'Aumale (€€)

Former hunting-lodge of the Duc d'Aumale, at the heart of the Forêt de Chantilly.
http:/relais-aumale.fr 37 place des Fêtes, Montgresin 60560 Orry la Ville 03 44 54 61 31 All year

Disneyland

RER Marne-la-Vallée/Chessy

Cheyenne (€–€€)

Each of the hotels has its own authentic American theme; this one is self-explanatory.
01 60 45 62 00; UK booking centre: 08705 03 03 03 All year

Disneyland Hotel (€€€)

This Victorian-style hotel is the most sophisticated and expensive of the six hotels in the Disneyland complex and the closest to the theme park.
01 60 45 65 00; UK booking centre: 08705 03 03 03 All year

Magny-le-Hongre

Kyriad Disneyland Resort Paris (€)

Family-style modern hotel belonging to the Kyriad Hotel chain, very close to the Disneyland theme parks; shuttle service.
77700 Magny-le-Hongre 01 60 43 61 61 All year

Fontainebleau

Gare de Lyon to Fontainebleau-Avon

Grand Hôtel de l'Aigle Noir (€€€)

Napoleon III-style decoration for this hotel facing the castle; fitness club, indoor swimming pool and very good restaurant.
www.hotelaiglenoir.fr 27 place Napoléon Bonaparte, 77300 Fontainebleau 01 60 74 60 00 All year

Drive in and Around the Forêt de Fontainebleau

Barbizon

Hôtel Les Charmettes (€)

Picturesque timber-framed Logis de France hotel.
www.lescharmettes.com 40 Grande-Rue, 77630 Barbizon 01 60 66 40 21 All year

Hostellerie de la Clé d'Or (€)

Former coaching-inn; rooms overlook the garden; terrace for summer meals.
73 Grande-Rue, 77630 Barbizon 01 60 66 40 96 All year

Hôtel Les Pléiades (€)

A former painter's house turned into a hotel in the

'painters' village! Splendid terrace for summer meals.
21 Grande-Rue, 77630 Barbizon **01 60 66 40 25** **All year**

Saint-Germain-en-Laye

RER Saint-Germain-en-Laye

Hôtel Cazaudehore-La Forestière (€€)
Relaxation is the keynote in this large hotel.
www.cazaudehore.fr **1 avenue du Président Kennedy, 78100 Saint-Germain-en-Laye** **Hotel: 01 39 10 38 38** **All year**

Hôtel Ermitage des Loges (€€)
There's music on Wednesday and Thursday nights in the hotel bar; excellent restaurant.
www.ermitage-des-loges.fr **11 avenue des Loges, 78100 Saint-Germain-en-Laye** **01 39 21 50 90** **All year**

Pavillon Henri IV (€€–€€€)
Historic building near the famous Grande Terrasse; great views.
www.pavillonhenri4.fr **19–21 rue Thiers, 78100 Saint-Germain-en-Laye** **01 39 10 15 15** **All year**

Versailles

Gare Saint-Lazare to Versailles Rive Droite; RER C to Versailles Rive Gauche

Relais de Courlande (€)
Attractive converted 16th-century farmhouse; hydrotherapy facilities.
23 rue de la Division Leclerc, 78350 Les Loges-en-Josas **01 30 83 84 00** **All year**

Sofitel Château de Versailles (€€€)
Luxury Château hotel next to Château de Versailles.
www.sofitel.com **2bis avenue de Paris, 78000 Versailles** **01 39 07 46 46** **All year**

Trianon Palace (€€€)
This luxury establishment, on the edge of the Parc de Versailles, boasts an exclusive fitness club, two tennis courts and golf and riding facilities. It is one of the top palace hotels in France.
www.trianonpalace.fr **1 boulevard de la Reine, 78000 Versailles** **01 30 84 50 00** **All year**

Drive through the Vallée De Chevreuse

Abbaye des Vaux de Cernay (€€–€€€)
A 12th-century Cistercian abbey, the setting for an unforgettable stay in the Vallée de Chevreuse; swimming pool, fitness club, tennis; musical evenings, *sons et lumières* show.
www.abbayedecernay.com **78720 Cernay-la-Ville (14km northeast of Rambouillet)** **01 34 85 23 00 and 01 34 85 11 59** **All year**

Auberge le Manet (€–€€)
A hotel in a former building of the 13th-century Abbaye de Port-Royal; set in its own grounds.
www.aubergedumanet.com **61 avenue du Manet, 78180 Montigny-le-Bretonneux (just north of the D91, ➤ 90, Vallée de Chevreuse drive)** **01 30 64 89 00** **All year**

Pavillon Henri IV
The lovely brick building of the Pavillon Henri IV, surmounted by a dome, is all that remains, together with another pavilion, of the Château Neuf erected at the beginning of the 17th century and demolished in the 18th century after being neglected for too long. King Louis XIV was actually born within its walls on 5 September 1638. The pavilion was turned into a hotel in 1836 and has subsequently attracted many famous guests.

Shopping in Paris

Opening Hours
Shops are usually open weekdays from 9–7. Some are closed on Mondays, others are open on Sundays. Smaller shops sometimes close for lunch. Food shops remain open later. Department stores close late on Thursdays (up to 10PM).

Duty-Free Shopping
Residents of non-EU countries are entitled to a VAT refund (about 12–13 per cent) if they spend over 175 euros in the same shop. Export receipts issued by shopkeepers must be presented on the day of departure to the Customs Officer, who may wish to see the goods. The refund will be credited within 30 days.
More information from: Centre de reuseignements des douanes ☎ 08 25 30 82 63 or Global Refund, www.globalrefund.com.

Department Stores

Bazar de l'Hôtel de Ville
Known as the BHV, this store is famous for its huge do-it-yourself department, which claims to be the place to find what you can't find anywhere else!
✉ 52–4 rue de Rivoli, 75001 Paris ☎ 01 42 74 90 00 Ⓜ Hôtel de Ville

Bon Marché Rive Gauche
The only department store on the Left Bank, and the first to open in Paris; famous for its Grande Epicerie, selling specialities from various countries and freshly prepared delicacies.
✉ 24 rue de Sèvres, 75007 Paris ☎ 01 44 39 80 00 Ⓜ Sèvres-Babylone

Galeries Lafayette
A few blocks away from Au Printemps, with designer ready-to-wear fashion and lingerie. Under a giant glass dome there is an enticing display of everything a home and its inhabitants need.
✉ 40 boulevard Haussmann, 75009 Paris ☎ 01 42 82 34 56 Ⓜ Chaussée d'Antin

Monoprix
Chain of department stores for the budget-conscious. There is a large branch at the back of Au Printemps.
✉ 52 avenue des Champs-Elysées, 75008 Paris ☎ 01 53 77 65 65 Ⓜ Franklin-D Roosevelt

Au Printemps
Three stores in one: Le Printemps de la Mode, including ready-to-wear designer fashion, Le Printemps de la Maison, including elegant tableware and hi-fi, record and stationery department in the basement, and Brummell, devoted to menswear.
✉ 64 boulevard Haussmann, 75009 Paris ☎ 01 42 82 50 00 Ⓜ Havre-Caumartin

Samaritaine
It lacks the stylishness of the boulevard Haussmann's stores but it offers a splendid view of Paris from the roof-top Toupary bistro.
✉ 19 rue de la Monnaie, 75001 Paris ☎ 01 40 41 20 20 Ⓜ Pont Neuf

Shopping Centres

Carrousel du Louvre
Elegant shopping centre located beneath the place du Carrousel and communicating with the Louvre; several boutiques connected with the arts, Virgin store and a number of bars serving food from different countries.
✉ 99 rue de Rivoli, 75001 Paris ☎ 01 43 16 47 47 Ⓜ Palais Royal

Drugstore Publicis
Unexpectedly situated at the top of the Champs-Elysées, a stone's throw from the Arc de Triomphe, this shopping mall has a restaurant and a selection of gift/souvenir shops.
✉ 133 avenue des Champs-Elysées, 75008 Paris ☎ 01 44 43 79 00 Ⓜ Charles de Gaulle-Etoile

Forum des Halles
Underground shopping centre on several floors including chain-store fashion boutiques and the new

Forum des Créateurs for young designers; also a huge FNAC store (► 107).
✉ 1–7 rue Pierre Lescot, 75001 Paris 🚇 Les Halles; RER Châtelet-Les Halles

Galeries Marchandes des Champs-Elysées
Several shopping malls link the Champs-Elysées and the parallel rue de Ponthieu between the Rond-Point des Champs-Elysées and the avenue George V; various boutiques including fashion and shoes.
✉ Avenue des Champs-Elysées, 75008 Paris 🚇 George V, Franklin-D Roosevelt

Marché Saint-Germain
Fashion and gift shops including clothes, shoes, leather goods, accessories, perfume, jewellery and gifts.
✉ Rue Clément, 75006 Paris 🚇 Mabillon

Trois Quartiers
Mainly traditional fashion boutiques in the exclusive Madeleine area.
✉ 23 boulevard de la Madeleine, 75001 Paris ☎ 01 42 97 80 12 🚇 Madeleine

Fashion – Haute Couture

Chanel
✉ 31 rue Cambon, 75001 Paris ☎ 01 42 86 28 00 🚇 Concorde

Christian Dior
✉ 30 avenue Montaigne, 75008 Paris ☎ 01 40 73 54 44 🚇 Champs-Elysées Clémenceau

Emmanuel Ungaro
✉ 2 avenue Montaigne, 75008 Paris ☎ 01 53 57 00 00 🚇 Alma-Marceau

Givenchy
✉ 3 avenue George V, 75008 Paris ☎ 01 44 31 50 00 🚇 Alma-Marceau

Pierre Cardin
✉ 27 avenue de Marigny, 75008 Paris ☎ 01 42 66 68 98 and 01 42 66 64 74 🚇 Champs-Elysées Clémenceau

Yves Saint-Laurent
✉ 7 avenue George V, 75008 Paris ☎ 01 56 62 64 00 🚇 Alma-Marceau

Fashion – Boutiques and Accessories

Hermès
Silk scarves, leather goods.
✉ 24 rue du Faubourg Saint-Honoré, 75008 Paris ☎ 01 40 17 47 17 🚇 Concorde

Jean-Paul Gaultier
Ready-to-wear fashion from this famous designer.
✉ 30 rue du Faubourg Saint-Antoine, 75012 Paris ☎ 01 44 68 84 84 🚇 Bastille

Madelios
Male fashion from city suits to casuals and accessories.
✉ 23 boulevard de la Madeleine, Paris 75001 ☎ 01 53 45 00 00 🚇 Madeleine

Nina Jacob
Trendy fashion and accessories.
✉ 23 rue des Francs-Bourgeois, 75004 Paris ☎ 01 42 77 41 20 🚇 Saint-Paul

raoul et curly
Designer accessories, jewellery, perfumes, cosmetics, leather goods.
✉ 47 avenue de l'Opéra, 75002 Paris ☎ 01 47 42 50 10 🚇 Opéra

Fashion
Most top fashion houses are located in the Concorde/Champs-Elysées area, in particular, avenue Montaigne, avenue Marigny and rue du Faubourg Saint-Honoré. Fashion boutiques selling ready-to-wear designer clothes are to be found in place des Victoires, in the Marais district (rue des Francs-Bourgeois), in the Palais-Royal area (rue Saint-Honoré), and in and around St-Germain-des-Prés (rue Saint-Sulpice, rue Bonaparte, rue de Rennes, rue de Sèvres and rue de Grenelle).

Shopping Arcades
A number of the covered shopping arcades built at the end of the 18th and the beginning of the 19th centuries still survive, retaining their old-world charm. Lined with boutiques and tea-rooms, they offer a moment's respite from the city's bustle. The most attractively decorated are the Galerie Vivienne, Galerie Colbert and Galerie Véro-Dodat, near the Palais-Royal. Others, such as the Passage Jouffroy along the Grands Boulevards, have a more exotic flavour.

Walter Steiger
Luxury shoes for men and women.
83 rue du Faubourg Saint-Honoré, 75008 Paris 01 42 66 65 08 Miromesnil

Yohji Yamamoto
Ready-to-wear clothes by the Japanese designer.
22 rue de Sèvres, 75007 Paris 01 45 44 29 32 St-Germain-des-Prés

High-Class Jewellers

Boucheron
26 place Vendôme, 75001 Paris 01 42 61 58 16 Opéra

Cartier
13 rue de la Paix, 75002 Paris 01 42 18 53 70 Opéra

Chaumet
12 place Vendôme, 75001 Paris 01 44 77 24 00 Opéra

Miscellaneous Gifts

Agatha
Fashion jewellery shop.
99 rue de Rivoli, 75001 Paris 01 42 96 03 09 Châtelet

Bernardaud
Porcelain, tableware, jewellery, original gifts.
11 rue Royale, 75008 Paris 01 47 42 82 86 Concorde, Madeleine

Lalique
Beautiful glass objects to suit every taste.
11 rue Royale, 75008 Paris 01 53 05 12 12 Concorde, Madeleine

Maison du Chocolat
Want to try the best chocolate in Paris?
225 rue du Faubourg Saint-Honoré, 75008 Paris 01 42 27 39 44 Ternes

Sic Amor
Fashion jewellery and accessories.
20 rue du Pont Louis-Philippe, 75004 Paris 01 42 76 02 37 Pont-Marie

Upla
Trendy gift shop.
5 rue St-Benoît, 75006 Paris 01 40 15 10 75 St-Germain des Prés

Art, Antiques and Handicrafts

Louvre des Antiquaires
This centre houses around 250 upmarket antique shops on three floors.
2 place du Palais-Royal, 75001 Paris 01 42 97 27 27 Palais-Royal

La Tuile à Loup
Handicrafts from various French regions.
35 rue Daubenton, 75005 Paris 01 47 07 28 90 Censier-Daubenton

Viaduc des Arts
Disused railway viaduct housing beneath its arches workshops and exhibitions displaying art and handicrafts.
9–129 avenue Daumesnil, 75012 Paris Bastille, Ledru-Rollin, Reuilly-Diderot

Village Saint-Paul
A group of small antique dealers established between rue Saint-Paul and rue Charlemagne.
Le Marais, 75004 Paris Saint-Paul

Village Suisse
Very expensive antiques displayed in the former Swiss pavilions of the 1900 World Exhibition.
78 avenue de Suffren, 54 rue de la Motte-Picquet, 75015 Paris
La Motte Picquet, Grenelle

Books, CDs, Videotapes and Hi-Fi

The Abbey Bookshop
New and second-hand books from Britain, Canada and the USA.
29 rue de la Parcheminerie, 75005 Paris 01 46 33 16 24
Saint-Michel

FNAC
Books, hi-fi, videos, CDs, cameras, computers, on several floors.
28 avenue des Ternes, 75017 Paris (other branches in Montparnasse, Les Halles and Bastille) 01 44 09 18 00
Ternes

Gibert Joseph
Stationery, new and second-hand books, CDs and videos.
26–30 boulevard Saint-Michel, 75006 Paris 01 44 41 88 88 Odéon, Cluny-la-Sorbonne, Luxembourg

Shakespeare & Company
New and second-hand books in English.
37 rue de la Bûcherie, 75005 Paris 01 43 26 96 50
Maubert-Mutualité

Village Voice
English-language bookshop.
6 rue Princesse, 75006 Paris 01 46 33 36 47 Mabillon

W H Smith
Branch of the famous British chain-store; reference and children's books; guidebooks in English and French.
248 rue de Rivoli, 75001 Paris 01 44 77 88 99
Concorde

Children's Shops

Agnès B Enfant
Smart children's clothes by the fashionable designer.
2 rue du Jour, 75001 Paris
01 40 39 96 88
Les Halles

La Boutique de Floriane
Elegant children's clothes; other branches in rue de Sèvres, rue du Faubourg Saint-Honoré, rue de Grenelle, rue de Longchamp.
17 rue Tronchet, 75008 Paris
01 42 65 25 95
Madeleine

Chantelivre
Specialist bookshop dealing with all the subjects that interest children.
13 rue de Sèvres, 75006 Paris 01 45 48 87 90
Sèvres-Babylone

La Maison des Bonbons
Delicious sweets in all shapes.
14 rue Mouton Duvernet 75014 Paris 01 45 41 25 55
Mouton Duvernet

Le Nain Bleu
The most famous toy shop in Paris.
408 rue Saint-Honoré, 75008 Paris 01 42 60 39 01
Concorde, Madeleine

Food and Wines

Dubois et Fils
This temple to an amazing range of cheese supplies Paris's top restaurants!

'Carré Rive Gauche'
The 'square' formed along the Left Bank by the quai Voltaire, rue de l'Université, rue du Bac and rue des Saints-Pères, which includes the rue de Verneuil, rue de Lille and rue de Beaune, is famous for its high concentration of antique dealers; every year in May, the area hosts the 'Cinq jours des objets extraordinaires', an exhibition of unusual antique objects.

Art and Antiques
Antique dealers and art galleries are often concentrated in the same area: in the Marais, stroll along rue Vieille-du-Temple, rue Debelleyme and rue Saint-Gilles. On the Left Bank, rue Jacob and rue des Saints-Pères are particularly interesting. You can't browse in the exclusive shops in the avenue Matignon and rue du Faubourg Saint-Honoré, since you need an appointment to see the dealers! The Bastille area is definitely avant-garde and artists often exhibit in their own studios.

Open Late
Some shops at the heart of the city are open until midnight or later every night, including Virgin Mégastore and Drugstore Publicis in the Champs-Elysées and the chain store Prisunic in rue de la Boétie near by.

✉ 80 rue de Tocqueville, 75017 Paris ☎ 01 42 27 11 38 Ⓜ Malesherbes

Berthillon
Mouth-watering ice cream in a wide range of flavours.
✉ 31 rue Saint-Louis-en-l'Ile, 75004 Paris ☎ 01 43 54 31 61 🕐 Closed Mon and Tue Ⓜ Pont-Marie

Les Caves Augé
For wine lovers. This is the oldest wine shop in Paris.
✉ 116 boulevard Haussmann, 75008 Paris ☎ 01 45 22 16 97 🕐 Closed one week in Aug Ⓜ École-Militaire

Fauchon and Hédiard
Strictly for gourmets! Two delicatessen shops with high-quality French regional products.
✉ Fauchon at No 26, Hédiard at No 21 place de la Madeleine, 75008 Paris ☎ Fauchon: 01 47 42 91 10; Hédiard: 01 43 12 88 88 Ⓜ Madeleine

La Grande Épicerie de Paris
This huge grocery store is every gourmet's dreamland!
✉ 38 rue de Sèvres, 75007, Paris ☎ 01 44 39 81 00 Ⓜ Sèvres-Babylone

Lenôtre
Succulent cakes that melt in the mouth!
✉ 15 bd. de Courcelles, 75008 Paris ☎ 01 45 63 87 63 Ⓜ Villiers

Boulangerie Poîlane
The most famous bakery in Paris! Long queues form outside this shop for traditionally baked bread.
✉ 8 rue du Cherche-Midi, 75006 Paris ☎ 01 45 48 42 59 Ⓜ Sèvres-Babylone

La Maison du Miel
Delicately flavoured honey from various regions of France.
✉ 24 rue Vignon, 75008 Paris ☎ 01 47 42 26 70 Ⓜ Madeleine

Nicolas
Chain-stores selling a wide range of good French wines; at least one store per *arrondissement*.
✉ 189 rue Saint-Honoré, 75001 Paris ☎ 01 42 60 80 12 Ⓜ Palais-Royal

Markets

Carreau du Temple
Covered market specialising in leather and second-hand clothes.
✉ 75003 Paris 🕐 Tue–Fri 9–1:30, Sat 9–6, Sun 9–2 Ⓜ Temple, Arts et Métiers

Marché aux Fleurs
Picturesque daily market (8–7) that becomes a bird market on Sundays (8–7).
✉ Place Louis Lépine, Ile de la Cité, 75004 Paris Ⓜ Cité

Marché aux Puces de Saint-Ouen
The largest flea market in Paris. Everything you can think of is for sale. Prices are often inflated, be prepared to bargain.
✉ Between Porte de Saint-Ouen and Porte de Clignancourt, 75017 Paris 🕐 Sat–Mon 8–6 Ⓜ Porte de Clignancourt

Marché aux Timbres
Stamp market for dealers and private collectors.
✉ Rond-Point des Champs-Elysées, 75008 Paris 🕐 Thu, Sat and Sun 9–7 Ⓜ Franklin-D Roosevelt

Shopping in the Ile de France

Meaux

Fromagerie de Meaux
Delicious Brie de Meaux and Coulommiers, two very tasty cheeses from Ile de France, made locally but famous nationwide.
4 rue du Général Leclerc, 77100 Meaux (11km north of Disneyland Paris) 01 64 34 22 82

Fontainebleau

Gare de Lyon to Fontainebleau-Avon, then A or B

Boutique du Musée National de Fontainebleau
For history buffs fascinated by Napoleon I and European history at the beginning of the 19th century.
Château de Fontainebleau, 77300 Fontainebleau 01 64 23 44 97

Drive in and Around the Forêt de Fontainebleau

Barbizon

Anabel's Galerie
Contemporary painting and sculpture.
Le Bornage, 77630 Barbizon
Fax: 01 60 69 23 96
Weekends only

Galerie d'Art Castiglione
One of more than 10 art galleries to be found in this popular artists' village.
Grande rue, 77630 Barbizon
01 60 69 22 12

Soisy-sur-Ecole

Verrerie d'Art de Soisy
The Verrerie d'Art de Soisy has demonstrations of glass-blowing by the traditional rod method. Visitors will also have an opportunity to purchase ornamental glassware.
Le Moulin de Noues, 91840 Soisy-sur-Ecole 01 64 98 00 03 Daily except Sun morning

Saint-Germain-en-Laye

RER Saint-Germain-en-Laye

Boutique du Musée des Antiquités Nationales
History books from prehistory to the early Middle Ages as well as reproductions of jewellery and various items from the museum's collections.
Place du Château, 78100 Saint-Germain-en-Laye
01 39 10 13 22

Les Galeries de Saint-Germain
Close to the RER and the Château, 42 boutiques in les Galeries de Saint-Germain sell fashion, articles for the home and gifts; famous names include Chanel and Yves Saint-Laurent.
10 rue de la Salle, 78100 Saint-Germain-en-Laye 01 39 73 70 67 Closed Mon

Versailles

Gare Saint-Lazare to Versailles Rive Droite; RER C to Versailles Rive Gauche

Librairie-Boutique de l'Ancienne Comédie
There are 2,000 titles connected with the castle, its gardens and its history, many with information on 17th-and 18th-century architecture.
Château de Versailles, passage des Princes, 78000 Versailles 01 30 83 76 90

Street Markets
It is a tradition in France to buy food, and in particular fresh vegetables and fruit, from a market stall and Paris is no exception. Each *arrondissement* has its covered market, but open-air ones are much more colourful and lively and their higgledy-piggledy displays are definitely more picturesque. To get the feel of these typical Parisian attractions, go to the rue Mouffetard (Monge), the rue de Buci (Odéon) and the rue Lepic (Abbesses). They are open daily except on Mondays.

Paris and the Ile de France

Eating Out
Some chain restaurants offer set junior menus, often for less than 7 euros. Batifol, Bistro Romain, L'entrecôte, Hippopotamus, Pomme de Pain, Pizza Hut (in Paris), Chantegrill, Côte à Côte, Courtepaille, Pizza del Arte (outside Paris). Any good restaurant will always suggest a choice of dishes for your children.

Interactive Museums
Most major museums organise themed visits and workshops for children from an early age, on Wed and Sat; in addition to the museums listed here, there are also the Carnavalet, Cognacq-Jay, Louvre, Mode et Costume, Orsay, and Palais de la Découverte museums in Paris, and the Château de Saint-Germain-en-Laye and Château de Versailles, outside Paris.

Paris

Museums

Cité des Sciences et de l'Industrie
Cité des Enfants: for the 3–5 and 5–12 age groups. Book as soon as you arrive.
Techno cité: 11 years upwards.
Cinaxe: very effective simulator.
✉ 30 avenue Corentin-Cariou, 75019 Paris ☎ Information: 01 40 05 80 00 ⌚ 10–6; closed Mon Ⓜ Porte de la Villette

Musée de la Magie
Fascinating demonstrations of magic; workshops during school holidays.
✉ 11 rue Saint-Paul, 75004 Paris ☎ 01 42 72 13 26 ⌚ Wed, Sat and Sun 2–7 Ⓜ Saint-Paul

Musée Grévin
Five hundred wax figures of the famous, from Henry VIII to Michael Jackson and Arnold Schwarzenegger!
✉ 10 boulevard Montmartre, 75009 Paris ☎ 01 47 70 85 05 ⌚ Mon–Fri 10–6:30; Sat–Sun 10–7 Ⓜ Rue Montmartre

Musée de la Marine
Shows for 8–12 year-olds, with titles such as *Treasure Island*, on Wednesdays.
✉ Palais de Chaillot, place du Trocadéro, 75016 Paris ☎ 01 53 65 69 69 ⌚ Wed 3PM Ⓜ Trocadéro

Musée National d'Histoire Naturelle
Spectacular procession of large and small animals in the Grande Galerie de l'Evolution.
✉ 57 rue Cuvier, 75005 Paris ☎ 01 40 79 30 00 ⌚ 10–6 ; closed Tue Ⓜ Jussieu, Gare d'Austerlitz

Musée d'Orsay
A tour and a workshop to initiate 5–10 year-olds to painting and sculpture.
✉ 62 rue de Lille, 75007 Paris ☎ 01 40 49 48 48 ⌚ Jul and Aug Wed, Sat, Sun; phone for details Ⓜ Solférino

Outdoor Activities

Aquaboulevard
Aqualand with slides, heated pool, waves, beaches etc.
✉ 4–6 rue Louis Armand, 75015 Paris ☎ 01 40 60 10 00 ⌚ 9AM–11PM (midnight on Fri and Sat) Ⓜ Balard

Jardin d'Acclimatation
Adventure park at the heart of the Bois de Boulogne.
✉ Bois de Boulogne, 75016 Paris ☎ 01 40 67 90 82 ⌚ 10–6; small train from Porte Maillot on Wed, Sat, Sun, hols 1:30–6 Ⓜ Sablons, Porte Maillot

Jardin des Enfants aux Halles
An adventure ground for 7–11 year-olds.
✉ Forum des Halles, 105 rue Rambuteau, 75001 Paris ☎ 01 45 08 07 18 ⌚ Oct–May 9–12 and 2–4 (Wed 10–4), closed Mon); Jul, Aug Tue, Thu, Fri 9–12 and 2–6; Wed, Sat 10–6, Sun 1–6 Ⓜ Les Halles

Parc des Buttes-Chaumont
Cave, waterfall, lake, island and suspended bridge. Play-grounds for smaller children.
✉ 5 rue Botzaris, 75019 Paris ☎ 01 42 38 02 63 ⌚ 7AM–9PM Ⓜ Buttes-Chaumont

Parc Zoologique de Paris
Located inside the Bois de Vincennes, this is much larger than the zoo of the Jardin des Plantes.

53 avenue de Saint-Maurice, 75012 Paris 01 44 75 20 10 (recorded information) 9–6 (6:30 Sun and bank hols) Porte Dorée

Shows

Circus shows

They are seasonal but there are always several available at any time in and around Paris; information is available in the weekly publications *Pariscope* and *l'Officiel des Spectacles,* both of which have a children's section.

Marionnettes du Champ-de-Mars

Indoor puppet show; two different shows every week.
Champ-de-Mars (next to the Eiffel Tower), 75007 Paris 01 48 56 01 44 3.15 and 4.15; closed one week in Aug École-Militaire

Paris-story

Audio-visual show illustrating the history of Paris through its monuments.
11bis rue Scribe, 75009 Paris 01 42 66 62 06 9–7 on the hour Opéra

Ile de France

Outdoor Activities

Beach

There is a lovely beach at L'Isle-Adam on the banks of the Oise River (May–Sep).
Plage de L'Isle-Adam, 95290 L'Isle-Adam (on the D922, ➤ 80) 01 34 69 41 99

Boat trips

Along the Oise, between l'Isle-Adam and Anvers.
Tourisme Accueil Val d'Oise 01 30 29 51 00 May–Sep

Fontainebleau

Rowing on the Etang des Carpes in the park; little train through the town and park; cycling through the forest (cycle hire at the station); riding (01 60 72 22 40).
Office du Tourisme, 4 rue Royale, 77300 Fontainebleau 01 60 74 99 99 Gare de Lyon to Fontainebleau-Avon

Mer de Sable

Lots to do for children of all ages, as well as shows inspired by the American Far West, magic shows, and spectacular horse-riding displays in the sand dunes.
60950 Ermenonville, A1 motorway, exit No 7 Survilliers-Ermenonville-Saint-Witz (close to Parc Astérix) 03 44 54 00 96 Apr–Sep 10:30–6:30 (variable, inquire beforehand) RER Roissy-Aéroport Charles de Gaulle, then shuttle to Ermenonville

Theme parks (see the individual entries for Disneyland Paris ➤ 81 and Parc Astérix ➤ 85)

Versailles

Cycle through the magnificent park (cycle hire at the end of the Grand Canal) or, for children, take a ride in the little train (departure from the Bassin de Neptune).
78000 Versailles Information: 01 30 83 78 00 7–sunset Gare Saint-Lazare-Versailles Rive Droite

Shows

Chantilly

Musée Vivant du Cheval: demonstration of dressage (daily) and horse show (1st Sun of every month).
Grandes Ecuries, 60500 Chantilly 03 44 57 40 40 Gare du Nord to Chantilly-Gouvieux

Le Guignol du Parc de Saint-Cloud

Take a look at the puppet show in the park.
Grille d'Orléans, route de Ville-d'Avray 01 48 21 75 37 Wed, Sun 3 and 4, Sat 4 Gare Saint-Lazare to Sèvres/Ville d'Avray

Monuments

The following are among children's favourites: Arc de Triomphe, Conciergerie (older children), Grande Arche de la Défense, Notre-Dame (the towers), Tour Eiffel, Château de Chantilly (stables), Château de Fontainebleau and Château de Versailles.
For further information: www.iledenfrance.com

Sea Life Val d'Europe

Situated in the newly developed Val d'Europe complex, close to Disneyland Paris in Marne-la-Ville, this interactive marine-life centre includes some 30 aquariums displaying marine fauna and flora from around the world and offering an insight into endangered species schemes. Spectacular 360 degree tunnel!
Centre Commercial International Val d'Europe, 14 cours du Danube, Serris, 77 Marne-la-Vallée. Take the A4 motorway towards Metz-Nancy, exit 14 01 60 42 33 66 10–9

Entertainment in Paris

Nightlife News
Several brochures keep you up-to-date with events:
Weekly – *Pariscope* (including a *Time Out* selection in English) and *l'Officiel des Spectacles* issued Wednesday.
Monthly – *Paris Voice,* a free magazine available from English-language bookshops, highlights what's on in Paris: dance, theatre, music, art exhibitions…and comments on the latest trends; *www.parisvoice.com.*
At any time on the internet – A weekly and monthly selection of events is available on the official website of the Office de Tourisme de paris, *www.paris-touristoffice.com;* in addition, *www.paris.org* has a very comprehensive 'Paris Calendar'.

Changing Fashion
Hip clubs come and go and DJs move around from one to the other, but some things remain constant: nothing really starts before midnight, some clubs have an entry fee that includes one drink, others charge more for their drinks. It pays to be smartly dressed to get past the door people; jeans and trainers are out.

Concert Venues

Cité de la Musique
This new temple of classical music regularly sets new trends with special commissions.
✉ 221 avenue Jean Jaurès, 75019 Paris ☎ 01 44 84 45 45 Ⓜ Porte de Pantin

Salle Pleyel
Traditional concert hall, named after one of France's most famous piano-makers, recently refurbished, and home to the Orchestre de Paris.
✉ 252 rue du Faubourg Saint-Honoré, 75008 Paris ☎ 01 45 61 53 00 Ⓜ Ternes, Charles de Gaulle-Etoile

Theâtre des Champs-Elysées
Paris's most prestigious classical concert venue with top international orchestras.
✉ 15 avenue Montaigne, 75008 Paris ☎ 01 49 52 50 50 Ⓜ Alma-Marceau

Théâtre du Châtelet
Classical concerts, opera performances, ballets and variety shows alternate in this 19th-century theatre that has welcomed great names such as Mahler and Diaghilev.
✉ 1 place du Châtelet, 75001 Paris ☎ 01 40 28 28 40 Ⓜ Châtelet

Zénith
This huge hall is the mecca of rock concerts, a privilege it shares with the Palais Omnisports de Paris Bercy (➤ 113).
✉ 211 avenue Jean Jaurès, 75019 Paris ☎ 01 42 08 60 00 Ⓜ Porte de Pantin

Cabaret and Music-Hall

Crazy Horse Saloon
One of the best shows in Paris with beautiful girls and striking colours and lights.
✉ 12 avenue George V, 75008 Paris ☎ 01 47 23 32 32 Ⓜ Alma-Marceau

Le Lido
The show put on by the famous Bluebell girls is still very effective. It is possible to have dinner on a *bateau-mouche* followed by a show at the Lido.
✉ 116 bis avenue des Champs-Elysées, 75008 Paris ☎ 01 40 76 56 10 Ⓜ George V

Moulin-Rouge
Undoubtedly the most famous of them all! The show still includes impressive displays of French can-can.
✉ 82 boulevard de Clichy, 75018 Paris ☎ 01 53 09 82 82 Ⓜ Blanche

Olympia
The most popular music-hall in France has been completely refurbished.
www.olympiahall.com
✉ 28 boulevard des Capucines, 75009 Paris ☎ 08 92 68 33 68 Ⓜ Opéra

Jazz Clubs

Bilboquet
Select establishment at the heart of St-Germain-des-Prés for serious jazz fans.
✉ 13 rue Saint-Benoît, 75006 Paris ☎ 01 45 48 81 84 Ⓜ St-Germain-des-Prés

Caveau de la Huchette
Jazz and rock mania let loose in medieval cellars!

5 rue de la Huchette, 75005 Paris 01 43 26 65 05
Saint-Michel

Nightclubs and Bars

Les Bains Douches
Hip rendezvous of models and VIPs, with different styles of music.
7 rue du Bourg-l'Abbé, 75003 Paris 01 48 87 01 80
Etienne Marcel

La Chapelle des Lombards
Salsa and Afro music; live shows mid-week.
19 rue de Lappe, 75011 Paris 01 43 57 24 24 Bastille

La Casbah
Acid jazz and house alternate on different days with dance, disco music. Exotic décor.
18–20 rue de la Forge-Royale, 75011 Paris 01 43 71 04 39 Faidherbe-Chaligny

Le Cithéa
Live music, disco, jazz, funk.
114 rue Oberkampf, 75011 Paris 01 40 21 70 95

Le Mambo Club
Exotic décor, Afro music, salsa...
20 rue Cujas, 75005 Paris 01 43 54 89 21
Cluny-la-Sorbonne

Zed Club
Rock, jazz, swing, salsa and 60s–90s pop.
20 rue des Anglais, 75005 Paris 01 43 54 93 78
Saint-Michel; Maubert-Mutalité

Rue Oberkampf
Music bars line this street, which teems with young Parisians in summer.
Parmentier

Sport

Piscine des Halles
Situated on Level 3 of Les Halles complex, this sports centre has a 50m-long underground swimming pool.
10 place de la Rotonde, 75001 Paris 01 42 36 98 44
Les Halles

Piscine Pontoise Quartier Latin
Fitness club with swimming pool, squash court, sauna.
19 rue de Pontoise, 75005 Paris 01 55 42 77 88
Maubert-Mutualité

Hippodrome d'Auteuil
Steeplechasing; Grand Steeplechase de Paris, mid-June.
Bois de Boulogne, 75016 Paris 01 40 71 47 47
Porte d'Auteuil

Hippodrome de Longchamp
Flat-racing; Grand Prix de Paris in late June, Prix de l'Arc de Triomphe in October.
Bois de Boulogne, 75016 Paris 01 44 30 75 00
Porte Maillot and 244

Hippodrome de Vincennes
Trotting races; Prix d'Amérique in late January.
2 route de la Ferme, 75012 Paris 01 49 77 17 17
Château de Vincennes

Palais Omnisports de Paris Bercy (POPB)
Around 150 international sporting events every year.
8 boulevard de Bercy, 75012 Paris 01 40 02 60 60
Bercy

Parc des Princes
The famous venue for national and international football and rugby matches.
24 rue du Commandant-Guilbaud, 75016 Paris 08 25 07 50 78 Porte de Saint-Cloud

Roland Garros
Venue every year in late May and early June for the tennis tournament.
2 avenue Gordon Bennett, 75016 Paris 01 47 43 48 00
Porte d'Auteuil

Free Concerts
The municipality of Paris organises free concerts in the city's parks and gardens between May and September (programmes from the Office de Tourisme de Paris). Organ concerts on the 3rd Sunday of every month in selected venues (01 42 76 67 00). Some church concerts are free, for instance in the Madeleine and the American Church on Sunday and in Saint-Merri on Saturday and Sunday. Concerts broadcast from La Maison de Radio-France are open to the public and the entrance is free (information and reservations 01 42 30 22 22).

Cinemas and Theatres
There are some 350 cinema screens in Paris. Most large cinemas show several films at once. On Friday and Saturday nights, there are long queues outside cinemas in the Champs-Elysées and the Grands Boulevards.
Paris is also well stocked with theatres from the grand Comédie Française (01 44 58 15 15), where French classics are performed, to the tiny local theatre where contemporary plays either hit the limelight or flop into oblivion.

Entertainment in the Ile de France

Tourist Offices
For information about the Ile de France, contact the following:

Espace du Tourisme d'Ile-de-France
Carrousel du Louvre, 99 rue de Rivoli, 75001 Paris 08 26 16 66 66 within France and 01 44 50 19 98 from abroad

Espace du Tourisme d'Ile-de-France et de Seine et Marne
Festival Disney, 77705 Marne-la-Vallée cedex 4
As for Espace du Touriseme above and www.pidf.com

Comité Départemental du Tourisme des Yvelines
2 place André Mignot, 78012 Versailles cedex
01 39 07 71 22, www.cg78.fr

Office National des Forêts, Direction Régionale Ile-de-France
Boulevard de Constance, 77300 Fontainebleau 01 60 74 92 40

La Haute Vallée de Chevreuse
The Parc Naturel Regional de la Haute Vallée de Chevreuse was created in 1984 over an area of 25,000 ha, including 12,000 ha of woodland. It is criss-crossed by footpaths offering many opportunities for walks of 1½ to 3 hours. Information and itineraries are available from the Maison du Parc in Chevreuse.

Outdoor Activities

Boat trips

Croisières sur l'Oise
River cruise through the beautiful countryside lying between L'Isle-Adam and Auvers-sur-Oise.
01 30 29 51 00 Sun and holidays in summer

Golf

Disneyland Paris (27 holes)
Conveniently located near to the theme park and the Disneyland hotels.
Allée de la Mare Houleuse, 77400 Magny le Hongre
01 60 45 68 90 RER to Marne-la-Vallée/Chessy

Fontainebleau (18 holes)
Route d'Orléans, 77300 Fontainebleau 01 64 22 22 95 Gare de Lyon to Fontainebleau-Avon

Saint-Germain-en-Laye (27 holes)
Built in the Forêt de Saint-Germain by the Englishman Harry Colt.
Route de Poissy, 78100 Saint-Germain-en-Laye
01 39 10 30 30 RER to Saint-Germain-en-Laye

Versailles: Golf de la Boulie (two 18-hole courses and one 9-hole course)
Route du Pont Colbert, 78000 Versailles 01 39 50 59 41
Gare Saint-Lazare to Versailles Rive Droite

Hiking

Comité Régional de Randonnée Pédestre en Ile-de-France
Information on hiking in the seven *départements* of the Ile de France.
40 rue de Paradis, 75010 Paris 01 48 01 81 51
Plaisance, Pernéty

Horse-Racing

Hippodrome de Chantilly
Prix du Jockey-Club and Prix de Diane-Hermès in June.
Route de l'Aigle, 60631 Chantilly 03 44 62 44 00
Gare du Nord to Chantilly-Gouvieux

Horse-Riding

Centre Equestre des Basses Masures
Poigny-la-Forêt, 78125
01 34 84 70 29

Haras du Croc Marin
Chemin rural des Trembleaux, 77690 Montigny-sur-Loing
01 64 45 84 01

Leisure Parks

Saint-Quentin-en-Yvelines
Rambling nature trails, a wide range of sporting activities, children's playground, cycle hire etc.
D912, 78190 Trappes (7km west of Versailles) 01 30 62 20 12 RER C to Saint-Quentin-en-Yvelines (10-minute walk)

Torcy
Cycling, pony-trekking, wind-surfing, canoeing etc.
Route de Lagny, 77200 Torcy (9km west of Disneyland Paris)
01 64 80 58 75 RER to Torcy then 421

Mountain Bike Trails

Several itineraries through the Forêt de Fontainebleau.
Office du Tourisme 4 rue Royale, 77300 Fontainebleau
01 60 74 99 99 Gare de Lyon to Fontainebleau-Avon

Nature Park

Parc Naturel Régional de la Haute Vallée de Chevreuse
Themed nature trails: obtain

information from the Maison du Parc in Chevreuse.
La Maison du Parc, Château de la Madeleine, 78460 Chevreuse (► 90) ☎ 01 30 52 09 09

Concerts

Festival de Sceaux
International festival of chamber music from July to mid-September.
Orangerie du Domaine de Sceaux, 92330 Sceaux ☎ 01 46 60 07 79

Saison Musicale de Royaumont
Concerts in the lovely 12th-century abbey from June to September.
Abbaye de Royaumont, 95270 Asnières-sur-Oise (► 80) ☎ 01 30 35 59 00

Soirées Musicales au Château de Versailles
Concerts of baroque music on Thursdays and Saturdays, from November to June in the Opera house and the Royal Chapel. Information from the Centre de Musique Baroque de Versailles.
22 avenue de Paris, 78000 Versailles ☎ 01 39 20 78 00

Shows

Disneyland Paris
Buffalo Bill's Wild West Show
A fast moving dinner-show in the company of Buffalo Bill busy conquering the American Wild West.
☎ Bookings: 01 60 45 71 00

Disney Village
Just outside the theme park, restaurants, clubs, bars and shops open late into the evening. Also, there is a multiple-screen cinema and regular live concerts.
Disneyland Paris, 77777 Marne-la-Vallée ☎ 01 60 30 60 30

Meaux (11km north of Disneyland Paris)
Fe'erie Historique de Meaux
Son et Lumière show on a historical theme, lasting 1½ hours June–September. Information and bookings from Office de Tourisme de la Ville de Meaux.
2 rue St-Rémy, 77100 Meaux ☎ 01 64 33 02 26

Vaux-le-Vicomte
Visites aux Chandelles
Tours of the Château de Vaux-le-Vicomte by candlelight take place every Saturday night from May to mid-October.
Château de Vaux-le-Vicomte, 77950 Maincy ☎ 01 64 14 41 90 Gare de Lyon to Melun then taxi

Versailles
Grandes Eaux Musicales
There is a popular display of fountains with music held in the beautiful park of the Château de Versailles, every Sunday afternoon from May to October.

Grande Fête de Nuit
Son et Lumière show illustrating Louis XIV's life in the Château de Versailles and ending in a magnificent fire-works display; takes place seven times during the summer. Contact the Office de Tourisme for information.
Grandes Écuries du Roy, 78000 Versailles ☎ 01 30 83 78 89 Gare Saint-Lazare to Versailles Rive Droite

Fountains in the Parc de Versailles
Louis XIV wanted all the fountains in the park to work simultaneously. In order to achieve this, Le Nôtre worked for ten years with several engineers, dug 60km of channels and laid 11km of underground piping linking 15 small lakes and eight artificial ones!

What's On When

Check First!
The venues of the events listed here are liable to change from one year to the next and in the case of major festivals, there is often more than one venue. Dates also vary slightly from year to year. Information and programmes are available from:

Office de Tourisme de Paris
✉ 127 avenue des Champs-Elysées, 75008 Paris ☎ 08 36 68 31 12, www.paris-touristoffice.com Ⓜ Charles de Gaulle-Etoile
Espace Régional du Tourisme Ile-de-France
✉ Carrousel du Louvre, 99 rue de Rivoli, 75001 Paris ☎ 08 03 81 80 00, www.paris-ile-de-france.com Ⓜ Palais-Royal

Paris

June
Festival Chopin: An annual tribute to the Romantic composer at the Orangerie de Bagatelle in the heart of the Bois de Boulogne.
Fête de la Musique: On 21 June, Paris's squares, gardens and streets become alive with hundreds of musicians.
Festival de théâtre: Open-air theatre in English and in French, Jardin de Pré Catelan in the Bois de Boulogne.

June–July
Paris Jazz Festival: Open-air concerts in the Parc Floral de Paris, Bois de Vincennes.
14 July: Military parade down the Champs-Elysées, fireworks and popular ball to celebrate National Day.

July–August
Fête des Tuileries: Jardin des Tuileries becomes a fair-ground (begins end of June).
Paris, Quartier d'Eté: Open-air music, plays and dance.

September
Biennale Internationale des Antiquaires: Biennial International antiques display,(even years); last two weeks of September.
La Villette Jazz Festival: Jazz in the Grande Halle and the Parc de la Villette.

October
Foire Internationale d'Art Contemporain: Exhibition of contemporary art.
Mondial de l'Automobile: International motor-car show every two years (even years).

November–December
Salon Nautique International: International boat show.

Ile-de-France

April–May
Salon des Antiquaires de Rambouiellet: Antique fair.

May–June
Festival de Saint-Denis: Symphonic concerts take place in Saint-Denis Basilica.
Festival d'Auvers-sur-Oise: Singing, piano and chamber music with famous artists.
Fête Médiévale: Medieval pageant, siege warfare demonstrations, tournaments in the historic city of Provins.
Le Mois Moière: Theatre, music and street entertainment in parts of the city of Versailles.

July–August
Fête des Loges de Saint-Germain-en-Laye: A fair held in Saint-Germain forest.

July–September
Festival de l'Orangerie de Sceaux: Chamber music festival in parc de Sceaux.

August
Fête de la Saint-Louis à Fontainebleau: An ancient royal tradition celebrated by fireworks at the Château.

September
Fête du Cheval Fontainebleau: International gathering of horse lovers.
Barbizon au temps des peintres... : Recalls 1848–70, when Forêt de Fontainebleau drew artists to Barbizon.

September–mid-October
Festival d'Ile-de-France: Concerts and shows in castles, abbeys and churches throughout the region.

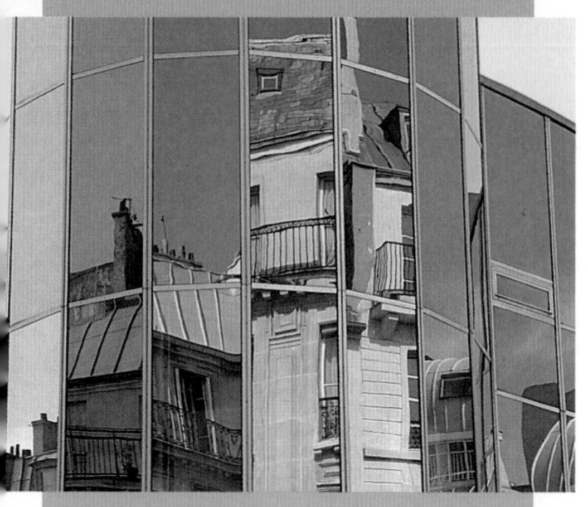

Practical Matters

Above: *Les Halles – old and new*
Right: *Egyptian obelisk, place de la Concorde*

TIME DIFFERENCES

GMT
12 noon

France
1PM

Germany
1PM

USA (NY)
7AM

Netherlands
1PM

Spain
1PM

BEFORE YOU GO

WHAT YOU NEED

● Required
○ Suggested
▲ Not required

Some countries require a passport to remain valid for a minimum period (usually at least six months) beyond the date of entry – contact their consulate or embassy or your travel agent for details.

	UK	Germany	USA	Netherlands	Spain
Passport/National Identity Card	●	●	●	●	●
Visa (Regulations can change – check before your journey)	▲	▲	▲	▲	▲
Onward or Return Ticket	▲	▲	▲	▲	▲
Health Inoculations	▲	▲	▲	▲	▲
Health Documentation (➤ 123, Health)	●	●	●	●	●
Travel Insurance	○	○	○	○	○
Driving Licence (national)	●	●	●	●	●
Car Insurance Certificate (if own car)	●	●	●	●	●
Car Registration Document (if own car)	●	●	●	●	●

WHEN TO GO

Paris

High season

Low season

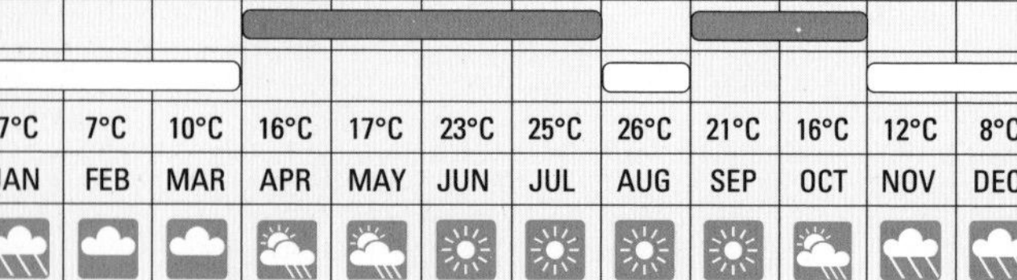

7°C	7°C	10°C	16°C	17°C	23°C	25°C	26°C	21°C	16°C	12°C	8°C
JAN	FEB	MAR	APR	MAY	JUN	JUL	AUG	SEP	OCT	NOV	DEC

 Wet
 Cloud
 Sun
 Sunshine & showers

TOURIST OFFICES

In the UK
French Tourist Office,
178 Piccadilly,
London W1J 9AL
☎ 09068 244123
Fax: (020) 7493 6594

In the USA
French Government
Tourist Office,
444 Madison Avenue,
16th floor,
New York NY10022
☎ 410 286 8310
Fax: 212/838 7855

French Government
Tourist Office,
9454 Wilshire Boulevard,
Suite 715,
Beverly Hills CA90212
☎ 310/271 6665
Fax: 310/276 2835

POLICE 17

FIRE 18

AMBULANCE 15

DOCTOR (24-hour call out) 01 47 07 77 77

WHEN YOU ARE THERE

ARRIVING

Paris has two main airports, Roissy-Charles-de-Gaulle (01 48 62 22 80), where most international flights arrive, and Orly (01 49 75 15 15). Eurostar trains, direct from London to Paris (☎ 0870 518 6186 in Britain, ☎ 08 92 35 35 39 in France), take 3 hours.

Roissy/Charles-de-Gaulle Airport
Kilometres to city centre

23 kilometres

Journey times

Train	45 minutes
Bus	50 minutes
Car	30–60 minutes

Orly Airport
Kilometres to city centre

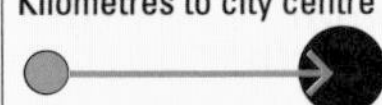

14 kilometres

Journey times

Train	40 minutes
Bus	30 minutes
Car	20–40 minutes

MONEY

The euro is the official currency of France. Euro banknotes and coins were introduced in January 2002. Banknotes are in denominations of 5, 10, 20, 50, 100, 200 and 500 euros and coins are in denominations of 1, 2, 5, 10, 20 and 50 cents, and 1 and 2 euros. Euro traveller's cheques are widely accepted, as are major credit cards. Credit and debit cards can also be used for withdrawing euro notes from cashpoint machines. Cashpoints are widely accessible throughout the city. France's former currency, the French franc, went out of circulation in early 2002.

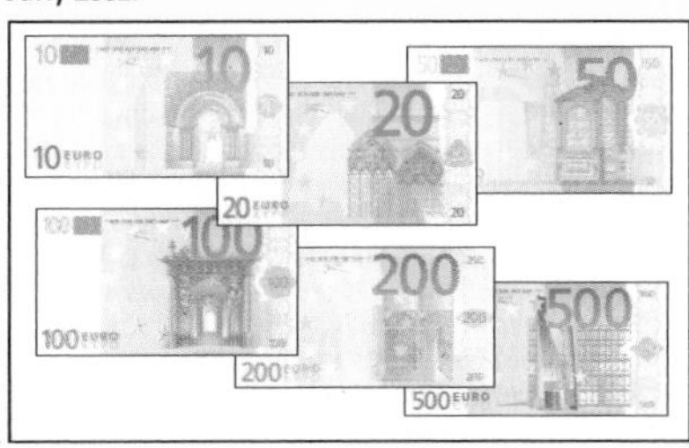

TIME

France is on Central European Time (GMT+1). From late March, when clocks are put forward one hour, until late October, French summer time (GMT +2) operates.

CUSTOMS

YES

From another EU country for personal use (guidelines):
up to 3,200 cigarettes, 400 cigarillos, 200 cigars, 3kg tobacco, 10 litres of spirits (over 22%), 20 litres of aperitifs, 90 litres of wine, 110 litres of beer.

From a non-EU country for personal use, the allowances are:
200 cigarettes OR 50 cigars OR 250g tobacco, 1 litre spirits (over 22%), 2 litres of wine, 2 litres of intermediary products (eg sherry) and sparkling wine, 50g perfume, 0.25 litres of eau de toilette. The value limit for goods is 175 euros.

Travellers under 17 years of age are not entitled to the tobacco and alcohol allowances.

NO

Drugs, firearms, ammunition, offensive weapons, obscene material, unlicensed animals.

UK	Germany	USA	Netherlands	Spain
01 44 51 31 00	01 53 83 45 00	01 43 12 22 22	01 40 62 33 00	01 44 43 18 00

WHEN YOU ARE THERE

TOURIST OFFICES

Head Office

- Office de Tourisme de Paris (Paris Tourism Bureau), 25 rue des Pyramides, 75001 Paris
  08 92 68 30 00 (omit the initial 0 when caling from outside France)
  Fax: 01 49 52 53 00
  www.paris-touristoffice.com

Branches

- Opéra-Grands Magasins
  Mon–Sat 9AM–6.30PM
- Gare de Lyon
  Mon–Sat 8AM–6PM
- Gare du Nord
  Daily 8AM–6PM
- Montmartre (place du Tertre)
  Daily 10AM–7PM
- Tour Eiffel (Eiffel Tower)
  May–Sep: daily 11AM–6:40PM

Paris Île-de-France

- Carrousel du Louvre (lower level)
  01 44 50 19 98/08 26 16 66 66
  www.pidf.com
  Daily 10AM–7PM
- Disneyland Resort Paris place des Passagers-du-Vent, Marne-la-Vallée, 77705
  01 60 43 33 33
  RER line A, Marne-la-Vallée–Parc Disneyland

NATIONAL HOLIDAYS

J	F	M	A	M	J	J	A	S	O	N	D
1		(1)	(1)	3(4)	(1)	1	1			2	1

1 Jan	New Year's Day
Mar/Apr	Easter Sunday and Monday
1 May	Labour Day
8 May	VE Day
May	Ascension Day
May/Jun	Whit Sunday and Monday
14 July	Bastille Day
15 Aug	Assumption Day
1 Nov	All Saints' Day
11 Nov	Remembrance Day
25 Dec	Christmas Day

Banks, businesses, museums and most shops (except boulangeries) are closed on these days.

OPENING HOURS

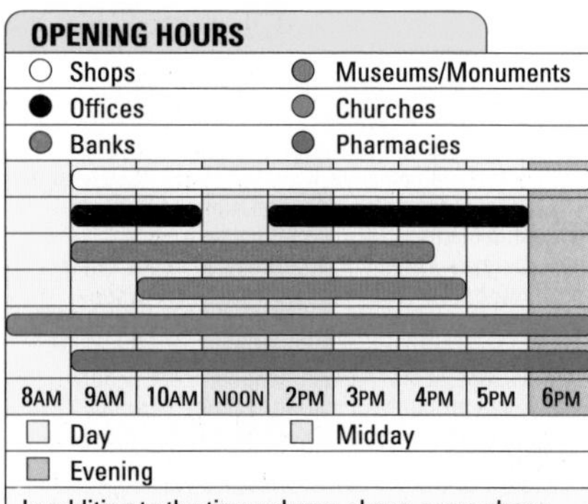

In addition to the times shown above, some shops close between noon and 2PM and all day Sunday and Monday. Large department stores open from 9:30AM to 6:30PM and until 9 or 10PM one or two days a week. Food shops open 7AM to 1:30PM and 4:30 to 8PM; some open Sunday until noon. Some banks are open extended hours, including Saturday morning but most banks close weekends. Museum and monument opening times vary but national museums close Tuesday (except the Musée d'Orsay, Versailles and the Trianon Palace which close Monday), while most other city museums usually close Monday.

PUBLIC TRANSPORT

Internal Flights Air France is the leading domestic airline – information (☎ 08 20 82 08 20). Daily departures from Orly and Roissy/Charles-de-Gaulle airports connect Paris with major French cities/towns in an average flight time of one hour.

RER The RER (pronounced 'ehr-oo-ehr') is the fast suburban rail service, which also serves the city centre. There are five lines (*lignes*): A, B, C, D and E and it is connected with the métro and SNCF suburban network. Services run 5:30AM to midnight, with trains every 12 minutes.

Métro Paris's underground with over 300 stations ensures you are never more than 500m from a métro stop. Lines are numbered 1 to 14 and are known by the names of the stations at each end. Follow the orange *correspondance* signs to change lines. The métro runs daily 5:30AM to 12:30AM.

Buses Buses are a good way of seeing Paris (especially route 24), although traffic can be very heavy. Bus stops show the numbers of buses that stop there. Buses run 6:30AM to 8:30PM with a reduced service on Sunday and after 8:30PM. Bus tickets are the same as those for the métro.

Boat The Batobus river shuttle (☎ 01 44 11 33 99) that plies the Seine from April to September provides an unusual view of Paris. It stops at the Eiffel Tower, Musée d'Orsay, the Louvre, Notre-Dame and the Hôtel de Ville; every 35 minutes, 10AM to 7PM (flat fare or all-day unlimited travel ticket).

CAR RENTAL

Car-rental companies have desks at Roissy/ Charles-de-Gaulle and Orly airports, and in Paris itself. Car hire is expensive but airlines and tour operators offer fly-drive, and French Railways (SNCF) – train/car, packages that are cheaper than hiring locally.

TAXIS

Taxis can be hailed if you see one with its roof light on. Taxis are metered with a surcharge for luggage, journeys after 10PM and before 6:30AM, and for going from and to stations and airports. Queues can be vast, particularly at railway stations.

DRIVING

Speed limits on toll motorways (*autoroutes*) **130kph (110kph** when wet). Non-toll motorways and dual carriageways: **110kph (100kph** when wet). Paris ring road (*périphérique*): **80kph**.

Speed limits on country roads: **90kph (80kph** when wet)

Speed limits on urban roads: **50kph**

Must be worn in front seats at all times and in rear seats where fitted.

Random breath-testing. Never drive under the influence of alcohol.

Leaded petrol is sold as *essence super* (98 octane). Unleaded is available in two grades: *essence sans plomb* (95 octane) and *essence super sans plomb* (98 octane). Diesel (*Gasoil* or *Gazole*) is also readily available. In Paris filling stations can be hard to spot, often consisting of little more than a few kerb-side pumps.

If your car breaks down in Paris, contact the 24-hour repair service (☎ 01 45 31 16 20). On motorways (*autoroutes*) use the orange-coloured emergency phones (located every 2km) to contact the breakdown service.

PERSONAL SAFETY

Petty crime, particularly theft of wallets and handbags is fairly common in Paris. Be aware of innocent, scruffy-looking children, they may be working the streets in gangs, fleecing unwary tourists. Report any loss or theft to the *Police Municipale* (blue uniforms). To be safe:

- Watch your bag on the métro, in busy tourist areas like Beaubourg and the Champs-Elysées and in museum queues.
- Cars should be well-secured.
- Keep valuables in your hotel safe.

Police assistance:
☎ **17 from any call box**

TELEPHONES

All telephone numbers in France comprise ten digits. Paris and Ile de France numbers all begin with 01. There are no area codes, simply dial the number. Most public phones use a phonecard (*télécarte*) sold in units of 50 or 120 from France Telecom shops, post offices, tobacconists and railway stations. Cafés have phones that take coins.

International Dialling Codes	
From France to:	
UK:	**00 44**
Germany:	**00 49**
USA:	**00 1**
Netherlands:	**00 31**
Spain:	**00 34**

POST

Post offices
Post offices are identified by a yellow or brown 'La Poste' or 'PTT' sign. Paris's main post office at 52 rue du Louvre is open 24 hours. ☎ 01 40 28 76 00. The branch at 71 avenue des Champs-Elysées opens Mon–Fri 9AM–7:30PM, Sat 10AM–7:30PM. Other branches: 🕒 8–7 (12 Sat); closed Sun

ELECTRICITY

The power supply in Paris is: 220 volts

Sockets accept two-round-pin (or increasingly three-round-pin) plugs, so an adaptor is needed for most non-Continental appliances and a voltage transformer for appliances operating on 100–120 volts.

TIPS/GRATUITIES

Yes ✓ No ✕		
Hotels (service included)	✓	(change)
Restaurants (service included)	✓	(change)
Cafés (service included)	✓	(change)
Taxis	✓	(1euro)
Tour guides	✓	(1 euro)
Porters	✓	(1 euro)
Usherettes	✓	(30c)
Hairdressers	✓	(1 euro)
Cloakroom attendants	✓	(15–30c)
Toilets	✓	(change)

PHOTOGRAPHY

What to photograph: Paris's monumental buildings and animated Parisians drinking in pavement cafés.
Where you need permission to photograph: certain museums will allow you to photograph inside. In churches with mural paintings and icons where flashlight is required permission must be sought first.
Where to buy film: shops and photo laboratories sell the most popular brands and types of film. Rapid film development is possible but quite expensive.

HEALTH

Insurance

Nationals of EU countries can obtain medical treatment at reduced cost in France with the relevant documentation (Form E111 for Britons), although private medical insurance is still advised and is essential for all other visitors.

Dental Services

As for general medical treatment (see above, **Insurance**), nationals of EU countries can obtain dental treatment at reduced cost. Around 70 per cent of standard dentists' fees are refunded. Still, private medical insurance is advised for all.

Sun Advice

July and August (when most Parisians leave the city) are the sunniest (and hottest) months. If 'doing the sights' cover up or apply a sunscreen and take on plenty of fluids. To escape the sun altogether spend the day visiting a museum.

Drugs

Pharmacies – recognised by their green cross sign – possess highly qualified staff able to offer medical advice, provide first-aid and prescribe a wide range of drugs, though some are available by prescription (*ordonnance*) only.

Safe Water

It is quite safe to drink tap water in Paris and all over France, but never drink from a tap marked *eau non potable* (not drinking water). Many prefer the taste of mineral water, which is fairly cheap and widely available in several brands.

CONCESSIONS

Students/Youths Holders of an International Student Identity Card (ISIC) are entitled to half-price admission to museums and sights and discounted air and ferry tickets, plus cheap meals in some student cafeterias. Those under 26, but not a student, with the International Youth Travel Card (or GO 25 Card) qualify for similar discounts as ISIC holders.

Senior Citizens Visitors over 60 can get discounts (up to 50 per cent) in museums, on public transport and in places of entertainment. Discounts apply to holders of the *Carte Senior*, which can be purchased from the *Abonnement* office of any main railway station. Without the card, show your passport and you may still get the discount.

CLOTHING SIZES

France	UK	Rest of Europe	USA	
46	36	46	36	Suits
48	38	48	38	
50	40	50	40	
52	42	52	42	
54	44	54	44	
56	46	56	46	
41	7	41	8	Shoes
42	7.5	42	8.5	
43	8.5	43	9.5	
44	9.5	44	10.5	
45	10.5	45	11.5	
46	11	46	12	
37	14.5	37	14.5	Shirts
38	15	38	15	
39/40	15.5	39/40	15.5	
41	16	41	16	
42	16.5	42	16.5	
43	17	43	17	
36	8	34	6	Dresses
38	10	36	8	
40	12	38	10	
42	14	40	12	
44	16	42	14	
46	18	44	16	
38	4.5	38	6	Shoes
38	5	38	6.5	
39	5.5	39	7	
39	6	39	7.5	
40	6.5	40	8	
41	7	41	8.5	

WHEN DEPARTING

- Contact the airport or airline on the day prior to leaving to ensure flight details are unchanged.
- It is advisable to arrive at the airport two hours before the flight is due to take off.
- Check the duty-free limits of the country you are entering before departure.

LANGUAGE

You will usually hear well-enunciated French in Paris, spoken quite quickly and in a myriad of accents as many Parisians come from the provinces. English is spoken by those involved in the tourist trade and by many in the centre of Paris – less so in the outskirts. However, attempts to speak French will always be appreciated. Below is a list of a few words that may be helpful. The gender of words is indicated by (m) or (f) for masculine and feminine. More extensive coverage can be found in the AA's *Essential French Phrase Book* which lists over 2,000 phrases and 2,000 words.

hotel	*hôtel (m)*	rate	*tarif (m)*
room	*chambre (f)*	breakfast	*petit déjeuner (m)*
..single/double	*une personne /deux personnes (f)*	toilet	*toilette (f)*
		bathroom	*salle de bain (f)*
...one/two nights	*une/deux nuits (f)*	shower	*douche (f)*
...per person/per room	*par personne/par chambre*	balcony	*balcon (m)*
		key	*clef/clé (f)*
reservation	*réservation (f)*	room service	*service de chambre*

bank	*banque (f)*	English pound	*livre sterling (f)*
exchange office	*bureau de change (m)*	American dollar	*dollar (m)*
		banknote	*billet (m)*
post office	*poste (f)*	coin	*pièce (f)*
cashier	*caissier (m)*	credit card	*carte de crédit (f)*
foreign exchange	*change (m)*	traveller's cheque	*chèque de voyage (m)*
currency	*monnaie (f)*	giro cheque	*chèque postal (m)*

restaurant	*restaurant (m)*	starter	*hors d'oeuvres (m)*
café	*café (m)*	main course	*plat principal (m)*
table	*table (f)*	dish of the day	*plat du jour (m)*
menu	*carte (f)*	dessert	*dessert (m)*
set menu	*menu (m)*	drink	*boisson (f)*
wine list	*carte des vins (f)*	waiter	*garçon (m)*
lunch	*déjeuner (m)*	waitress	*serveuse (f)*
dinner	*dîner (m)*	the bill	*addition (f)*

aeroplane	*avion (m)*	...first/second class	*première/deuxième classe (f)*
airport	*aéroport (m)*		
train	*train (m)*	ticket office	*guichet (m)*
...station	*gare (f)*	timetable	*horaire des départs et des arrivées (m)*
bus	*l'autobus (m)*		
...station	*gare routière (f)*		
ferry	*bateau (m)*	seat	*place (f)*
...port	*port (m)*	non-smoking	*non-fumeurs*
ticket	*billet (m)*	reserved	*réservée*
...single/return	*simple/retour*	taxi!	*taxi! (m)*

yes	*oui*	help!	*au secours!*
no	*non*	today	*aujourd'hui*
please	*s'il vous-plaît*	tomorrow	*demain*
thank you	*merci*	yesterday	*hier*
hello	*bonjour*	how much?	*combien?*
goodbye	*au revoir*	expensive	*cher*
goodnight	*bonsoir*	closed	*fermé*
sorry	*pardon*	open	*ouvert*

INDEX

Acknowledgements

The Automobile Association would like to thank the following photographers, libraries and associations for their assistance in the preparation of this book.

DACS *Femmes a Leur Toilette*, Pablo Picasso, © Succession Picasso/DACS 1997 67; **MARY EVANS PICTURE LIBRARY** 10c, 14l, 14r, 35b; **ROBERT HARDING PICTURE LIBRARY** 1; **HULTON ARCHIVE** 11; **PARK ASTERIX** 85c; **SPECTRUM COLOUR LIBRARY** 122b; **www.euro.ecb.int/** 119 (euro notes)

The remaining photographs are held in the Association's own library (**AA WORLD TRAVEL LIBRARY**) with contributions from: **P ENTICKNAP** 20b, 60, 61b; **P KENWARD** 27t, 28, 29, 30, 33t, 34, 35t, 36t, 40tl, 41t, 43t, 44tl, 45t, 45c, 49tr, 50tl, 51tr, 52t, 53tl. 53tr, 54, 55, 57t, 58, 63t, 65t, 66t, 70tl, 73tr; **E MEACHER** 37c; **R MOSS** 83b, 122r; **D NOBLE** 78, 79 80tl, 80tr, 81, 83, 83t, 84t, 85t, 86t, 86b, 87t, 87c, 88/89, 89t, 91t, 90c; **K PATERSON** 5t, 6t, 6c, 7t, 8t, 9t, 9c, 9b, 10t, 12t, 12b, 13t, 14t, 16c, 18b, 19b, 24c, 25b, 27b, 38, 39, 40tr, 49tl, 50b, 51b, 52b, 57c, 61t, 62, 64, 65c, 66c, 71, 75t, 89c, 91b, 117t, 117b, 122t; **B RIEGER** 5b, 7c, 8c, 13b, 37tl, 37b, 43b, 47, 48, 63c, 84bl. 84br; **A SOUTER** 2, 6b, 15t, 15b, 16t, 17t, 17c, 18t, 19t, 20t, 22t, 22c, 23t, 23b, 24t, 25t, 26t, 26c, 31, 32, 33c, 36b, 41c, 42, 44tr, 46, 50c, 51tl, 56, 59, 65b, 67, 68, 69, 70b, 72, 74, 76/77, 91t, 92/116; **J A TIMS** 21, 75b; **W VOYSEY** 17b, 70tc

Abbreviations for the above – (t) top; (b) bottom; (c) centre; (l) left; (r) right

Author's Acknowledgements

The author would like to thank Mairie de Paris, Office de Tourisme de Paris, and Comité Régional du Tourisme d'Ile de France.

Contributors

Updated by Elisabeth Morris **Copy editor:** Sheila Hawkins
Page Layout: Design 23 **Indexer:** Marie Lorimer

Questionnaire

Dear Traveler

Your comments, opinions and recommendations are very important to us. So please help us to improve our travel guides by taking a few minutes to complete this simple questionnaire.

Send to: Essential Guides,
MailStop 64, 1000 AAA Drive, Heathrow, FL 32746–5063

Your recommendations...

We always encourage readers' recommendations for restaurants, nightlife or shopping – if your recommendation is added to the next edition of the guide, we will send you a FREE AAA Essential Guide of your choice. Please state below the establishment name, location and your reasons for recommending it.

____

____

____

____

____

Please send me AAA Essential ______________________

About this guide...

Which title did you buy?

______________________________ **AAA Essential**

Where did you buy it? ______________________

When? m m / y y

Why did you choose a AAA Essential Guide? ______________________

____

____

____

Did this guide meet with you expectations?

Exceeded ☐ **Met all** ☐ **Met most** ☐ **Fell below** ☐

Please give your reasons ______________________

____

____

____

continued on next page...

Were there any aspects of this guide that you particularly liked? ______

Is there anything we could have done better? ______

About you...

Name (Mr/Mrs/Ms) ______

Address ______

______ **Zip** ______

Daytime tel nos. ______

Which age group are you in?

Under 25 ☐ **25–34** ☐ **35–44** ☐ **45–54** ☐ **55–64** ☐ **65+** ☐

How many trips do you make a year?

Less than one ☐ **One** ☐ **Two** ☐ **Three or more** ☐

Are you a AAA member? **Yes** ☐ **No** ☐

Name of AAA club ______

About your trip

When did you book? m m / y y **When did you travel?** m m / y y

How long did you stay? ______

Was it for business or leisure? ______

Did you buy any other travel guides for your trip? **Yes** ☐ **No** ☐

If yes, which ones? ______

Thank you for taking the time to complete this questionnaire.

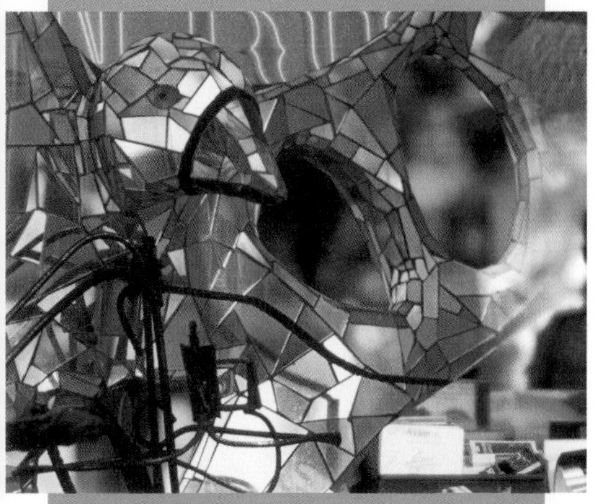

The Atlas

Acknowledgements
All pictures are from AA World Travel Library with contributions from the following photographers:
Bertrand Rieger: Paris by night
Clive Sawyer: street stall, Montparnasse Cemetery
Tony Souter: abstract sculpture by Centre Georges Pompidou, Moulin Rouge, neon signs

ROUGE
LIN ROU

www.theAA.com
The Automobile Association's website offers comprehensive and up-to-the-minute information covering AA-approved hotels, guest houses and B&Bs, restaurants and pubs in the UK; airport parking, insurance, European breakdown cover, European motoring advice, a ferry planner, European route planner, overseas fuel prices, a bookshop and much more.

www.aaa.com
AAA's website offers comprehensive information covering AAA-approved hotels and restaurants in the US. In addition, AAA can assist US citizens with obtaining a passport, reservations and tickets for cruise, tour, motorcoach, rail and air travel. AAA provides information on independent or escorted tours for individuals or groups and offers benefits on cruises, tours and travel packages.

The Foreign and Commonwealth Office
Country advice, traveller's tips, before-you-go information, checklists and more.
www.fco.gov.uk

French Government Tourist Office
www.franceguide.com

GENERAL
UK Passport Service
www.ukpa.gov.uk

US passport information
www.travel.state.gov

BBC – Holiday
www.bbc.co.uk/holiday

The Full Universal Currency Converter
www.xe.com/ucc/full.shtml

Flying with Kids
www.flyingwithkids.com

www.thingstodo-paris.com
www.discover-paris.info
www.paris-tourist-information.co.uk

TRAVEL
Rail and flights
www.eurostar.com
www.railbookers.com
www.raileurope.com
www.cheapflights.co.uk
www.thisistravel.co.uk
www.ba.com
www.continental.com
www.worldairportguide.com

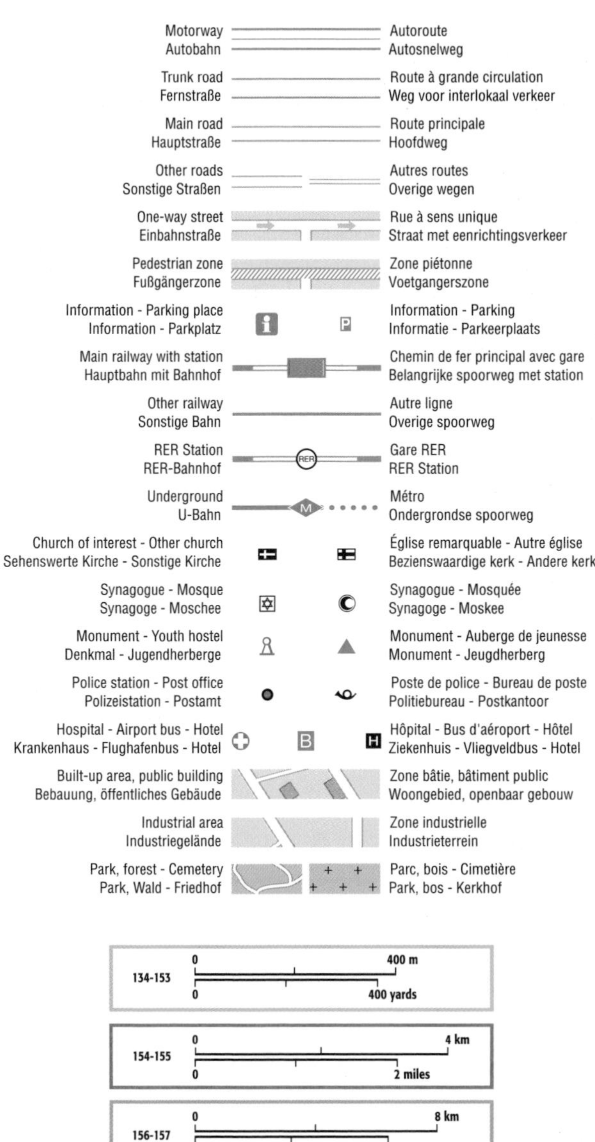
Motorway
Autobahn
Autoroute
Autosnelweg
Trunk road
Fernstraße
Route à grande circulation
Weg voor interlokaal verkeer
Main road
Hauptstraße
Route principale
Hoofdweg
Other roads
Sonstige Straßen
Autres routes
Overige wegen
One-way street
Einbahnstraße
Rue à sens unique
Straat met eenrichtingsverkeer
Pedestrian zone
Fußgängerzone
Zone piétonne
Voetgangerszone
Information - Parking place
Information - Parkplatz
Information - Parking
Informatie - Parkeerplaats
Main railway with station
Hauptbahn mit Bahnhof
Chemin de fer principal avec gare
Belangrijke spoorweg met station
Other railway
Sonstige Bahn
Autre ligne
Overige spoorweg
RER Station
RER-Bahnhof
RER
Gare RER
RER Station
Underground
U-Bahn
M
Métro
Ondergrondse spoorweg
Church of interest - Other church
Sehenswerte Kirche - Sonstige Kirche
Église remarquable - Autre église
Bezienswaardige kerk - Andere kerk
Synagogue - Mosque
Synagoge - Moschee
Synagogue - Mosquée
Synagoge - Moskee
Monument - Youth hostel
Denkmal - Jugendherberge
Monument - Auberge de jeunesse
Monument - Jeugdherberg
Police station - Post office
Polizeistation - Postamt
Poste de police - Bureau de poste
Politiebureau - Postkantoor
Hospital - Airport bus - Hotel
Krankenhaus - Flughafenbus - Hotel
B
H
Hôpital - Bus d'aéroport - Hôtel
Ziekenhuis - Vliegveldbus - Hotel
Built-up area, public building
Bebauung, öffentliches Gebäude
Zone bâtie, bâtiment public
Woongebied, openbaar gebouw
Industrial area
Industriegelände
Zone industrielle
Industrieterrein
Park, forest - Cemetery
Park, Wald - Friedhof
Parc, bois - Cimetière
Park, bos - Kerkhof
134-153
0
400 m
0
400 yards
154-155
0
4 km
0
2 miles
156-157
0
8 km
0
4 miles

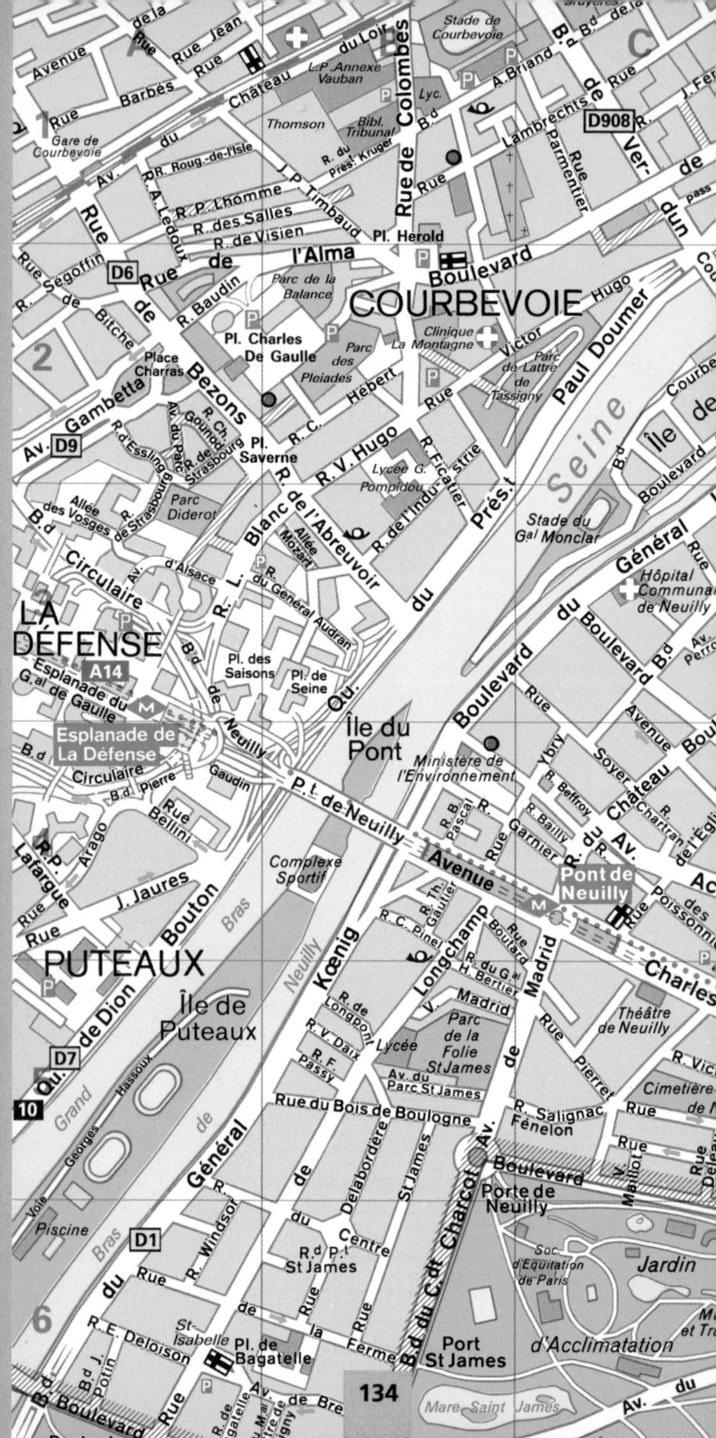
A
B
C
1
2
6
5
10
COURBEVOIE
LA DÉFENSE
PUTEAUX
Stade de Courbevoie
Gare de Courbevoie
L.P. Annexe Vauban
Thomson
Bibl. Tribunal
Lyc.
D908
D6
D9
D7
D1
A14
Rue de la Barbès
Rue Jean
Avenue
Rue du Château
du Loir
Rue de Colombes
Bd A. Briand
Bd de Verdun
Rue Lambrechts
Rue Parmentier
J. Fer
R. du Prés. Kruger
R. Roug.-de-l'Isle
R. A. Ledoux
R. P. Lhomme
R. des Salles
R. de Visien
J.P. Timbaud
Pl. Herold
Rue de l'Alma
Boulevard Victor Hugo
Rue Segoffin
R. de Bitche
Rue de Bezons
R. Baudin
Parc de la Balance
Pl. Charles De Gaulle
Parc des Pleiades
Clinique La Montagne
Parc de Lattre de Tassigny
Paul Doumer
Place Charras
Av. Gambetta
R. Ch. Gounod
Av. du Parc
R. d'Essling
R. de Strasbourg
Pl. Saverne
R. C. Hébert
Rue
R. V. Hugo
R. Ficatier
Lycée G. Pompidou
R. de l'Industrie
Seine
Île de
Courbe
Bd
Boulevard
Stade du Gal Monclar
Parc Diderot
Allée des Vosges
R. de Strasbourg
Bd Circulaire
Av. d'Alsace
R. L. Blanc
Allée Mozart
R. de l'Abreuvoir
Qu. du Prés.
R. du Général Audran
Général
Rue
Hôpital Communal de Neuilly
Boulevard du Boulevard
Bd
Av. Perro
Pl. des Saisons
Pl. de Seine
Bd de Neuilly
Esplanade du G.al de Gaulle
Esplanade de La Défense
Île du Pont
Rue Ybry
Avenue Soyer
Boul
Ministère de l'Environnement
Bd Circulaire
Bd Pierre
Gaudin
Pt de Neuilly
R. Beffroy
Av. du Château
R. Chartran
R. de l'Églis
R. B. Pascal
R. Garnier
R. Bailly
R. du
Rue Bellini
R. P. Lafargue
Arago
Complexe Sportif
Avenue
Pont de Neuilly
Ac
Rue des Poissonniers
J. Jaures
Rue
Bouton
Bras
R. Th. Gautier
R. C. Pinel
Rue Boutard
Charles
Koenig
Longchamp
R. du Gal H. Bertier
Rue de Madrid
Neuilly
V. Madrid
Théâtre de Neuilly
Île de Puteaux
Qu. de Dion
R. de Longpont
R. V. Daix
Lycée
Parc de la Folie St James
Rue Pierret
R. Vic
R. F. Passy
Av. du Parc St James
Cimetière de N
Hassoux
Grand
Rue du Bois de Boulogne
R. Salignac Fénelon
Rue
Rue
Georges
de
Delabordère
St James
Av.
Boulevard
V. Maillot
Rue Delean
Voie
Général
R. Windsor
de
du Centre
Porte de Neuilly
Piscine
Bras
Rd Pt St James
Soc. d'Equitation de Paris
Jardin
du
Rue
Rue
Rue
Bd du Cdt Charcot
R. E. Deloison
Ste-Isabelle
Pl. de Bagatelle
de la Ferme
Port St James
d'Acclimatation
Bd J. Potin
Rue
R. de Bagatelle
Av. de Bre
Av. du Mal
Bd
Boulevard
Mare Saint James
Av. du

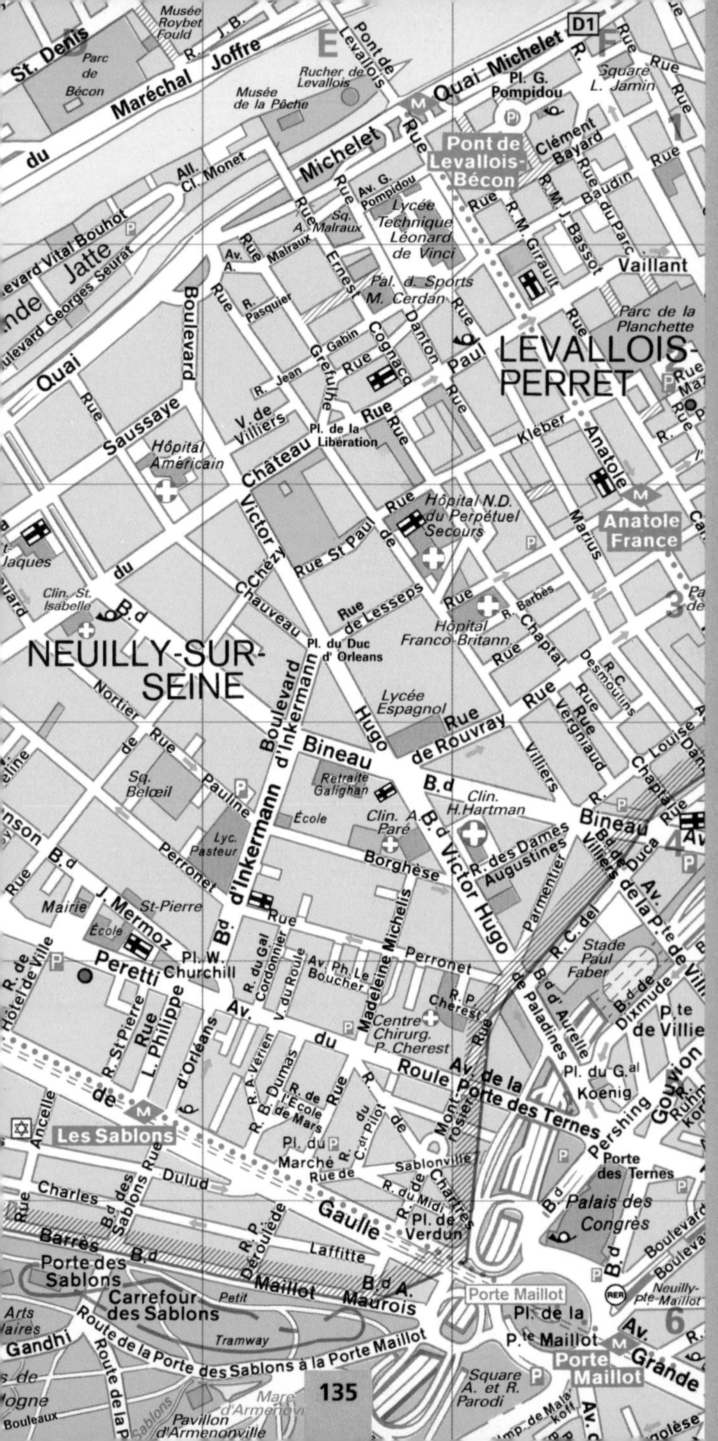

D1
E
F
1
3
4
6
Musée Roybet Fould
Parc de Bécon
St. Denis
Maréchal Joffre
du
R. J. B.
Pont de Levallois
Rucher de Levallois
Musée de la Pêche
Quai Michelet
Michelet
Pl. G. Pompidou
Square L. Jamin
Clément Bayard
Pont de Levallois-Bécon
All. Cl. Monet
Av. G. Pompidou
Sq. A. Malraux
Lycée Technique Léonard de Vinci
Rue Baudin
Rue du Parc
R. M. J. Bassot
R. M. Girault
Vaillant
Boulevard Vital Bouhot
Jatte
Boulevard Georges Seurat
Av. A. Malraux
Rue Ernest
Pal. d. Sports M. Cerdan
Parc de la Planchette
LEVALLOIS-PERRET
Boulevard
R. Pasquier
Quai
Rue Gabin
Rue Cognacq
Rue Danton
Rue Paul
Rue Greffulhe
R. Jean
Rue Kléber
Rue Anatole
Rue Saussaye
V. de Villiers
Pl. de la Libération
Rue Château
Hôpital Américain
Hôpital N.D. du Perpétuel Secours
Anatole France
Rue de
Rue St Paul
Victor
Chézy
Marius
Jaques
du
Chauveau
Rue de Lesseps
R. Barbès
Clin. St. Isabelle
B.d
Hôpital Franco-Britann.
Chaptal
NEUILLY-SUR-SEINE
Pl. du Duc d' Orleans
R. C. Desmoulins
Nortier
Boulevard d'Inkermann
Hugo
Lycée Espagnol
Rue de Rouvray
Rue Vergniaud
Villiers
Louise
Bineau
Chaptal
Sq. Belœil
Rue Pauline
Retraite Galighan
B.d
Clin. H.Hartman
Bineau
Clin. A. Paré
École
Lyc. Pasteur
Borghèse
R. des Dames Augustines
B.d de Villiers
Duca
Perronet
B.d d'Inkermann
B.d Victor Hugo
Parmentier
Av. de la P.te de Villiers
Mairie
St-Pierre
J. Mermoz
École
Rue
R. C. del
Stade Paul Faber
R. de Hôtel de Ville
Peretti
Pl. W. Churchill
R. du G.al Cordonnier
V. du Roule
Av. Ph. Le Boucher
Madeleine Michelis
Perronet
R. P. Cherest
B.d de Dixmude
P.te de Villiers
Av.
B.d de Paladines
B.d d'Aurelle
R. St Pierre
Rue L. Philippe
d'Orléans
R. A. Verien
R. B. Dumas
R. de l'École de Mars
du
Centre Chirurg. P. Cherest
Roule
Av. de la Porte des Ternes
Pl. du G.al Koenig
Pershing
Gouvion
de
Les Sablons
Ancelle
Pl. du Marché
R. du C.dt Pilot
R. de Mont-rosier
Rue de Sablonville
Porte des Ternes
Rue Dulud
Charles
R. du Midi
R. de Chartres
Pl. de Verdun
B.d Palais des Congrès
Boulevard
Rue Barrès
B.d des Sablons
R. P. Déroulède
Gaulle
Laffitte
B.d
Porte des Sablons
Maillot
B.d A. Maurois
Porte Maillot
Neuilly-P.te Maillot
Carrefour des Sablons
Petit
Arts
Gandhi
Route de la Porte des Sablons à la Porte Maillot
Tramway
Pl. de la P.te Maillot
Av. Grande
Route de la
Mare d'Armenonville
Square A. et R. Parodi
Bouleaux
Pavillon d'Armenonville
Sablons

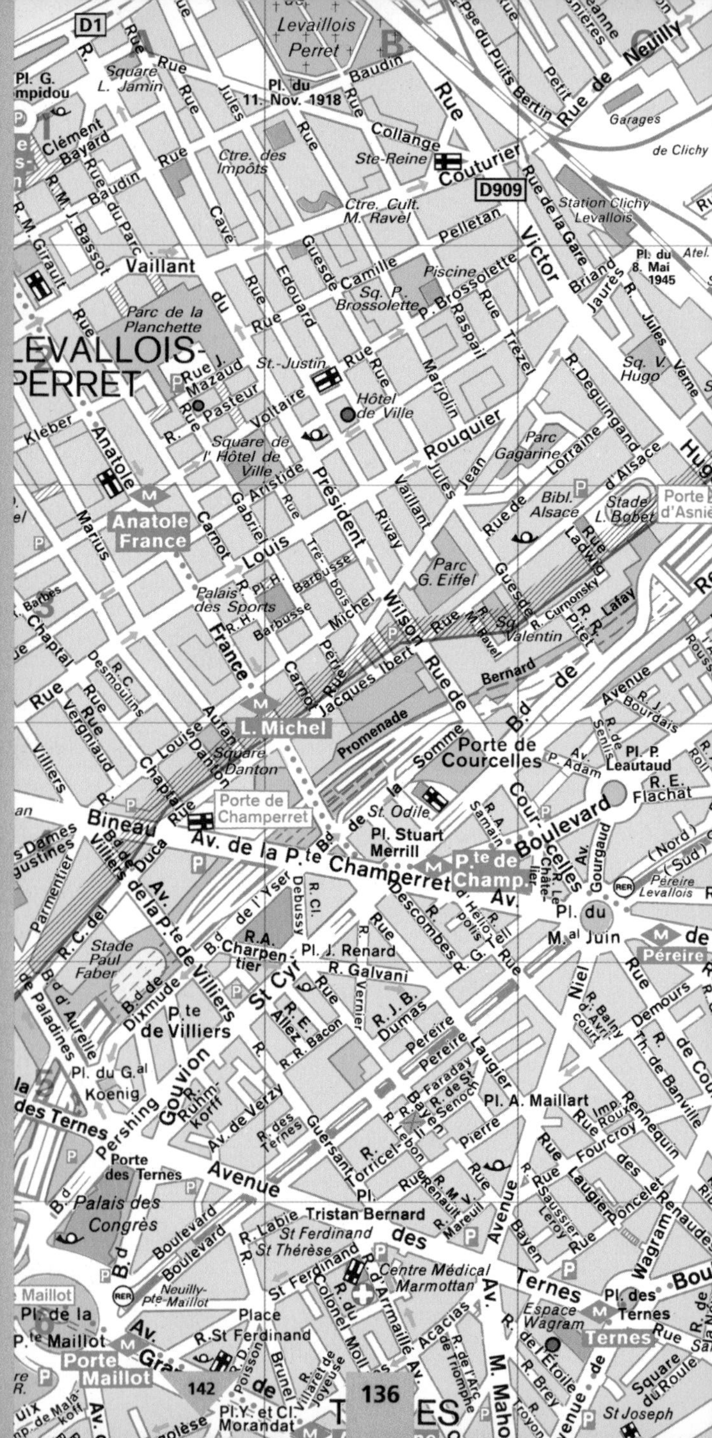
D1
Levallois Perret
Pl. G. Pompidou
Square L. Jamin
Pl. du 11. Nov. 1918
Rue Baudin
Rue Collange
Ste-Reine
Couturier
D909
Rue de Neuilly
Garages
de Clichy
Pge du Puits Bertin
Clément Bayard
Ctre. des Impôts
Ctre. Cult. M. Ravel
Station Clichy Levallois
R. M. Girault
R. M. J. Bassot
Rue du Parc
Rue Cavé
Rue Jules Guesde
Rue Edouard Vaillant
Pelletan
Rue de la Gare
Victor
Pl. du 8. Mai 1945
Atel.
Camille
Piscine
Sq. P. Brossolette
P. Brossolette
Raspail
Trézel
Briand
Jaurès
R. Jules Verne
Sq. V. Hugo
Parc de la Planchette
LEVALLOIS-PERRET
Rue J. Mazaud
R. Pasteur
St.-Justin
Hôtel de Ville
Voltaire
Marjolin
R. Deguingand
Kléber
Anatole
Square de l' Hôtel de Ville
Aristide
Rouquier
Parc Gagarine
Lorraine
d'Alsace
Hugo
Anatole France
Marius
Carnot
Gabriel
Président
Rivay
Jules Jean
Bibl. Alsace
Rue de Ladwig
Stade L. Bobet
Porte d'Asnières
Louis
Pl. H. Barbusse
Tré-bois
Parc G. Eiffel
Guesde
Palais des Sports
R. H. Barbusse
Michel
Wilson
R. Curnonsky
R. R. Pitet
Lafay
Sq. Valentin
Chaptal
R. C. Desmoulins
France
Carnot
Rue Jacques Ibert
Rue de Rue
Bernard
Bd. de
Avenue
R. J. Bourdais
Rue Vergniaud
Villiers
Louise
Aufan
Danton
Square Danton
L. Michel
Promenade
Somme
Porte de Courcelles
Av. P. Adam
Pl. P. Leautaud
R. E. Flachat
Chaptal
Porte de Champerret
St. Odile
R. A. Samain
Bineau
Bd. de Villiers
Duca
Av. de la P.te Champerret
Pl. Stuart Merrill
P.te de Champ.
Boulevard
Courcelles
Av. Gourgaud
(Nord)
(Sud)
Péreire Levallois
Parmentier
Av. de la P.te de Villiers
Bd. de l'Yser
Debussy
R. Cl.
Descombes
d'Héliopolis
R. G. Tell
Pl. du M.al Juin
Péreire
R. C. del
Stade Paul Faber
R.A. Charpentier
Pl. J. Renard
R. Galvani
Vernier
Niel
Rue Demours
Bd. d'Aurelle de Paladines
Bd. de Dixmude
P.te de Villiers
St Cyr
R. E. Allez
R. R. Bacon
R. J. B. Dumas
Pereire
Laugier
R. Balny d'Avricourt
R. Th. de Banville
Pl. du G.al Koenig
Pershing
Gouvion
R. Ruhmkorff
Av. de Verzy
R. des Ternes
Guersant
R. Faraday
R. de St. Senoch
R. Bayen
R. Lebon
Pl. A. Maillart
Imp. Roux
Rue Rennequin
Rue Fourcroy
des Ternes
Porte des Ternes
Avenue
R. Torricelli
Pierre
Rue Renault
R. M. Mareuil
Rue Laugier
R. Saussier Leroy
Poncelet
des Renaudes
Bd.
Palais des Congrès
Boulevard
R. Labie
Tristan Bernard
St Ferdinand
St Thérèse
des
Avenue Bayen
Wagram
Pl. St Ferdinand
Centre Médical Marmottan
R. d'Armaillé
Neuilly-P.te-Maillot
Maillot
Pl. de la P.te Maillot
Porte Maillot
Av. Grande
Place
R. St Ferdinand
R. du Colonel Moll
Acacias
R. de l'Arc de Triomphe
Ternes
Pl. des Ternes
Espace Wagram
R. de l'Étoile
Rue Saint-Senoch
Square du Roule
Brunel
Villaret de Joyeuse
Poisson
M. Maho
R. Brey
Troyon
St Joseph
Pl. Y. et Cl. Morandat
142
136

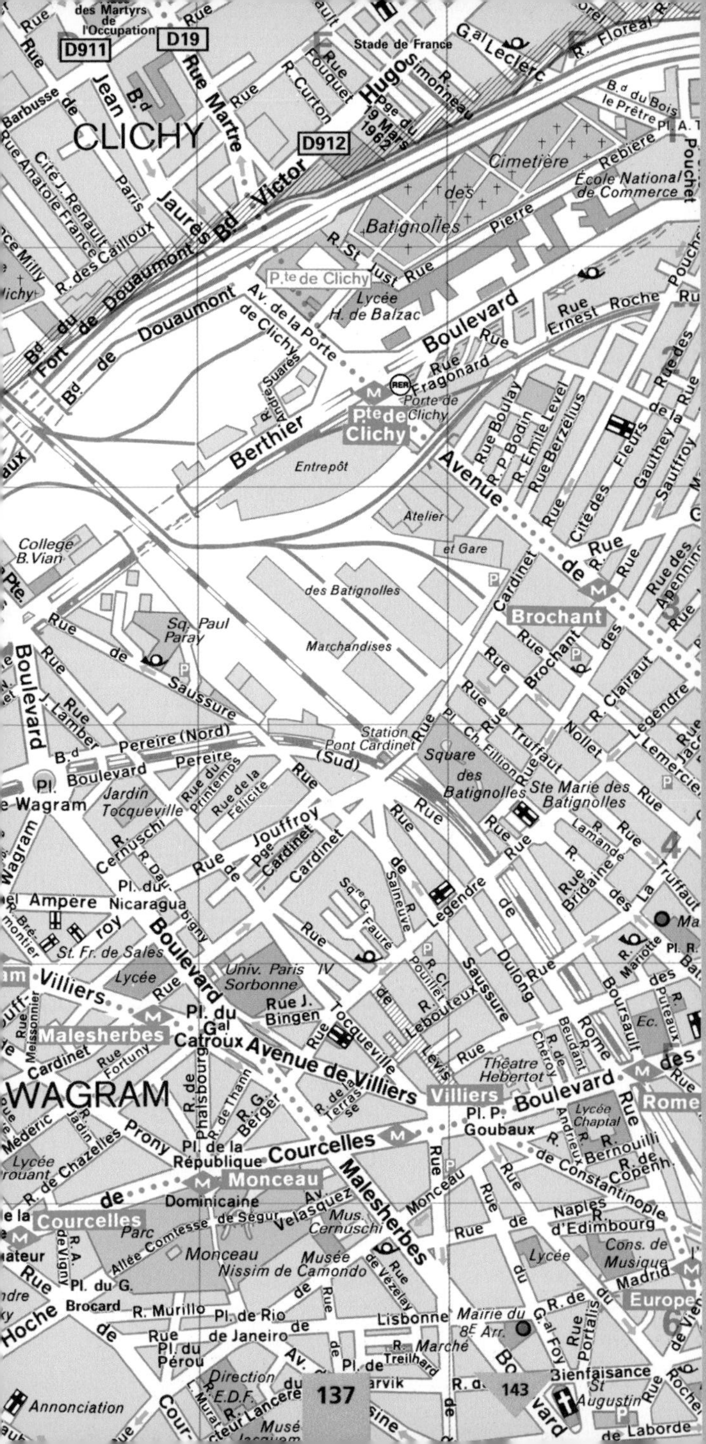

CLICHY
WAGRAM
D911
D19
D912
Stade de France
Bd. Victor Hugo
Bd. Jean Jaurès
Rue Martre
Rue Fouquet
R. Curton
R. Simonneau
Pge du 19 Mars 1962
G.al Leclerc
R. Floréal
B.d du Bois le Prêtre
Pl. A. T.
Rue Pouchet
Cimetière des Batignolles
Rue Rebière
École National de Commerce
Rue Pierre
R. St Just
Rue Barbusse
Rue Anatole France
Cité J. Renault
Paris
R. des Cailloux
Bd. du Fort de Douaumont
Bd. de Douaumont
P.te de Clichy
Lycée H. de Balzac
Av. de la Porte de Clichy
Boulevard Berthier
Rue Ernest Roche
Rue Fragonard
Porte de Clichy
Pte de Clichy
R. André Suarès
Entrepôt
Atelier et Gare des Batignolles
Marchandises
Avenue de Clichy
Rue Boulay
R. P. Bodin
R. Émile Level
Rue Berzélius
Cité des Fleurs
Rue Gauthey
Rue Sauffroy
Rue des Apennins
Rue de la Jonquière
College B. Vian
Rue de Saussure
Sq. Paul Paray
Boulevard Pereire (Nord)
Rue Cardinet
Brochant
Rue Brochant
Rue des Moines
R. Clairaut
Rue Legendre
Rue Nollet
Rue Lemercier
Rue Truffaut
Rue Jacquemont
Station Pont Cardinet
(Sud)
Pl. Ch. Fillion
Square des Batignolles
Ste Marie des Batignolles
Pl. Wagram
Boulevard Pereire
Jardin Tocqueville
Rue du Printemps
Rue de la Félicité
R. Cernuschi
R. Dardanelles
Rue Jouffroy
Pge Cardinet
Rue de Tocqueville
Rue de Saussure
Rue Dulong
R. Lamandé
R. Bridaine
Rue des Dames
Rue La Condamine
Sq. G. Fauré
Rue de Sainteville
Rue Legendre
Pl. du Nicaragua
Ampère
Rue Brémontier
St. Fr. de Sales
Boulevard Malesherbes
Avenue de Villiers
Lycée
Univ. Paris IV Sorbonne
Rue J. Bingen
Pl. du G.al Catroux
Malesherbes
Rue Meissonnier
Rue Fortuny
R. de Phalsbourg
R. de Thann
R. G. Berger
R. de la Terrasse
R. Cl. Pouillet
R. Lebouteux
Rue de Lévis
Théâtre Hébertot
R. de Chéroy
R. Beudant
R. de Rome
Rue Boursault
R. Mariotte
Pl. R.
Rue des Batignolles
R. des Puteaux
Ec.
Villiers
Boulevard des Batignolles
Rome
Lycée Chaptal
R. Andrieux
R. Bernouilli
R. de Copenh.
R. de Constantinople
Pl. P. Goubaux
Rue Médéric
R. Jadin
R. de Chazelles
Rue de Prony
Pl. de la République Dominicaine
Boulevard de Courcelles
Monceau
Courcelles
Rue de Monceau
Rue de Naples
Rue d'Édimbourg
Cons. de Musique
Lycée Carnot
Av. Velasquez
Mus. Cernuschi
Musée Nissim de Camondo
Allée Comtesse de Ségur
Parc Monceau
R. A. de Vigny
Pl. du G. Brocard
R. Murillo
Rue de Vézelay
Rue Hoche
Rue de Lisbonne
Pl. de Rio de Janeiro
Rue du Pérou
Mairie du 8E Arr.
R. du Marché
Pl. de Treilhard
R. de Madrid
Europe
R. du G.al Foy
Rue Portalis
Rue de Vienne
Rue de la Bienfaisance
St Augustin
Rue du Rocher
Rue de Laborde
Direction E.D.F.
R. Murat
Annonciation
Musée
R. de Narvik
137
143

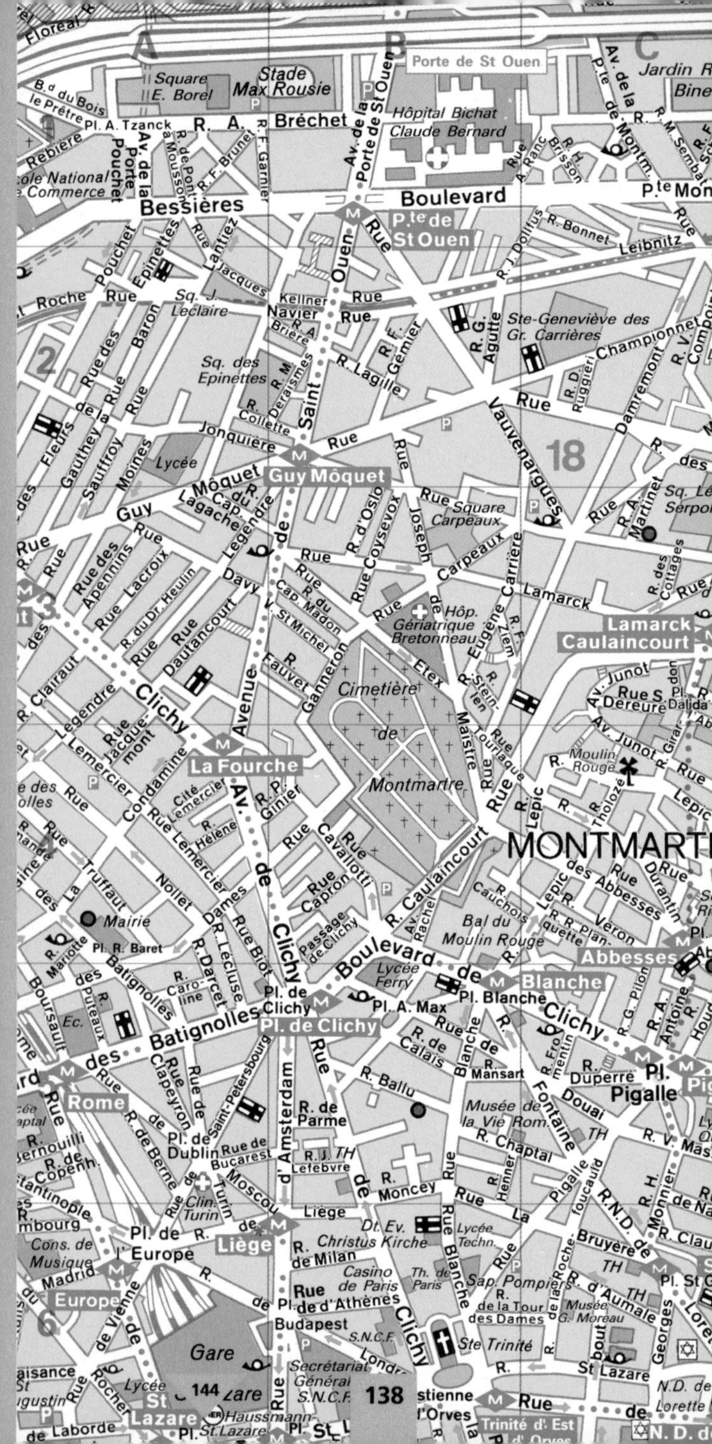

A
B
C
Porte de St Ouen
Square E. Borel
Stade Max Rousie
Hôpital Bichat Claude Bernard
Jardin R
Boulevard
Bessières
P.te de St Ouen
Av. de la Porte de St Ouen
Av. de la Porte Pouchet
R. A. Bréchet
Pl. A. Tzanck
B.d du Bois le Prêtre
Rebière
Ecole National de Commerce
R. Bonnet
Leibnitz
R. J. Dollfus
Rue Pouchet
Rue des Epinettes
Rue Lantiez
Sq. J. Leclaire
Rue Navier
R. A. Brière
Rue Kellner
Rue Jacques
Rue Roche
2
Sq. des Epinettes
R. M. Deraismes
R. Collette
R. Lagille
R. F. Gémier
R. G. Agutte
Ste-Geneviève des Gr. Carrières
Championnet
R. D. Ruggieri
Rue Damrémont
R. V. Compoint
Rue Vauvenargues
18
Rue de Saint Ouen
Rue Jonquière
Guy Môquet
Rue Guy Môquet
Rue des Fleurs
Rue Gauthey
Rue Sauffroy
Rue des Moines
Lycée
R. Cap. Lagache
R. du Cap. Lagache
Rue Legendre
Avenue de St Ouen
R. d'Oslo
Rue Coysevox
Rue Joseph de Maistre
Rue Carpeaux
Square Carpeaux
Rue Lamarck
R. A. Martinet
Sq. Léon Serpollet
R. des Cottages
Lamarck Caulaincourt
Rue des Apennins
Rue Lacroix
R. du Dr. Heulin
Rue Davy
Rue Dautancourt
R. du Cap. Madon
V. St Michel
R. Fauvet
Rue Ganneron
Rue Etex
Hôp. Gériatrique Bretonneau
R. Eugène Carrière
R. F. Ziem
R. Steinlen
Av. Junot
Rue S. Dereure
Pl. Dalida
Rue Tourlaque
Cimetière de Montmartre
R. Clairaut
3
Avenue de Clichy
Rue Legendre
Rue Lemercier
Rue Jacquemont
La Fourche
Rue Condamine
Cité Lemercier
R. Hélène
R. P. Ginier
Rue Cavallotti
Rue Caulaincourt
R. Lepic
R. Tholozé
Moulin Rouge
Rue Lepic
MONTMARTRE
Rue des Abbesses
Rue Durantin
R. Véron
R. Cauchois
Rue Lemercier
Rue Nollet
Rue Truffaut
Mairie
Pl. R. Baret
Rue des Dames
R. Darcet
R. Lécluse
Rue Biot
Rue Capron
Passage de Clichy
Av. Rachel
Bal du Moulin Rouge
Abbesses
Rue Mariotte
Rue des Batignolles
R. Caroline
Boulevard de Clichy
Lycée Ferry
Pl. de Clichy
Pl. A. Max
Pl. Blanche
Blanche
R. G. Pilon
R. A. Antoine
Rue des Puteaux
Rue Boursault
Batignolles
Ec.
Rue Clapeyron
R. de Calais
Rue Blanche
R. Fromentin
R. Duperré
Pl. Pigalle
Pigalle
Rome
Rue de Rome
Rue de Saint-Pétersbourg
Rue d'Amsterdam
R. de Parme
R. Ballu
R. Mansart
Musée de la Vie Rom.
Rue Fontaine
Douai
R. Chaptal
R. V. Massé
R. de Berne
Pl. de Dublin
Rue de Bucarest
R. J. Lefebvre
R. de Copenh.
Rue de Constantinople
Rue de Moscou
R. Moncey
R. Henner
Rue La Rochefoucauld
R.N.D. de Lorette
R. H. Monnier
Rue de Turin
Clin. Turin
Liège
Rue de Clichy
Dt. Ev. Christus Kirche
Lycée Techn.
Rue Bruyère
R. d'Aumale
R. Clauzel
Cons. de Musique
Pl. de l'Europe
R. de Liège
R. de Milan
Casino de Paris
Th. de Paris
Sap. Pompiers
Musée G. Moreau
Pl. St Georges
Madrid
Europe
6
Rue de Vienne
Rue d'Athènes
Budapest
S.N.C.F.
R. de la Tour des Dames
Ste Trinité
Rue Rochechouart
Rue Saint Georges
R. de Londres
Gare St Lazare
144
Secrétariat Général S.N.C.F.
Estienne d'Orves
Rue St Lazare
N.D. de Lorette
Rue de Laborde
Lycée
Haussmann-St.Lazare
Pl. St Augustin
Trinité d'Est d'Orves
Rue N.D. de Lorette

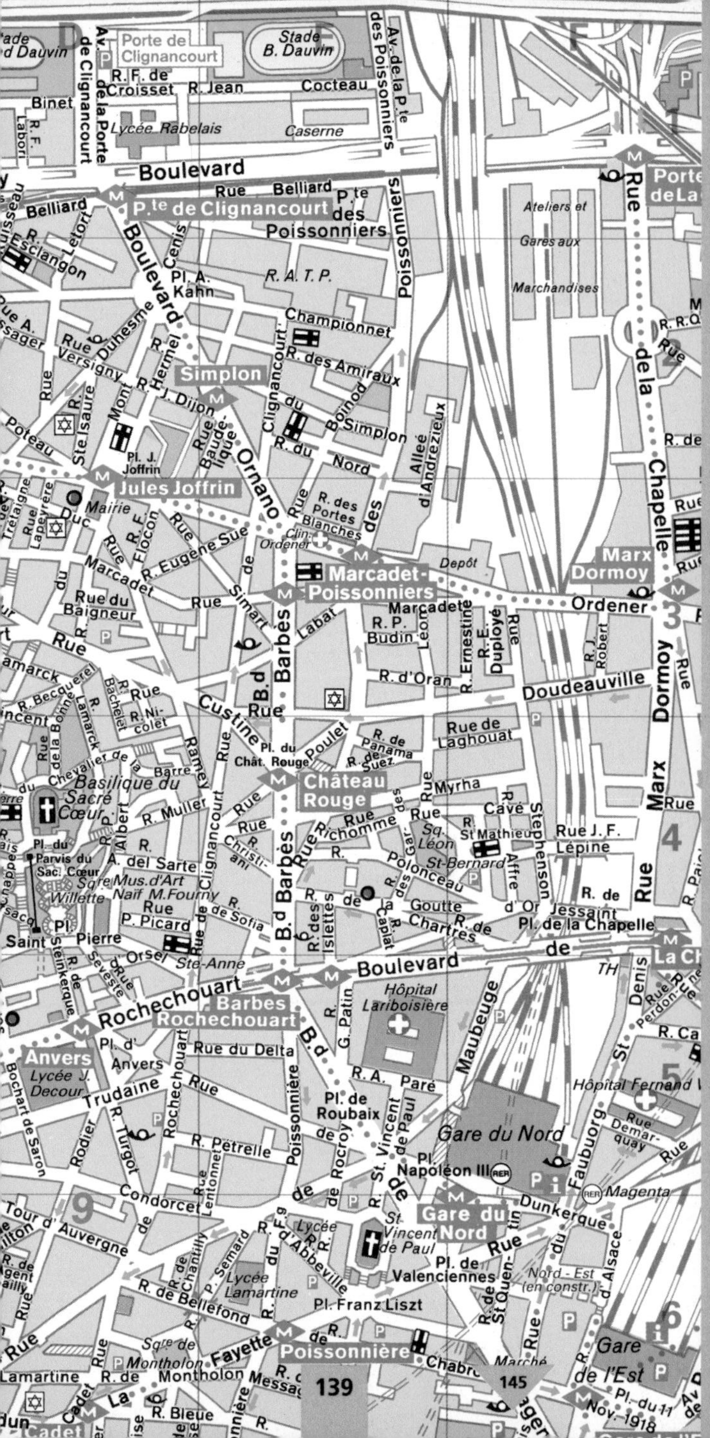

Porte de Clignancourt
Stade B. Dauvin
Av. de la P.te des Poissonniers
Av. de la Porte de Clignancourt
R. F. de Croisset
R. Jean Cocteau
Binet
Lycée Rabelais
Caserne
Boulevard
Rue Belliard
Belliard
P.te de Clignancourt
P.te des Poissonniers
R. Esclangon
Letort
Boulevard Ornano
Cenis
Pl. A. Kahn
R.A.T.P.
Poissonniers
Championnet
Rue Duhesme
Rue Versigny
R. Hermel
Simplon
R. des Amiraux
Clignancourt
R. J. Dijon
Rue Baudelique
R. du Simplon
Boinod
Allée d'Andrézieux
Ateliers et Gares aux Marchandises
Rue de la Chapelle
Poteau
R. Ste Isaure
R. Mont
Pl. J. Joffrin
Jules Joffrin
R. du Nord
R. des Portes Blanches
Mairie
Rue Lapeyrère
Rue Duc
R. F. Flocon
Rue Eugène Sue
Marcadet
Rue de Simart
Clin. Ordener
Marcadet-Poissonniers
Dépôt
Marx Dormoy
Ordener
Rue du Baigneur
Labat
R. P. Budin
Léon
R. Ernestine
R. E. Duployé
R. J. Robert
Rue Dormoy
Rue Custine
B.d Barbès
R. d'Oran
Doudeauville
R. Becquerel
R. Bachelet
R. Nicolet
Rue Lamarck
Rue de la Bonne
Rue Ramey
Pl. du Chât. Rouge
Poulet
R. de Panama
R. de Suez
Rue de Laghouat
Château Rouge
Rue Myrha
R. du Chevalier de la Barre
Basilique du Sacré Cœur
R. Muller
R. P. Albert
Rue Richomme
Rue des Gardes
Sq. Léon
R. Cavé
R. St Mathieu
Rue J. F. Lépine
Stephenson
Marx
Pl. du Parvis du Sac. Cœur
R. A. del Sarte
R. Christiani
R. Polonceau
St-Bernard
Affre
Sqre Willette
Mus. d'Art Naïf M. Fourny
R. de Sofia
R. des Islettes
R. de la Goutte d'Or
R. Capiat
R. de Chartres
R. de Jessaint
Pl. de la Chapelle
Rue P. Picard
Saint Pierre
R. Steinkerque
R. d'Orsel
Ste-Anne
Rue Sevestre
Boulevard de Rochechouart
Barbès Rochechouart
Hôpital Lariboisière
R. G. Patin
Maubeuge
Rue St Denis
Rue Perdonnet
Anvers
Pl. d'Anvers
Rue du Delta
Lycée J. Decour
Rue Trudaine
Rue Rochechouart
R. A. Paré
Pl. de Roubaix
Hôpital Fernand Widal
Rue Demarquay
Bochart de Saron
R. Turgot
Rodier
R. Pétrelle
Rue de Rocroy
R. St. Vincent de Paul
Gare du Nord
Pl. Napoléon III
Magenta
Condorcet
Rue Lentonnet
Gare du Nord
Rue de Dunkerque
Faubourg
Tour d'Auvergne
Lycée R. d'Abbeville
St Vincent de Paul
Pl. de Valenciennes
Nord-Est (en constr.)
R. d'Alsace
R. de Chantilly
P. Semard
Lycée Lamartine
R. de Bellefond
R. du Fg Poissonnière
Pl. Franz Liszt
R. de St Quentin
Gare de l'Est
Sqre de Montholon
Fayette
Poissonnière
Chabrol
Marché
Lamartine
R. de Montholon
Messageries
R. Bleue
Cadet
Pl. du 11 Nov. 1918
145

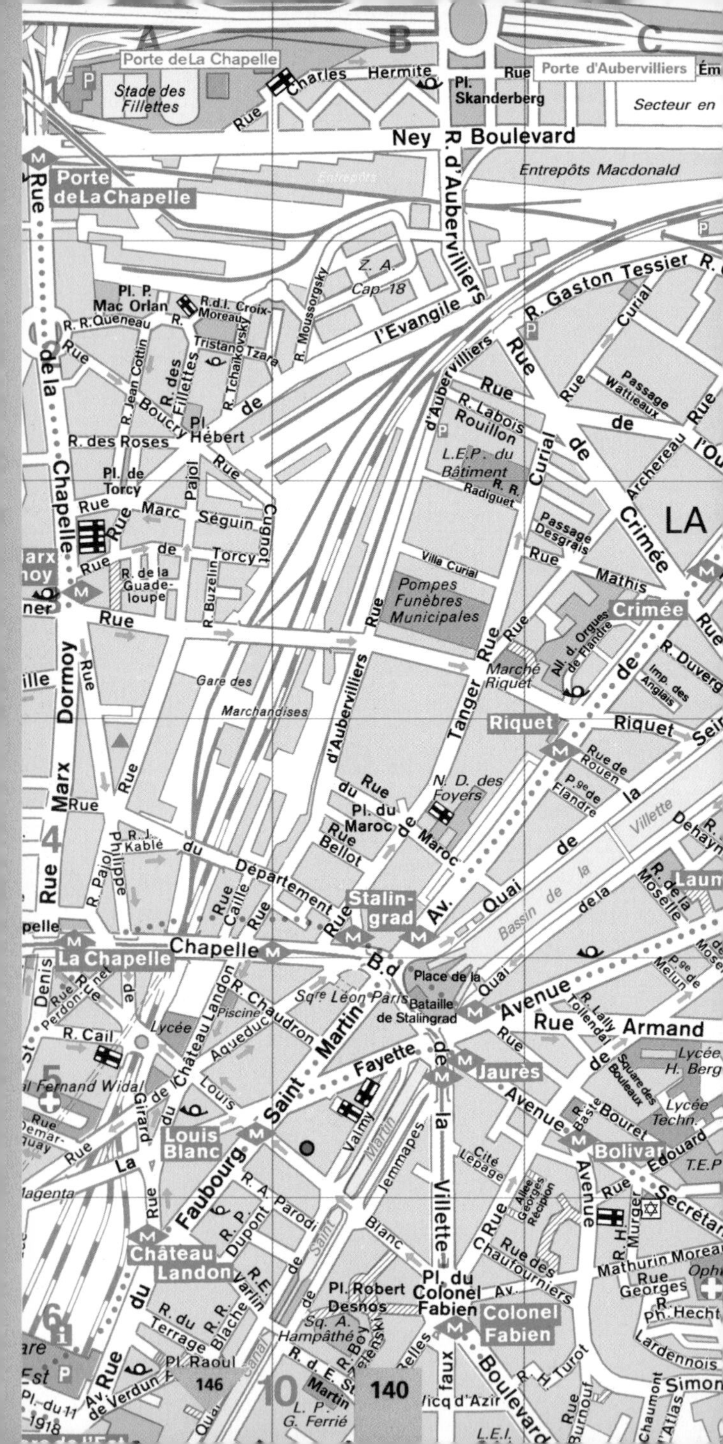

A
B
C
1
Porte de La Chapelle
Stade des Fillettes
Rue Charles Hermite
Pl. Skanderberg
Porte d'Aubervilliers
Secteur en
Ney Boulevard
R. d'Aubervilliers
Entrepôts Macdonald
Porte de La Chapelle
Z. A. Cap 18
R. Gaston Tessier
Pl. P. Mac Orlan
R. d. l. Croix-Moreau
R. R. Queneau
R. Moussorgsky
Rue de l'Evangile
Tristan Tzara
R. Tchaikovsky
R. Jean Cottin
R. des Fillettes
Rue Boucry
Pl. Hébert
R. des Roses
Rue de la Chapelle
Rue Curial
Passage Wattieaux
Rue de l'Ourcq
R. Labois Rouillon
L.E.P. du Bâtiment
R. R. Radiguet
Rue de Crimée
Rue Archereau
LA
Pl. de Torcy
Rue Marc Séguin
Rue Pajol
Rue Cugnot
Rue de Torcy
R. de la Guadeloupe
R. Buzelin
Passage Desgrais
Villa Curial
Rue Mathis
Pompes Funèbres Municipales
Crimée
All. d. Orgues de Flandre
Rue Riquet
Rue Tanger
Marché Riquet
R. Duvergier
Imp. des Anglais
Riquet
Gare des Marchandises
Rue Dormoy
Rue Marx Dormoy
Rue d'Aubervilliers
Rue de Rouen
P.ge de Flandre
N. D. des Foyers
Rue du Maroc
Pl. du Maroc
Rue Bellot
Rue de la Villette
Rue Dehaynin
4
R. J. Kablé
Rue Philippe
R. Pajol
Rue du Département
Rue Caillé
Stalingrad
Av.
Quai de la Seine
Bassin de la Villette
R. de la Moselle
Laumière
Rue de la Chapelle
La Chapelle
Bd de la Chapelle
Place de la Bataille de Stalingrad
Rue Perdonnet
R. Chaudron
Sq.re Léon Paris
Piscine
R. Château Landon
Aqueduc
Avenue Jean Jaurès
Quai de la Loire
P.ge de Melun
R. Lally Tollendal
Rue Armand
Lycée H. Berg
R. Cail
Lycée
Rue Louis Blanc
Rue Saint Martin
Rue La Fayette
Jaurès
5
Fernand Widal
Rue Girard
Valmy
Canal Saint Martin
Rue de Meaux
Square des Bouleaux
R. Baste
Rue Bouret
Lycée Techn.
Rue Demarquay
Louis Blanc
Faubourg
Jemmapes
Cité Lepage
Bolivar
Avenue Secrétan
Edouard
T.E.P.
Magenta
R. A. Parodi
R. P. Dupont
Blanc
Allée Georges Récipon
Rue H. Murger
Château Landon
R.E. Varlin
Rue des Chaufourniers
Mathurin Moreau
Pl. du Colonel Fabien
Rue Georges
R. Ph. Hecht
Ophtal.
6
Rue du Terrage
R. R. Blache
Pl. Robert Desnos
Sq. A. Hampâthé
R. Boy Zelenski
Colonel Fabien
Rue Lardennois
Est
Pl. Raoul
Rue de Verdun
146
10
R. d. E. St Martin
140
Vicq d'Azir
Rue Burnouf
R. H. Turot
Boulevard
Simon
Chaumont
Atlas
Pl. du 11 nov. 1918
Av. de Verdun
L. P. G. Ferrié
L.E.I.

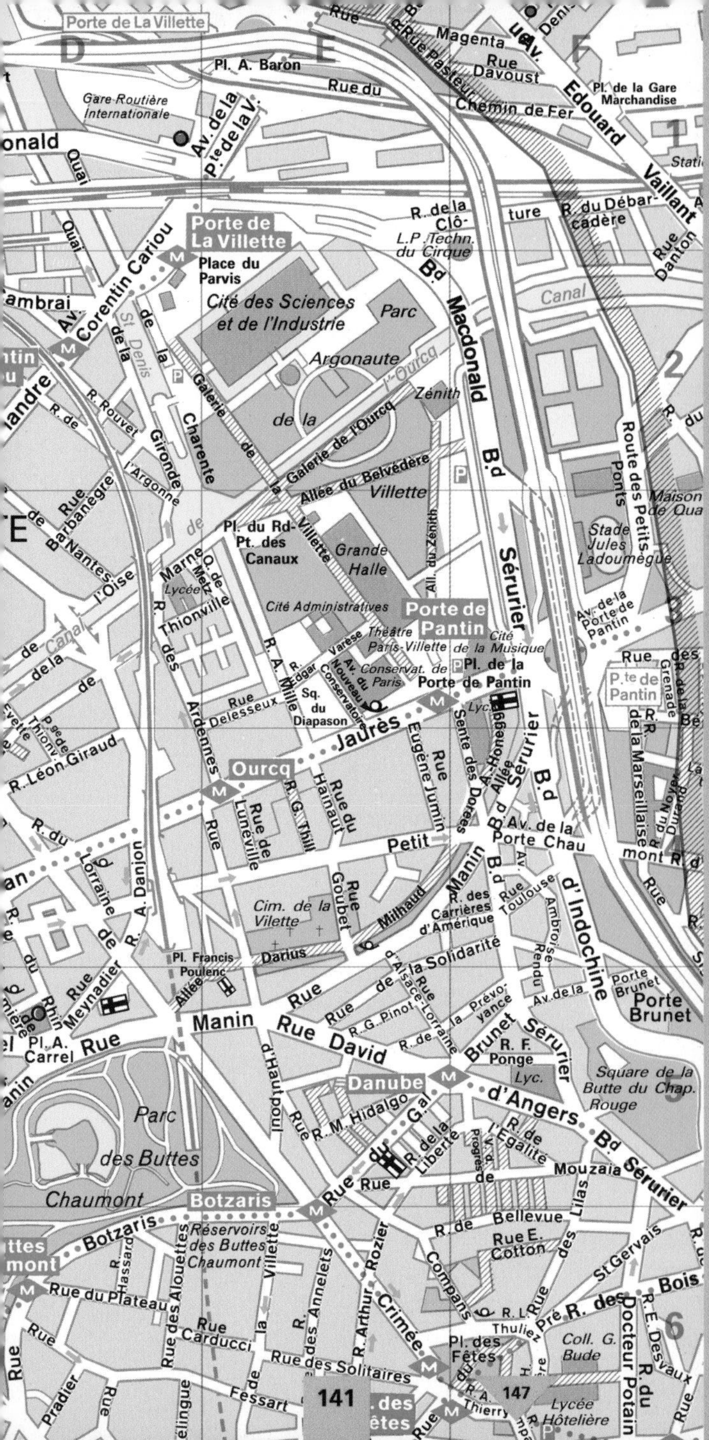

Porte de La Villette
Pl. A. Baron
Gare Routière Internationale
Porte de La Villette
Place du Parvis
Cité des Sciences et de l'Industrie
Parc
Argonaute
Zénith
de la
Villette
Grande Halle
Cité Administratives
Porte de Pantin
Théâtre Paris-Villette
Cité de la Musique
Conservat. de Paris
Pl. de la Porte de Pantin
Sq. du Diapason
Ourcq
Cim. de la Vilette
Pl. Francis Poulenc
Danube
Parc des Buttes Chaumont
Botzaris
Réservoirs des Buttes Chaumont
Stade Jules Ladoumègue
Square de la Butte du Chap. Rouge
Porte Brunet
Coll. G. Bude
Lycée Hôtelière
Pl. des Fêtes
Bd Macdonald
Bd Sérurier
Bd d'Indochine
Canal
Rue Manin
Rue David d'Angers
Rue Petit
Rue de Crimée
Rue des Alouettes
Rue du Plateau
Rue des Solitaires
Rue Fessart
141
147

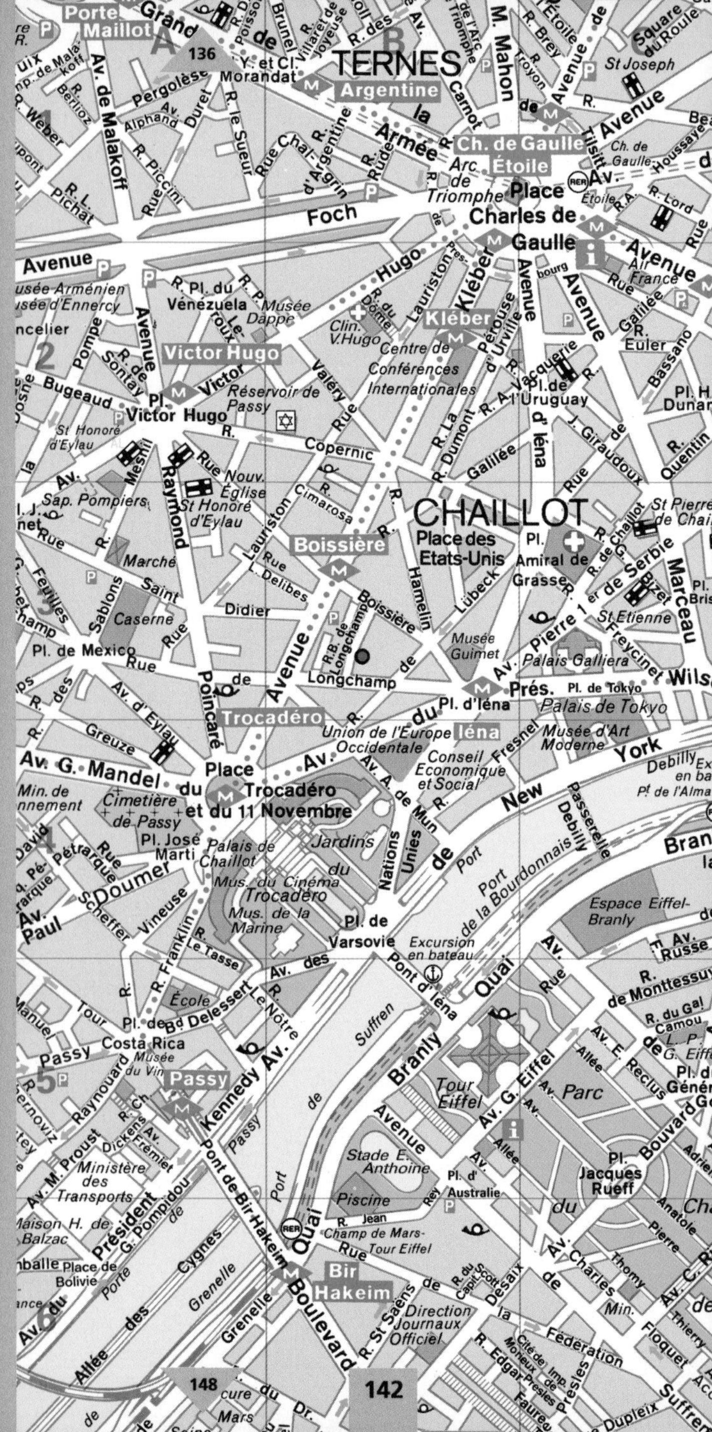
Porte Maillot
136
TERNES
Argentine
Av. de Malakoff
Pergolèse
Y. et Cl. Morandat
Av. de la Grande Armée
Ch. de Gaulle Étoile
Arc de Triomphe
Place Charles de Gaulle
Avenue Foch
Avenue Hugo
Avenue Kléber
Avenue d' Iéna
Kléber
St Joseph
Square du Roule
Avenue de Tilsitt
Air France
Musée Arménien
Musée d'Ennery
Pl. du Vénézuela
Musée Dappe
Clin. V.Hugo
Centre de Conférences Internationales
Victor Hugo
Pl. Victor Hugo
Réservoir de Passy
R. Copernic
St Honoré d'Eylau
Sap. Pompiers
Nouv. Église St Honoré d'Eylau
Rue Lauriston
R. Cimarosa
Boissière
CHAILLOT
Place des Etats-Unis
Pl. Amiral de Grasse
Marché Saint Didier
Caserne
Pl. de Mexico
Rue de Longchamp
Musée Guimet
Av. Pierre 1er de Serbie
Palais Galliera
Av. Marceau
Pl. d'Iéna
Pl. de Tokyo
Palais de Tokyo
Musée d'Art Moderne
Iéna
Trocadéro
Union de l'Europe Occidentale
Conseil Economique et Social
Av. de New York
Av. G. Mandel
Place du Trocadéro et du 11 Novembre
Cimetière de Passy
Pl. José Marti
Palais de Chaillot
Mus. du Cinéma
Mus. de la Marine
Jardins du Trocadéro
Av. des Nations Unies
Pl. de Varsovie
Passerelle Debilly
Port de la Bourdonnais
Espace Eiffel-Branly
Quai Branly
Excursion en bateau
Pont d'Iéna
Av. Paul Doumer
R. Franklin
École
Bd Delessert
Pl. de Costa Rica
Musée du Vin
Passy
Av. Kennedy
Av. de Suffren
Tour Eiffel
Av. G. Eiffel
Parc du Champ de Mars
Pl. Jacques Rueff
Stade E. Anthoine
Piscine
Pl. d' Australie
Champ de Mars-Tour Eiffel
Ministère des Transports
Av. du Président G. Pompidou
Maison H. de Balzac
Place de Bolivie
Pont de Bir Hakeim
Bir Hakeim
Boulevard de Grenelle
Allée des Cygnes
Port de Grenelle
Direction Journaux Officiel
R. de la Fédération
Av. de Suffren
148

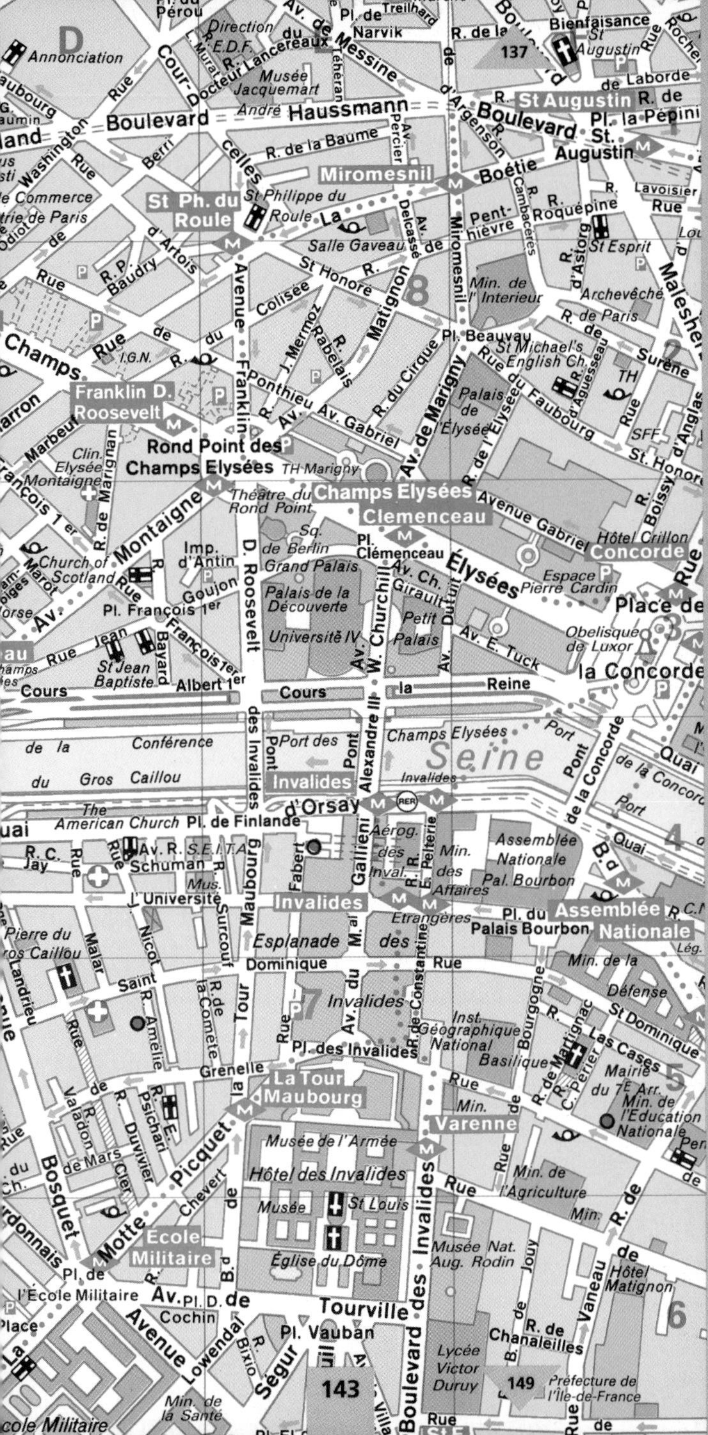
D
Annonciation
Pérou
Direction E.D.F.
R. Murat
Docteur Lancereaux
Av. de Messine
Pl. de Narvik
Treilhard
R. de la
Boulevard
137
Bienfaisance
St Augustin
Musée Jacquemart André
Téhéran
de Laborde
R. St Augustin R. de
Boulevard Haussmann
Av. Percier
d'Argenson
Boulevard St. Augustin
Pl. la Pépinière
Washington
Rue Berri
R. de la Baume
celles
Miromesnil
Boétie
Cambacérès
R. Roquépine
Lavoisier
Rue
de Commerce
St Ph. du Roule
St Philippe du Roule
La
Av. Delcassé
Pent-hièvre
R. d'Astorg
St Esprit
Salle Gaveau
de
Miromesnil
R. P. Baudry
d'Artois
St Honoré
Malesherbes
Avenue
Colisée
Matignon
8
Min. de l'Interieur
Archevêché
R. de Paris
Rue
J. Mermoz
R. Rabelais
Pl. Beauvau
St Michael's English Ch.
R. d'Aguesseau
Surène
Champs
Rue de
I.G.N.
R. du
Franklin
Ponthieu
R. du Cirque
Av. de Marigny
Rue du Faubourg
Palais de l'Élysée
TH
R. de l'Élysée
SFF
d'Anglas
Franklin D. Roosevelt
Av. Gabriel
St. Honoré
Marbeuf
Clin. Elysée Montaigne
R. de Marignan
Rond Point des Champs Elysées
TH Marigny
François 1er
Montaigne
Théâtre du Rond Point
Champs Elysées Clemenceau
Avenue Gabriel
R. Boissy
Hôtel Crillon
Concorde
Imp. d'Antin
Sq. de Berlin
Pl. Clémenceau
Élysées
Church of Scotland
Rue
Goujon
D. Roosevelt
Grand Palais
Palais de la Découverte
Av. Ch. Girault
Av. Dutuit
Espace Pierre Cardin
Place de
Pl. François 1er
François 1er
Petit Palais
Université IV
Av. W. Churchill
Av. E. Tuck
Obelisque de Luxor
3
Rue Jean
Bayard
St Jean Baptiste
Albert 1er
la Concorde
Cours
Cours la Reine
de la Conférence
du Gros Caillou
des Invalides
Port des Invalides
Pont Alexandre III
Champs Elysées
Seine
Port
Pont de la Concorde
Quai
de la Concorde
Invalides
Invalides
d'Orsay
The American Church
Pl. de Finlande
Port
Quai
R. C. Jay
Rue
Av. R. Schuman
S.E.I.T.A.
Mus.
Maubourg
Fabert
Gallieni
Aérog. des Inval.
R. E. Pelterie
R. R.
Min. des Affaires Etrangères
Assemblée Nationale
Pal. Bourbon
B.d
4
l'Université
Invalides
Pl. du Palais Bourbon
Assemblée Nationale
Pierre du Gros Caillou
Malar
Nicot
Surcouf
Esplanade des
M.al
Dominique
Rue
Min. de la Défense
Landrieu
Saint
R. Amélie
R. de la Comète
Tour
7
Invalides
Av. du
R. de Constantine
Inst. Géographique National
Bourgogne
R. de Martignac
St Dominique
Las Cases
Rue
Pl. des Invalides
Basilique
Grenelle
La Tour Maubourg
R. C. Périer
Mairie du 7E Arr.
5
Rue de
R. Valadon
R. Duvivier
R. E. Psichari
la
Rue
Min.
Varenne
Min. de l'Education Nationale
de Mars
Cler
Picquet
Musée de l'Armée
Hôtel des Invalides
Rue
Min. de l'Agriculture
Bosquet
Chevert
de
Musée
St Louis
Invalides
Min.
R. de
de
Motte
Ecole Militaire
Église du Dôme
Musée Nat. Aug. Rodin
Jouy
Hôtel Matignon
Pl. de l'École Militaire
Av.
B.d
Pl. D. Cochin
de
Tourville
Vaneau
6
Place
Avenue
Lowendal
R. Bixio
Pl. Vauban
Ségur
Boulevard des
de
R. de Chanaleilles
Lycée Victor Duruy
149
Préfecture de l'Île-de-France
143
Min. de la Santé
École Militaire
Rue
de

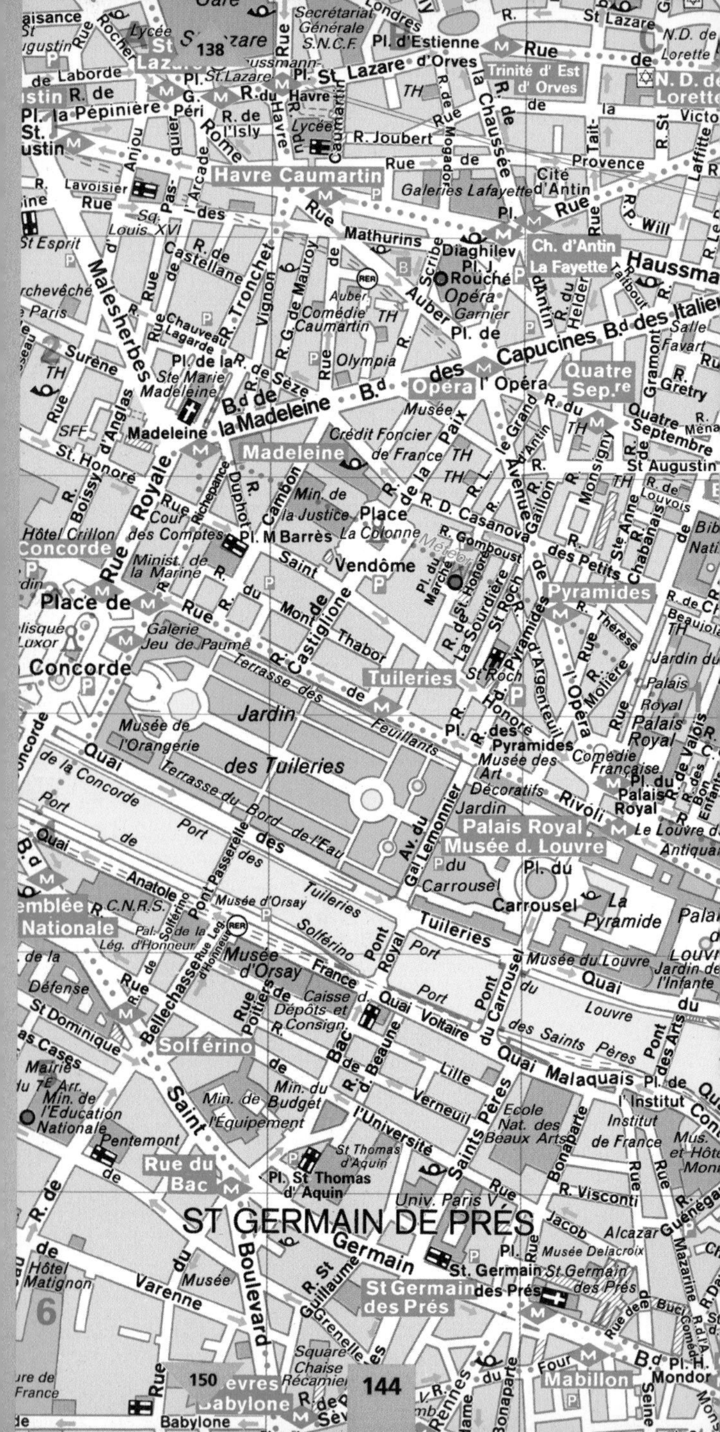
138
Secrétariat Générale S.N.C.F.
Londres
St Lazare
Rue St Lazare
N.D. de Lorette
Lycée
Pl. d'Estienne d'Orves
Trinité d' Est d' Orves
N. D. de Lorette
R. de Laborde
Pl. St Lazare
Havre
Pl. G. Péri
R. du Havre
TH
R. de Mogador
Rue de la Chaussée d'Antin
Pl. la Pépinière
R. de l'Isly
Rue de Rome
Lycée Caumartin
R. Joubert
Rue de Provence
R. Tait-bout
R. St Lafitte
St. Augustin
Rue Pasquier
Rue d' Anjou
Rue de l' Arcade
Havre Caumartin
Galeries Lafayette
Cité d'Antin
R. Lavoisier
Sq. Louis XVI
Rue des Mathurins
Pl. Diaghilev
Rue Haussmann
R.P. Will
Ch. d'Antin La Fayette
St Esprit
R. de Castellane
Rue Tronchet
Vignon
R. G. de Mauroy
Rue Scribe
Pl. J. Rouché
Opéra Garnier
R. du Helder
R. Taitbout
Archevêché de Paris
Bd Malesherbes
Rue Chauveau Lagarde
Rue Auber
Comédie Caumartin
TH
Pl. de l' Opéra
Bd des Capucines
Bd des Italiens
Salle Favart
R. Gramont
Surène
TH
Pl. de la Madeleine
Ste Marie Madeleine
R. de Sèze
Olympia
Opéra
Quatre Sep.re
R. Grétry
Bd de la Madeleine
Bd des
Musée
R. du Quatre Septembre
R. Ménars
SFF
Madeleine
Rue d' Anglas
Crédit Foncier de France
TH
R. de la Paix
Rue de St Augustin
Rue Monsigny
R. St Honoré
R. Boissy
Rue Royale
R. Richepance
R. Duphot
R. Cambon
Min. de la Justice
Place Vendôme
La Colonne
R. D. Casanova
R. L. le Grand
R. Gaillon
Avenue de l'Opéra
R. de Louvois
Ste Anne
R. Chabanais
Bib. Nati.
Hôtel Crillon
Rue Cour des Comptes
Pl. M Barrès
R. Gomboust
Concorde
Minist. de la Marine
Saint
R. du Marché St Honoré
R. des Petits
Pyramides
Place de
R. de la Concorde
Rue de Castiglione
R. du Mont Thabor
R. de la Sourdière
R. St Roch
R. de Beaujolais
Obélisque Luxor
Galerie Jeu de Paume
Thérèse
Rue Molière
Jardin du Palais Royal
Concorde
Terrasse des Feuillants
Tuileries
St Roch
Rue de Valois
Musée de l'Orangerie
Jardin des Tuileries
Pl. des Pyramides
Rue Richelieu
Rue de l'Opéra
R. d'Argenteuil
Palais Royal
Comédie Française
Pl. du Palais Royal
R. des Bons Enfants
Quai de la Concorde
Port de la Concorde
Terrasse du Bord de l'Eau
Musée des Art Décoratifs
Rivoli
Jardin
Palais Royal Musée d. Louvre
Le Louvre des Antiquaires
Av. du Gal Lemonnier
Pl. du Carrousel
Quai Anatole France
Port des Tuileries
Pont Passerelle Solférino
Carrousel
La Pyramide
Palais du Louvre
Assemblée Nationale
C.N.R.S.
Musée d'Orsay
Pal. de la Lég. d'Honneur
Rue Leg. d'Honneur
Port Solférino
Pont Royal
Quai des Tuileries
Musée du Louvre
Jardin de l'Infante
Rue de Bellechasse
Rue Poitiers
Caisse des Dépôts et Consign.
Port
Quai Voltaire
Pont du Carrousel
Quai du Louvre
Pont des Arts
R. de la Défense
St Dominique
Rue de Lille
Port des Saints Pères
Solférino
Las Cases
Rue du Bac
R. de Beaune
Quai Malaquais
Pl. de l'Institut
Quai Conti
Mairie du 7E Arr.
Min. de l'Education Nationale
Min. de l'Équipement
Min. du Budget
Rue de Verneuil
Rue des Saints Pères
Ecole Nat. des Beaux Arts
Institut de France
Mus. et Hôtel de la Monnaie
Pentemont
Boulevard Saint Germain
R. de l'Université
St Thomas d'Aquin
Rue Bonaparte
Rue de Seine
Rue Mazarine
Rue du Bac
Pl. St Thomas d' Aquin
Univ. Paris V
R. Visconti
R. Guénégaud
ST GERMAIN DE PRÉS
Rue Jacob
Alcazar
Musée Delacroix
R. Dauphine
de Varenne
Hôtel Matignon
Musée
R. St Guillaume
Pl. St. Germain des Prés
St Germain des Prés
Rue de Buci
6
R. de Grenelle
Boulevard Raspail
Square Chaise Récamier
Four
Mabillon
Bd St Germain
Pl. H. Mondor
Centre de France
150
Sèvres Babylone
Rue de Babylone
R. de Sèvres
Rue de Rennes
R. du Vieux Colombier
Rue Bonaparte
Seine

Poissonnière
Chabrol
Marché
Gare de l'Est
R. de Montholon
Fayette
Lamartine
R. des Messageries
139
Pl. du 11 Nov. 1918
Cadet
Musée
R. Bleue
Gare de l'Est
Trévise
Cité de Trévise
Poissonnière
Cité Paradis
R. de Paradis
Musée du Cristal
Mus. Baccarat
Paradis
R. de la Fidélité
R. St Laurent
Pge des Récollets
R. Saulnier
Folies Bergère
L.E.C. Ch. de Gaulle
R. d'Hauteville
R. Jarry
P. ge Dubail
R. Richer
R. d. Petites Écuries
R. Martel
Strasbourg
B. de St Martin
R. d. Vi
R. G. Laumain
R. de Montyon
R. Ste Cécile
R. Bergère
F. g Montmartre
Château d'Eau
R. de Nancy
Musée Grévin
Grds. Boulevards
R. d'Enghien
Mairie du 10E Arr.
Bd. Montmartre
TH
B.d Poissonnière
R. de l'Échiquier
R. du F.g
R. de Metz
B.d de
Faubourg
R. du Château
Cité Riverin
Jacq Bonse
Pl. J. Bo
TH des Variétés
R. d'Uzès
Bd. d. Bonne Nouvelle
Strasbourg St Denis
TH Ant.
R. Bouchardon
Marché
2
R. St Fiacre
Sentier
Bonne Nouvelle
R. Beauregard
Pt. St. Denis
B.d St Denis
St Martin
Th. de la Renaiss.
René
Pl. J. Strauss
R. des Jeûneurs
R. du Croissant
R. St Joseph
R. de Cléry
R. Blondel
Boulevard St Martin
R. d'Aboukir
R. d'Alexandrie
Sébastopol
R. du Sentier
P. Lelong
Mairie du 2E Arr.
R. du Caire
Rue Notre Dame de Nazareth
Républi
R. du Mail
Réaumur Sébastopol
Sq. Emile Chaut.
Conservatoire National des Arts et Métiers
R. du Vertbois
Lycée
R. Volta
Turbigo
R. L. Bellan
R. St Sauveur
Palais de la Jeunesse
Arts et Métiers
R. Bachaumont
R. Mandar
Montorgueil
Greneta
R. de Palestro
R. Ste Élisabeth
Louvre
R. M. Stuart
R. Tiquetonne
Réaumur
Hôtel des Postes
Montmartre
Étienne
É. Marcel
R. au Maire
Spe du Temp
R. Coq Héron
St Eustache
Marcel
R. d. B. Abbé
R. aux Ours
R. des Gravilliers
Mairie du 3E Arr.
Pl. R. Cassin
Bourse de Commerce
R. de Montmorency
Chapon
MARA
Les Halles
Rambuteau
P. Lescot
R. du Grenier St Lazare
R. M. Le Comte
Mus. Poupée
3
Pastourelle
Forum
Pl. des Halles
Châtelet-les-Halles
RER
Quincampoix
Brantôme
Rambuteau
Archives
Mus. de la Chasse et de Nature
Rue Berger
M. Quentin
St Honoré
Jardin St. Aignan
Temple
Centre Georges Pompidou
Mus. du Judaïsme
R. d. Braque
Pal. Soubise
Archives Nat.
R. du Roule
R. du Pont Neuf
R. d. Bourdonnais
Halles
Pl. G. Pompidou
Rue du Renard
R. des Blancs Manteaux
Hôtel de Rohan
R. de l'Arbre Sec
R. de la Monnaie
R. des Lombards
St. Merri
R. Brisemiche
Boulevard
Crédit Municipal
Vieille du Temple
Châtelet
R. Pernelle
R. St Bon
R. Ste Croix de la Bretonnerie
R. Aubriot
R. des Blancs Manteaux
Marché d.
École
Quai de la Mégisserie
Av. Th. du Châtelet
Tour St Jacques
Voie
Excursion en bateau
Pl. du Châtelet
Théâtre de la Ville
Hôtel de Ville
R. de la Verrerie
Cognac
R. d. Rosiers
Pl. du Quai de l'Horloge
Pont Neuf
R. Victoria
Pl. de l'Hôtel de Ville
Rivoli
R. des Écouffes
R. F. Duval
R. du Roi de Sicile
Centre Malher
ÎLE DE
Palais de Justice
Conciergerie
Ste Chap.
Pont au Change
Quai
Cité
Quai de Gesvres
Hôtel de Ville de Paris
Mairie
Quai de
R. de Lobau
R. St Gervais
R. du Pont L. Philippe
R. G. l'Asnier
R. Fr. Miron
St Paul
St. P
Lycée S. Germ.
B.d du Palais
Pont Notre Dame
R. de la Corse
Pont d'Arcole
Hôtel Dieu
Port de l'Hôtel de Ville
Pont L. Philippe
Quai de l'Hôtel de Ville
Pont Marie
R. Charlem
Hôtel de Sens
Préf. de Police
Orfèvres
Qu. du Marché Neuf
Qu. St Michel
Pont St Michel
LA CITÉ
Pl. du Parvis Notre D.
R. d'Arcole
R. du Cloître Notre Dame
Qu. aux Fleurs
Pont St Louis
Quai de Bourbon
R. Pont Marie
Quai d'Anjou
Quai des Célestins
Av. Marie
Pompidou
Grands Augustins
Dame
RTIER LATIN
Harpe
St Michel Notre Dame
St-Séverin
R. du Petit Pont
Quai de Montebello
Double
145
Quai d'Orléans
St. Louis
ÎLE
151
St-Julien le-Pauvre
ST LOUIS

140
10
B
C
Pl. Raoul Follereau
Av. de Verdun
Pl. du 11 Nov. 1918
Gare de l'Est
Square Villemin
R. d. St Laurent
R. Récollets
Pge des Récollets
Pge Dubail
R. d. Vinaigriers
R. Lucien Legouvé
R. Lancry
Quai de Jemmapes
Quai de Valmy
Quai
R. de l'Hôpital St. Louis
R. de la Grange aux Belles
R. d. E. St. Martin
L. P. G. Ferrié
L.P.M. Laurencin
Sam-paix
Hôpital St Louis
Pl. du Dr. A. Fournier
R. Vicq d'Azir
R. J. Dodu
Vellefaux
Av. Claude Vellefaux
Boulevard de la Villette
R. H. Turot
Rue Burnouf
L.E.I. C.Ader
R. de Sambre et Meuse
Pl. Ste Marthe
R. Ste Marthe
R. du Chalet
Pge Hébrard
R. du Buisson St Louis
Cité St. Chaumont
Rue de l'Atlas
Simon Bolivar
Rue de Rébeva
Sq. de Rébeva
Pl. J. Rostand
Pl. du Gal Ingold
Belleville
Canal Saint Martin
Av. Richerand
St. Louis
R. Alibert
Piscine
R. Louvel Tessier
R. Tesson
Avenue Parmentier
R. Bichat
R. J.
R. de Marseille
R. Yves
R. A. Thomas
R. Beaurepaire
R. Dieu
Jacques Bonsergent
Pl. J. Bonsergent
Château d'Eau
Marché
Pl. J. Strauss
Magenta
Rue d'Eau
Bourse du Travail
Douanes
R. L. Jouhaux
R. Toudic
Palais des Glaces
Goncourt
Rue du Fg du Temple
R. Darboy
St. Joseph
R. Deguerry
R. de la Présentation
R. L. Bonnet
l'Orillon
R. J. Verne
Rue de l'Orillon
R. de Vaucouleurs
Rue au Morand
Rue Saint Maur
Boulanger
St Martin
République
Place de la République
Meslay
R. de Nazareth
Vertbois
Turbigo
Temple
Rue de Malte
B.d J Ferry
R. de la Fontaine au Roi
R. de la P. Levée
R. des Trois Bornes
Rue Jean Pierre Timbaud
Av. de la République
Rue des Trois Bornes
Parmentier
Ste Elisabeth
Th. Dejazet
R. D. Thouars
R. Dupuis
Béranger
Bd du Temple
Boulevard
R. de Malte
R. J. P. Timbaud
Bd R. Lenoir
Folie Méricourt
Avenue de la République
Lycée
Spre du Temple
R. E. Spuller
R. Perrée
R. Charlot
Mairie du 3e Arr.
Saintonge
Oberkampf
Cirque d'Hiver
Pl. Pasdeloup
R. Ternaux
Pge Beslay
Pge Commun
St. Ambroise
MARAIS
de Bretagne
Filles du Calvaire
Bd du Calvaire
Bd des Filles
Rue Amelot
Pge St. P. Amelot
Sq. R. Lenoir
R. Pasteur
Marché
Pastourelle
R. de Poitou
Archives
Mus. de la Chasse et de Nature
Froissart
Pge St Sébastien
St. Sébastien
R. Lenoir
St Sébastien Froissart
Piscine
St Ambroise
Ste Croix de Paris
Lycée
Turenne
R. St Claude
Amelot
R. de l'Asile Popincourt
R. Moufle
4 Fils
Hôtel de Rohan
Musée Picasso
R. de Thorigny
St Denis du St Sacrement
R. Pelée
Allée-Verte
R. G. Sylvia
Richard Lenoir
Vieille du Temple
Barbette
Musée
R. du Parc Royal
Villehardouin
Sq. B. Sabin
Villa Marcès
Bréguet
Sedaine
Musée Cognacq-Jay
R. Payenne
Sévigné
R. St Gilles
Rue St Sabin
Bréguet Sabin
Chemin Vert
R. d. Minimes
R. du Foin
Musée Carnavalet
Bourgeois
Biblio-thèque
R. Froment
R. Boulle
11
Rosiers
R. F. Duval
Centre Malher
de Sicile
R. Malher
Pl. du Marché Ste Catherine
Pl. des Vosges
Sqre Louis XIII
Beaumarchais
Rue des Tournelles
Sq. Br.-Sabin
N. D. d'Esperance
Pge Charles Dallery
Th. de la Bastille
Paul
St. Paul-Germ. St. Louis
Lycée
R. Charlemagne
Hôtel de Sens
Rue St Paul
Caisse Nat.
Maison de Victor Hugo
R. Daval
Rue de la Roquette
R. des Taillandiers
Lycée Techn.
Pge d. l. Thiére
Café Danse
Rue de Lappe
Keller
Bastille
Place de la Bastille
Colonne de Juillet
St Antoine
R. Beautreillis
R. St Charles V
Ave Marie
Mus. de la Magie
Quai des Célestins
Musc
École
Cour St Louis
Rue du Fg St Antoine
Ledru Rollin
152
146
Henri IV
Opéra
LOUIS

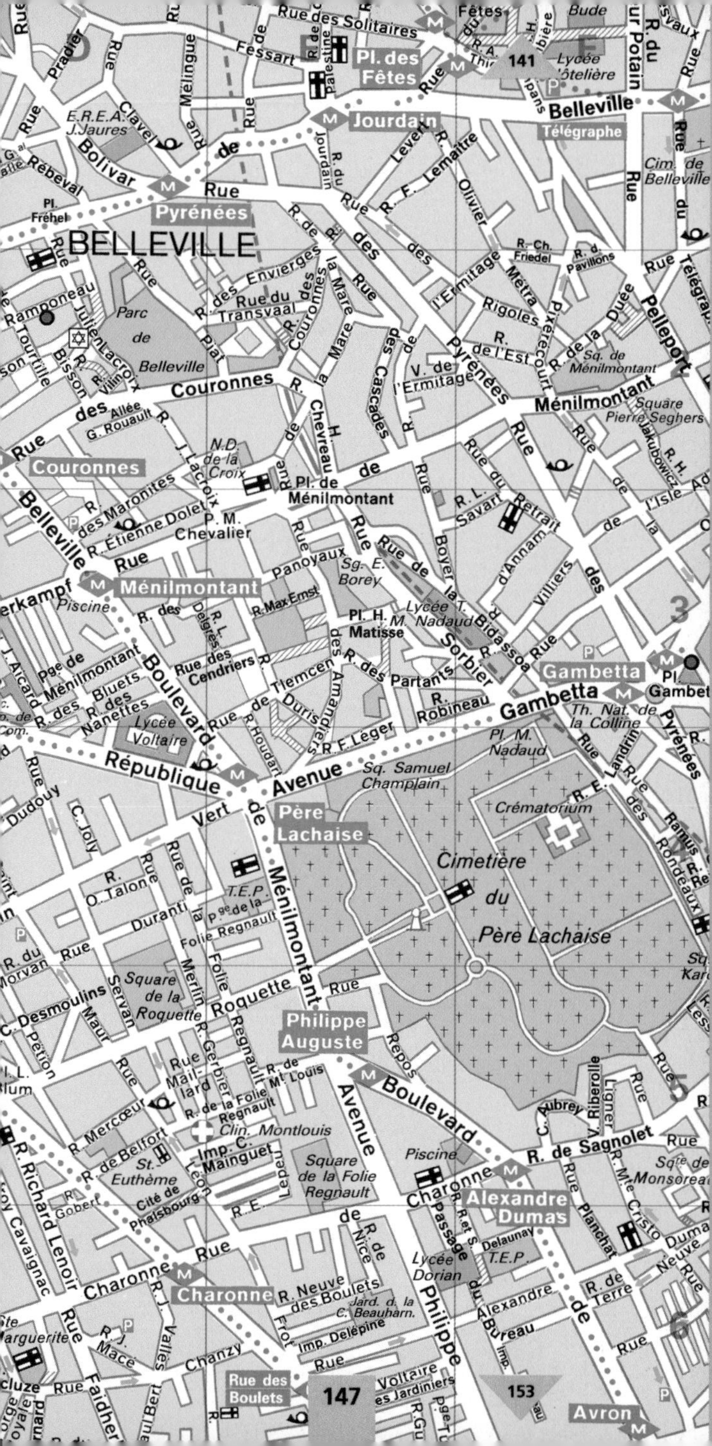

141
147
153
BELLEVILLE
Rue des Solitaires
Fessart
R. de Palestine
Pl. des Fêtes
Fêtes
Bude
R. du
Potain
Lycée Hôtelière
Rue Pradier
Rue Clavel
Rue Mélingue
E.R.E.A. J.Jaures
Rue Bolivar
Rue Rébeval
Pl. Fréhel
Rue de Belleville
Jourdain
R. du Jourdain
Pyrénées
Belleville
Télégraphe
Levert
R. F. Lemaître
Olivier
Cim. de Belleville
Rue du Télégraphe
Rue des Pyrénées
R. de R.
R. des Envierges
Rue du Transvaal
R. des Couronnes
la Mare
Rue de la Mare
R. Ch. Friedel
R. d. Pavillons
l'Ermitage
Métra
Rigoles
Pixérécourt
R. de l'Est
R. de la Duée
Sq. de Ménilmontant
Pelleport
Ramponeau
Julien Lacroix
Parc de Belleville
R. Vilin
Bisson
Tourtille
Plat
Rue des Couronnes
R. des Cascades
V. de l'Ermitage
Ménilmontant
Square Pierre Seghers
Jakubowicz
R. H.
Allée G. Rouault
R. J. Lacroix
N.D. de la Croix
Pl. de Ménilmontant
Rue de Ménilmontant
H. Chevreau
Rue Boyer
Rue du Retrait
R. L. Savart
Rue de l'Isle Adam
Couronnes
Boulevard de Belleville
R. des Maronites
R. Étienne Dolet
P. M. Chevalier
Panoyaux
Sq. E. Borey
Rue de la Bidassoa
Rue Sorbier
R. d'Annam
Villiers
Rue des Gâtines
Oberkampf
Ménilmontant
Piscine
R. des Maronites
R. L. Delgrès
R. Max Ernst
Pl. H. Matisse
Lycée T. M. Nadaud
Gambetta
Pl. Gambetta
J. Aicard
Pge de Ménilmontant
R. des Bluets
R. des Nanettes
Rue des Cendriers
R. de Tlemcen
Duris
R. des Amandiers
R. des Partants
R. Robineau
Avenue Gambetta
Th. Nat. de la Colline
Lycée Voltaire
Boulevard de Ménilmontant
Rue Houdart
R. F. Léger
Pl. M. Nadaud
Rue Landrin
Rue des Pyrénées
République
Avenue de la République
Vert
Sq. Samuel Champlain
R. E. Landrin
Crématorium
Rue des Rondeaux
Ramus
Dudouy
C. Joly
Père Lachaise
Rue de Ménilmontant
Cimetière du Père Lachaise
R. O. Talon
Rue Duranti
Rue de la Folie Regnault
T.E.P.
Pge de la Folie Regnault
R. du Morvan
Rue Servan
Square de la Roquette
Merlin
Rue de la Roquette
C. Desmoulins
Maur
Pétion
Philippe Auguste
Rue du Repos
L. Blum
Rue Mercœur
Rue Mailllard
R. Gerbier
Regnault
R. de Mt Louis
R. de la Folie Regnault
Clin. Montlouis
Boulevard de Charonne
Avenue Philippe Auguste
C. Aubrey
V. Riberolle
Ligner
R. de Sagnolet
Rue de Bagnolet
Sqre de Monsoreau
R. Richard Lenoir
R. de Belfort
St. Euthème
Imp. C. Mainguet
Léon
Lepeu
Square de la Folie Regnault
Piscine
R. Mercœur
R. Gobert
Cité de Phalsbourg
R. E.
R. de Nice
Charonne
Alexandre Dumas
R. Planchat
R. Mt Cristo
Passage
R. R. et S. Delaunay
T.E.P.
Lycée Dorian
Rue de Charonne
Cavaignac
R. J. Vallès
Charonne
R. Neuve des Boulets
Jard. d. la C. Beauharn.
Frot
Imp. Delépine
Alexandre
Bureau
R. de Terre Neuve
Rue
Ste Marguerite
R. J. Macé
Chanzy
Rue Faidherbe
Rue des Boulets
Voltaire
Avron

142
148
GRENELLE
15
Place de Brazzaville
Place St Charles
Sq. Pablo Casals
Piscine
L. P. Beaugrenelle
Dupleix
Place Dupleix
La Motte Picquet Grenelle
Av. É. Zola
Charles Michels
Pl. Ch. Michels
Av. Émile Zola
Place du Commerce
Commerce
Pl. Violet
Sq^re Violet
Félix Faure
Boucicaut
Hôpital Boucicaut
Lourmet
Convention
Cim. de Vaugirard
Lycée Tech. Louis Armand
Dépôt R.A.T.P.
N.D. de Charité
Square St Lambert
Pl. Hubert Monmarché
Hôpital St Michel
Vaugirard
Parc des Expositions
Palais des Sports
P^te de Versailles
Porte de la Plaine
P^te de Plaisance
Objets Trouvés
Four Municipale
Parc Georges Brassens
Théâtre Silvia Monfort
Sq. des Périchaux
Sq. du Calmette
Sq. des Varennes
Boulevard Lefebvre
Rue de la Convention
Rue Lecourbe
Rue de Vaugirard
Rue du Commerce
Rue des Entrepreneurs
Rue St Charles
Rue de Javel
Rue de l'Abbé Groult
Rue Desnouettes
Boulevard Victor
Av. E. Renan
Rue du Quatre Septembre
Av. de l'Industrie

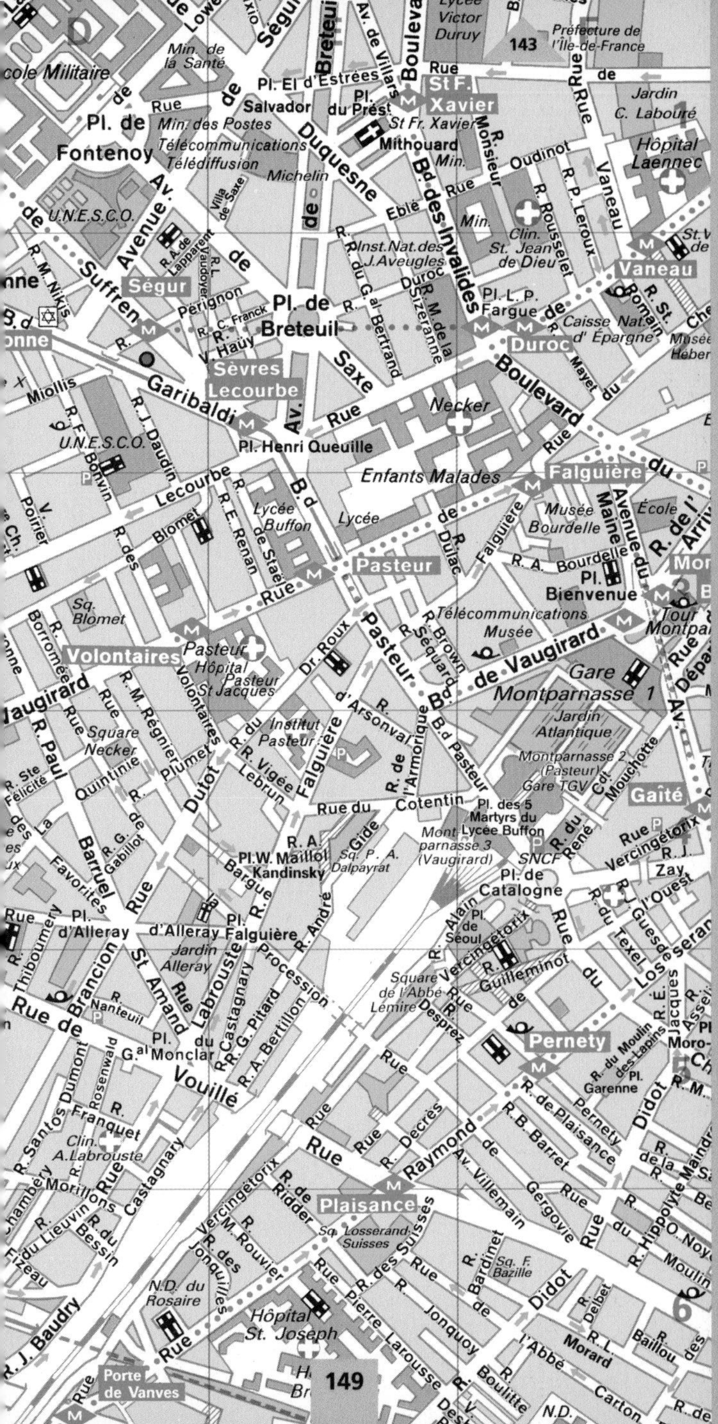

143
Lycée Victor Duruy
Préfecture de l'Île-de-France
École Militaire
Min. de la Santé
Pl. El d'Estrées
Pl. Salvador du Prést
St F. Xavier
St Fr. Xavier
Mithouard
Pl. de Fontenoy
Min. des Postes Télécommunications Télédiffusion
Michelin
U.N.E.S.C.O.
Avenue de Ségur
Av. de Suffren
Av. de Saxe
Bd des Invalides
Av. de Breteuil
Av. de Villars
Av. Duquesne
Rue Eblé
Rue Oudinot
R. Monsieur
R. Rousselet
R. P. Leroux
Rue Vaneau
Jardin C. Labouré
Hôpital Laennec
Vaneau
Clin. St. Jean de Dieu
Inst. Nat. des J. Aveugles
R. Duroc
R. du G.al Bertrand
R. M. de la Sizeranne
Villa de Saxe
R. A. de Lapparent
R. L. Vaudoyer
Ségur
R. Pérignon
R. C. Franck
R. V. Haüy
Pl. de Breteuil
Pl. L. P. Fargue
Duroc
Caisse Nat. d'Épargne
R. St. Romain
Rue de Sèvres
Musée Hébert
R. Mayet
Boulevard du Montparnasse
Sèvres Lecourbe
Bd Garibaldi
R. Miollis
R. M. Nikis
R. J. Daudin
R. F. Bonvin
U.N.E.S.C.O.
Pl. Henri Queuille
Necker
Enfants Malades
Falguière
Musée Bourdelle
École
Avenue du Maine
R. de l'Arrivée
Rue Lecourbe
R. E. Renan
Lycée Buffon
R. de Staël
Lycée
R. Dulac
R. Falguière
R. A. Bourdelle
Pl. Bienvenue
Rue Blomet
R. des Volontaires
V. Poirier
Pasteur
Sq. Blomet
R. Borromée
Volontaires
Pasteur
Hôpital Pasteur St Jacques
R. Dr. Roux
Bd Pasteur
R. Séguard
R. Brown
Télécommunications Musée
Bd de Vaugirard
Tour Montparnasse
Gare Montparnasse 1
Jardin Atlantique
Montparnasse 2 (Pasteur) Gare TGV
R. d'Arsonval
R. de l'Armorique
B.d Pasteur
Institut Pasteur
Rue Vaugirard
R. Paul Barruel
R. M. Régnier
Rue Square Necker
R. Quintinie
R. Plumet
R. Dutot
R. du R. Vigée Lebrun
R. Falguière
Rue du Cotentin
Pl. des 5 Martyrs du Lycée Buffon
Mont-parnasse 3 (Vaugirard)
SNCF
Cdt. Mouchotte
R. du Cdt. René Mouchotte
Gaîté
Rue Vercingétorix
R. J. Zay
R. Ste Félicité
R. des Favorites
R. G. Gabillot
R. de la Bargue
R. A. Gide
Pl. W. Maillol Kandinsky
Sq. P. A. Dalpayrat
Pl. de Catalogne
R. de l'Ouest
R. J. Guesde
R. du Texel
Rue Losserand
Rue Thiboumery
Pl. d'Alleray
d'Alleray
Pl. Falguière
Jardin Alleray
R. André
R. de la Procession
R. Alain
Pl. de Séoul
R. Vercingétorix
R. Guilleminot
R. Brancion
R. Nanteuil
Rue St Amand
Rue Labrouste
R. Castagnary
R. G. Pitard
R. A. Bertillon
Square de l'Abbé Lémire
Rue Desprez
Rue de l'Ouest
Pernety
R. du Moulin des Lapins
Pl. Garenne
R. É. Jacques
Moro-Giafferi
Rue de Vouillé
Pl. G.al Monclar
R. Rosenwald
R. Santos Dumont
R. Franquet
Clin. A. Labrouste
R. Morillons
Rue Castagnary
R. de Plaisance
R. Pernety
R. B. Barret
Rue Decrès
Rue Raymond Losserand
Rue de Gergovie
Didot
R. de la Sablière
R. Hippolyte Maindron
R. Chambéry
R. du Lieuvin
R. du Bessin
R. Fizeau
Vercingétorix
R. de Ridder
Plaisance
Sq. Losserand Suisses
Av. Villemain
R. des Suisses
R. M. Rouvier
R. des Jonquilles
R. Bardinet
Sq. F. Bazille
Rue Didot
R. Delbet
R. O. Noyer
Rue du Moulin
R. Baillou
R. L. Morard
R. J. Baudry
N.D. du Rosaire
Hôpital St. Joseph
Rue Pierre Larousse
Rue Jonquoy
Rue de l'Abbé Carton
R. Boulitte
R. V. Desh.
N.D.
Porte de Vanves
149

MONTPARNASSE
Jardin du Luxembourg
Cimetière du Montparnasse
Montparnasse Bienvenue
Vavin
Raspail
Edgar Quinet
Denfert Rochereau
Mouton Duvernet
Gaîté
St Placide
N.-D. des Champs
Rennes
St Sulpice
Vaneau
Mabillon
Alésia
St Jacques
Boulevard du Montparnasse
Boulevard Raspail
Rue de Vaugirard
Av. du Général Leclerc
Observatoire de Paris
Palais du Luxembourg (Sénat)
Hôpital Laennec
Bon Marché
Tour Montparnasse
144
150

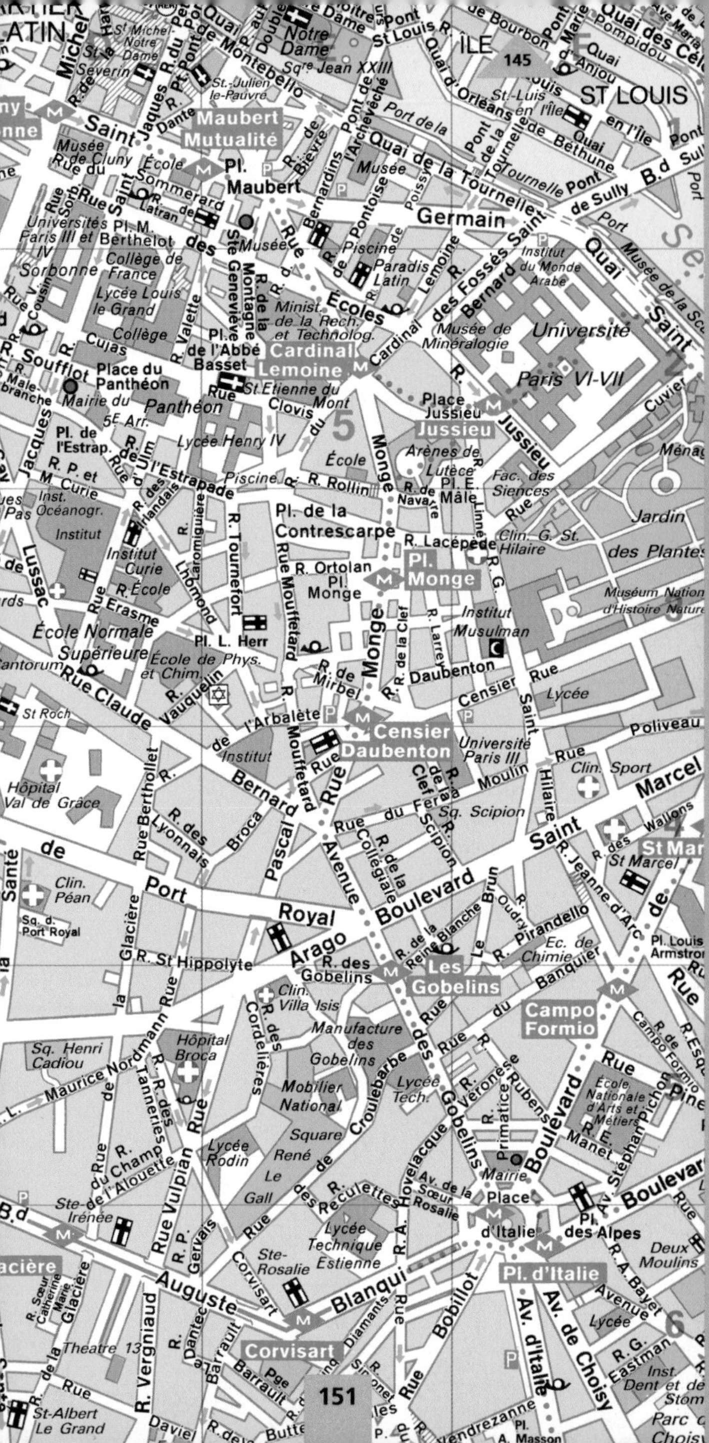
LATIN
Notre Dame
Sq^re Jean XXIII
ÎLE
145
ST LOUIS
Quai des Célestins
Pompidou
Quai d'Anjou
Quai d'Orléans
St.-Luis en l'Île
Quai de Béthune
Pont de Sully
B.d
Port
Quai de Montebello
St.-Julien le-Pauvre
St Michel-Notre-Dame
St. Séverin
Maubert Mutualité
Musée de Cluny
École
Pl. Maubert
Quai de la Tournelle
Pont de la Tournelle
Port de la Tournelle
Pont de l'Archevêché
Musée
Piscine
Paradis Latin
Germain
Saint
Institut du Monde Arabe
Quai Saint Bernard
Musée de la Sculpture
Universités Paris III et IV
Pl. M. Berthelot
Sorbonne
Collège de France
Lycée Louis le Grand
Collège
Ste Geneviève
R. de la Montagne
Musée
Minist. de la Rech. et Technolog.
Écoles
R. des Fossés Saint Bernard
R. Cardinal Lemoine
Musée de Minéralogie
Université Paris VI-VII
R. Cujas
R. Soufflot
Place du Panthéon
Pl. de l'Abbé Basset
Cardinal Lemoine
St.Etienne du Mont
Rue Clovis
Mairie du 5E Arr.
Panthéon
Lycée Henry IV
5
Place Jussieu
Jussieu
R. Jussieu
Cuvier
Pl. de l'Estrap.
R. de l'Estrapade
R. P. et M. Curie
Inst. Océanogr.
Piscine
R. Rollin
École
Monge
Arènes de Lutèce
R. de Navarre
Pl. E. Mâle
Fac. des Siences
Jardin des Plantes
Institut
Pl. de la Contrescarpe
R. Lacépède
Clin. G. St. Hilaire
Institut Curie
R. Ortolan
Pl. Monge
Pl. Monge
Muséum National d'Histoire Naturelle
Rue Erasme
École Normale Supérieure
R. Tournefort
Rue Mouffetard
R. de la Clef
R. Larrey
Institut Musulman
Pl. L. Herr
École de Phys. et Chim.
R. Vauquelin
R. de Mirbel
R. Daubenton
Rue Censier
Lycée
Rue Claude Bernard
St Roch
l'Arbalète
Censier Daubenton
Université Paris III
Rue Poliveau
Institut
Hôpital Val de Grâce
Rue Berthollet
R. des Lyonnais
Broca
Pascal
Avenue des Gobelins
R. du Fer à Moulin
Sq. Scipion
Clin. Sport
Boulevard Saint Marcel
Rue Collégiale
R. Scipion
R. Jeanne d'Arc
R. des Wallons
St Marcel
St Marcel
Santé
Boulevard de Port Royal
Clin. Péan
Sq. d. Port Royal
Boulevard Arago
R. de la Reine Blanche
R. Pirandello
Ec. de Chimie
Pl. Louis Armstrong
R. St Hippolyte
R. des Gobelins
Les Gobelins
Rue du Banquier
Campo Formio
R. de Campo Formio
Clin. Villa Isis
R. des Cordelières
Manufacture des Gobelins
Hôpital Broca
Sq. Henri Cadiou
Maurice Nordmann
Mobilier National
Lycée Tech.
R. Véronèse
R. Rubens
Boulevard de l'Hôpital
École Nationale d'Arts et Métiers
R. Primatice
R. E. Manet
Rue Pinel
Square René Le Gall
Lycée Rodin
R. des Tanneries
Rue Vulpian
R. du Champ de l'Alouette
Rue Croulebarbe
Rue des Reculettes
Rue Corvisart
R. Hovelacque
Av. de la Sœur Rosalie
Mairie
Place d'Italie
Pl. des Alpes
Boulevard Vincent Auriol
Deux Moulins
Ste-de l'Irénée
B.d Auguste Blanqui
R. P. Gervais
Lycée Technique Estienne
Ste-Rosalie
Pl. d'Italie
R. A. Bayet
Avenue
Lycée
Glacière
R. Sœur Catherine Marie
R. Vergniaud
Theatre 13
R. Dantec
R. Barrault
Pge Barrault
Corvisart
Diamants
R. Bobillot
Av. d'Italie
Av. de Choisy
R. G. Eastman
Inst. Dent et de Stom.
6
Parc de Choisy
St-Albert Le Grand
Daviel
Butte
Pl. A. Masson

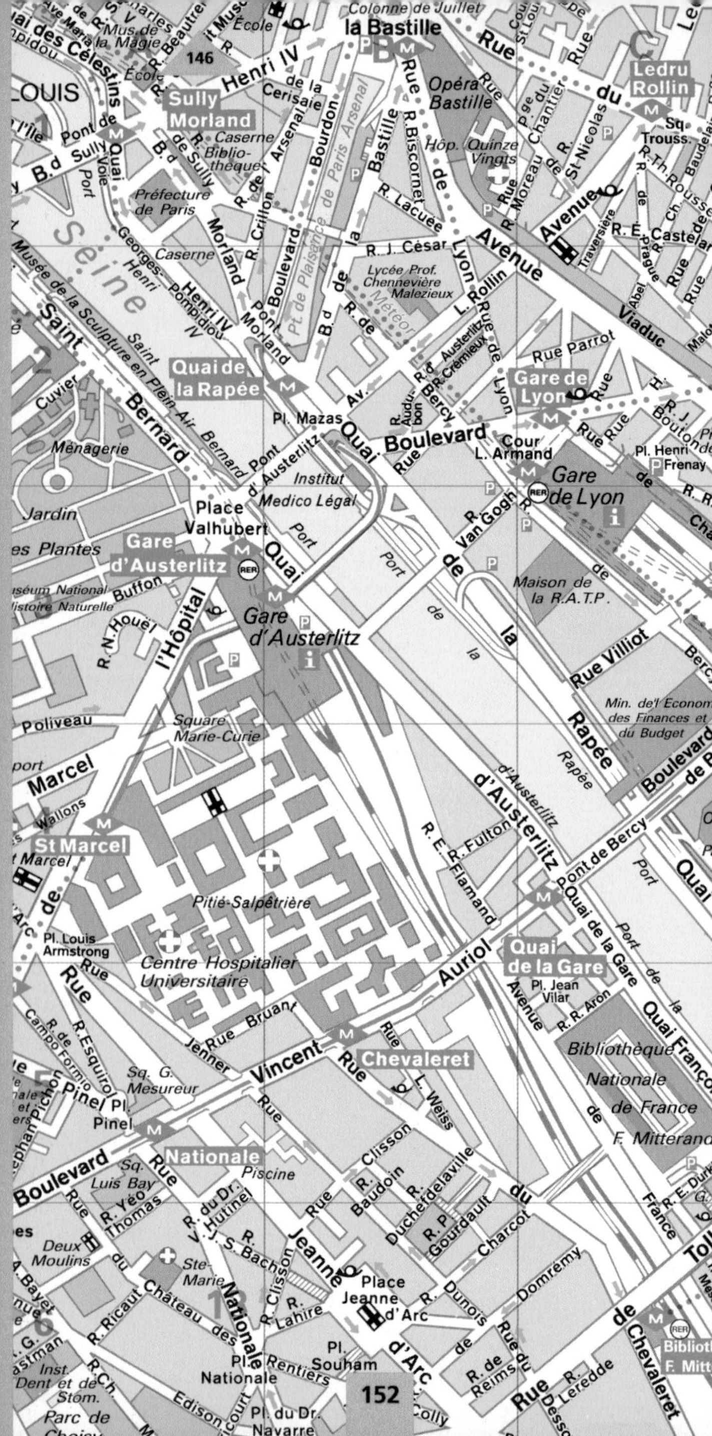
146
la Bastille
Colonne de Juillet
Sully Morland
Quai de la Rapée
Gare de Lyon
Ledru Rollin
Gare d'Austerlitz
Opéra Bastille
Préfecture de Paris
Seine
Jardin des Plantes
Ménagerie
Pitié-Salpêtrière
Centre Hospitalier Universitaire
St Marcel
Quai de la Gare
Chevaleret
Nationale
Bibliothèque Nationale de France F. Mitterand
Maison de la R.A.T.P.
Min. de l'Econom. des Finances et du Budget
Square Marie-Curie
Institut Medico Légal
Place Valhubert
Pl. Mazas
Place Jeanne d'Arc
Pl. Nationale
Boulevard Vincent Auriol
Quai d'Austerlitz
Quai de la Rapée
Boulevard de Bercy
Avenue Daumesnil
Rue de Lyon
Boulevard de l'Hôpital
Rue Jeanne d'Arc
Rue Nationale
Rue de Tolbiac
Rue du Chevaleret
Boulevard Marcel
Musée de la Sculpture en Plein Air
Lycée Prof. Chennevière Malezieux
Hôp. Quinze Vingts
Pont d'Austerlitz
Pont de Bercy
Pont de Sully

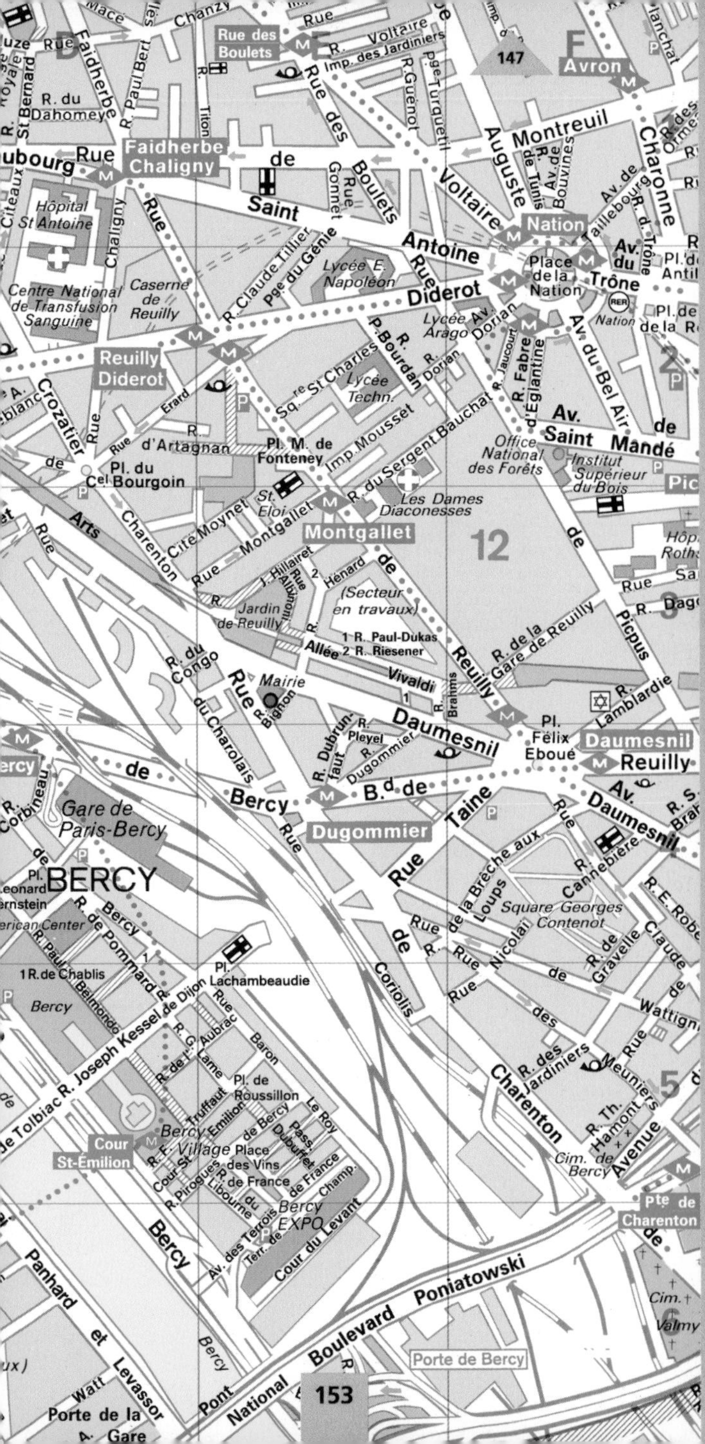

147
Rue des Boulets
Faidherbe Chaligny
Nation
Avron
Reuilly Diderot
Montgallet
Daumesnil
Dugommier
Cour St-Émilion
Porte de Bercy
Pte de Charenton
Rue du Faubourg Saint Antoine
Bd Diderot
Bd Voltaire
Rue des Boulets
Rue de Charonne
Rue de Montreuil
Av. du Trône
Place de la Nation
Av. du Bel Air
Av. de Saint Mandé
Rue de Picpus
Av. Daumesnil
Rue de Reuilly
Rue de Charenton
Bd de Bercy
Rue de Bercy
Boulevard Poniatowski
Pont National
Hôpital St Antoine
Centre National de Transfusion Sanguine
Caserne de Reuilly
Lycée E. Napoléon
Lycée Arago
Lycée Techn.
Office National des Forêts
Institut Supérieur du Bois
Les Dames Diaconesses
Jardin de Reuilly
Mairie
(Secteur en travaux)
Gare de Paris-Bercy
BERCY
Bercy Village
Bercy EXPO
Square Georges Contenot
Cim. de Bercy
Cim. Valmy
12
153

Les Arrondissements de Paris

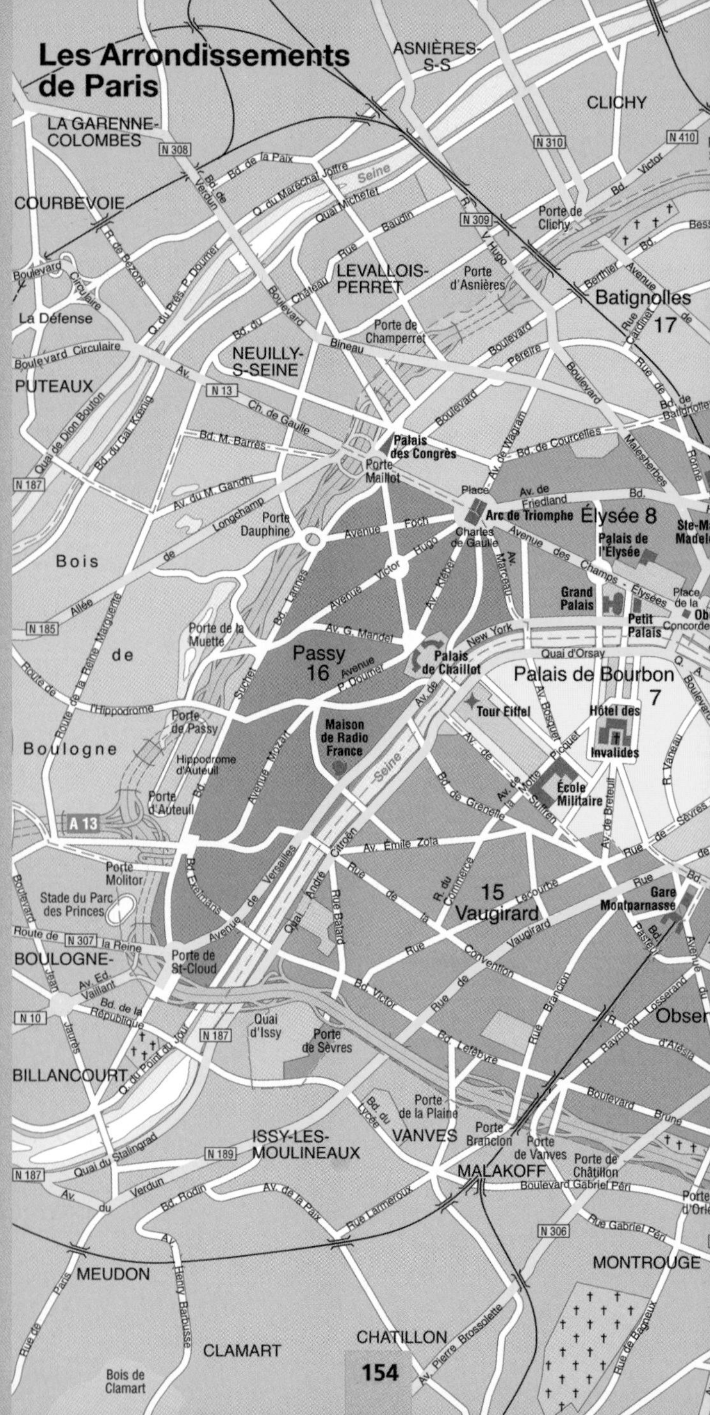

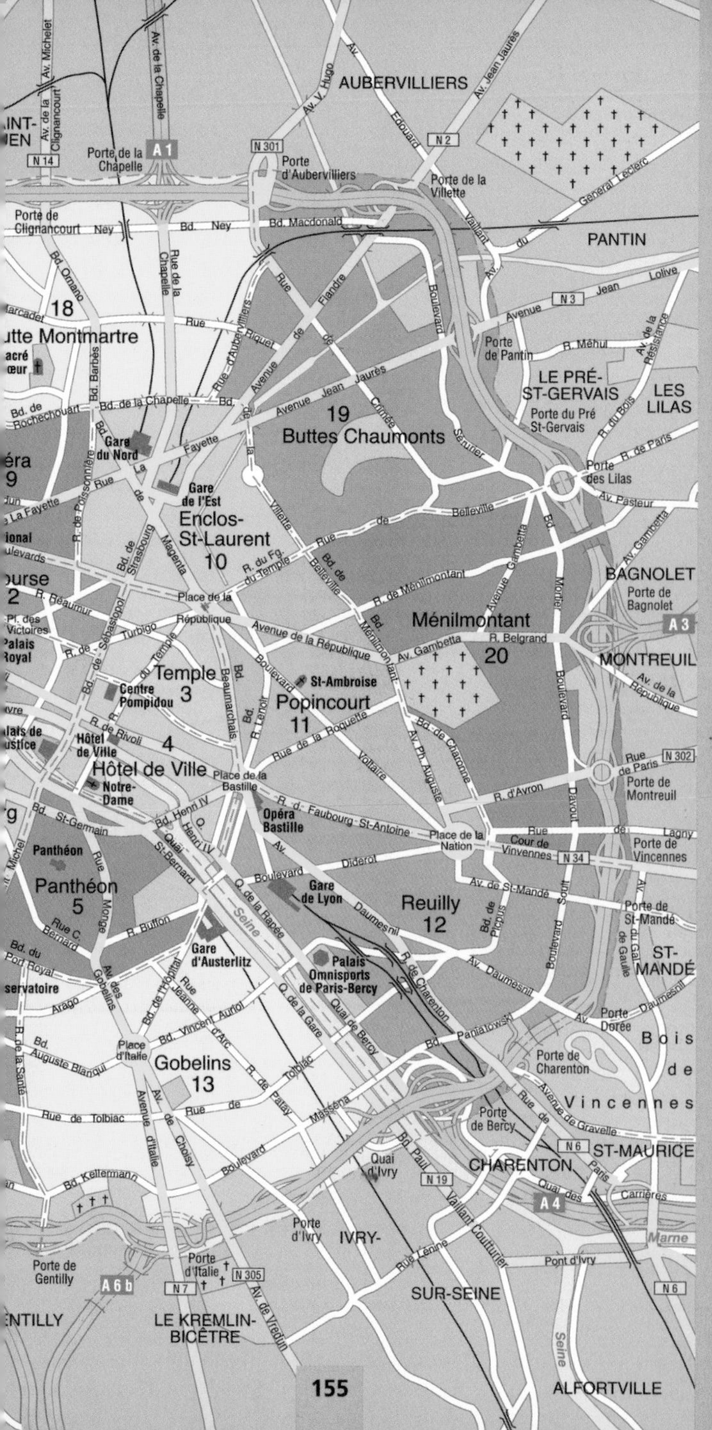
AUBERVILLIERS
PANTIN
LE PRÉ-ST-GERVAIS
LES LILAS
BAGNOLET
MONTREUIL
ST-MANDÉ
ST-MAURICE
CHARENTON
IVRY-SUR-SEINE
ALFORTVILLE
LE KREMLIN-BICÊTRE
18
19
Buttes Chaumonts
Enclos-St-Laurent
10
Ménilmontant
20
Temple
3
Popincourt
11
Hôtel de Ville
4
Panthéon
5
Reuilly
12
Gobelins
13
Bois de Vincennes
Gare du Nord
Gare de l'Est
Gare de Lyon
Gare d'Austerlitz
Centre Pompidou
Opéra Bastille
Palais Omnisports de Paris-Bercy
Notre-Dame
Place de la République
Place de la Bastille
Place de la Nation
Place d'Italie
Seine
Marne

Paris Street Index